DR. FRANK MINIRTH, DR. PAUL MEIER,
DR. ROBERT HEMFELT, DR. SHARON SNEED,
AND DR. DON HAWKINS

LOVE HUNGER WEIGHT-LOSS WORKBOOK

A
JANET
THOMA
BOOK

THOMAS NELSON PUBLISHERS
Nashville

A Division of Thomas Nelson, Inc.
www.ThomasNelson.com

Published in Nashville, Tennessee, by Thomas Nelson, Inc.
The case examples presented in this book are fictional constructs fabricated to illustrate recovery principles. Any resemblance between these fictional characters and actual persons is coincidental and unintentional.

Scripture quotations noted NKJV are taken from THE NEW KING JAMES VERSION. Copyright © 1979, 1980, 1982, 1990, Thomas Nelson, Inc., Publishers.

Library of Congress Cataloging-in-Publication Data Available

ISBN 0-7852-6022-6

Printed in the United States of America

04 05 06 07 08 — 5 4 3 2 1

CONTENTS

PART ONE

UNDERSTANDING
THE PROBLEM

CHAPTER 1

LOVE HUNGER

Valerie Henderson had just moved into a new house. Her life was hectic, her schedule impossible, the kids cranky, and she and her husband, Todd, had both managed to gain more than twenty pounds. If this had been their only weight concern, the task before them would not have seemed so monumental. But, added to the preexistent thirty- to forty-pound excess they already needed to lose, morale was running low in the Henderson household.

Valerie was thankful to be settling into a routine once again even though she wasn't totally familiar with her new surroundings. As she unpacked a carton of old photos, her eye caught sight of her now fourteen-year-old wedding portrait. *Will I ever be a size ten again?* she wondered. The crumpled newspaper, which she had used to carefully wrap this special memory, actually showed a diet studio advertisement for a place that had promised her "quick and painless" weight loss. Six long months ago, she had signed up for this nonprofessional program and two thousand dollars later she had indeed lost twelve pounds. The program did not focus on Valerie's real problems, however, and with the onset of a rather frustrating holiday season, she eventually regained that twelve pounds, plus three more. Valerie's mind was flooded with the unanswered questions of every yo-yo dieter. *Why can't I stop eating? What's wrong with me, anyway? Why can't I find permanent answers?*

Tired of the quick-fix approach, Valerie and Todd made a decision to seek professional guidance. Dr. Hemfelt began a family and emotional dynamics assessment with the Hendersons and helped them see that they were taking out many of their frustrations in life with a knife and fork. Todd was an underpaid but dedicated high school English teacher. He enjoyed his students and his job on most days. But his lifelong desire to attend graduate school had grown from a gentle yearning to an unrequited obsession as year after year rolled by. Now with two children and a new and more costly house payment, fulfillment of this dream seemed like a mirage in the distance.

Valerie was quite happy in her part-time job as an interior decorator, although she astutely recognized that her fifty-plus pound excess was a liability, albeit unfair, in obtaining certain jobs which required a sleek, designerlike, personal appearance. The Hendersons seemed to be working harder than ever; free time was becoming a luxury. Add their current frustrations to the negative messages from each of their childhoods, and the result was two very insecure and frustrated people looking for some way to anesthetize their emotional pain. Being committed to children and a quality life, they chose food as their medicator instead of alcohol, drugs, or some other addictive substance or behavior. Todd rationalized in this way, "What harm can come from a quart of ice cream? At least it's not alcohol; and, anyway, I like ice cream. That can't be an addiction."

Valerie's weight problem had begun as an emotionally driven addiction to food. For five years, however, she had tried repeatedly and earnestly to lose weight. Something seemed different and unresponsive about her body. The thirty pounds she had collectively gained with the two pregnancies seemed, to use her words—"glued on." It wasn't budging. No way. No how. Not with any diet. In fact, when her new weight loss instruction sessions began with Dr. Sneed, she unequivocally stated that there was nothing new to learn about dieting. What she soon came to realize was that her desire for an unrealistically fast weight loss had led her down the dead-end alley of many a failed, fad diet. Dr. Sneed showed her how to cut the caloric content of almost any recipe by one-fourth to even one-half without substantially affecting the flavor of the product. She also learned that a low-fat diet was not synonymous with a low-taste diet and in many cases was more satisfying than other food choices she had made in her past.

A COMPLEX AND PERVASIVE PROBLEM

Compulsive overeating is a complex and pervasive problem. A one-dimensional approach to weight loss has rarely worked, but it has somehow taken a long time to realize this fact. Different people are overweight for different reasons, and most people have several factors feeding their obesity problems. This workbook is patterned after the national bestseller, *Love Hunger: Recovery from Food Addiction* (Thomas Nelson, 1990), written by Drs. Minirth, Meier, Hemfelt, and Sneed. The focus of this book is the psychological dependence on food which has swept the nation. It has affected men and women of all ages, as food addiction is not bound by chronological or sexual barriers. Many parts of *Love Hunger* and even this workbook are about recovery from other forms of addiction and the whole issue of codependency. If you're not sure whether or not you are a food addict, keep reading.

Valerie and Todd eventually lost their extra poundage and have been successful in keeping that weight off. They participated in the twelve-week course presented in this workbook with follow-up visits until they had both reached their ideal body weights. The important thing is that they have not only recovered physically, they have experienced a deep healing within the body, mind, and soul; one which will last. This same healing is within reach for you.

USING THE LOVE HUNGER WORKBOOK

The multifaceted approach to "diet" presented in this book is designed to help you develop life-long, lifestyle changes. Every possible weight loss aid has been explored as we discuss your body, mind, and soul.

Each weekly lesson has been divided into these same three categories.

In the Body sections, all aspects of nutrition, diet, foods, and food preparation and even a little physiology are discussed to help you understand the workings of fat cells.

In the Mind portions, you are helped to understand the feelings driving you to overeat so that they can no longer be a threat to your success in life.

In the Soul sections, we have provided daily meditations structured around the twelve steps of Alcoholics Anonymous: one step for each of the twelve weeks of the Love Hunger diet program. No addiction recovery program is complete without a thoughtful understanding of what is needed to feed your innermost being. In these sections you will look at your relationship with God and the undercurrent of strength which can be found in Him, a strength which will see you through to the end of this program and far beyond.

As you work through this book (it is indeed a true "workbook"), the following suggestions will help ensure your weight loss success.

1. Be receptive. Understand the Love Hunger concept. Dieting is far more than what you eat. It involves why you eat. Are you eating because you are tense or angry, or are you truly hungry? Don't be afraid to explore your innermost feelings about why you eat. This is crucial to your treatment program.

2. Be thoughtful. Complete all fill-in-the-blanks. When you approach your weekly worksheets, you should be alone or with a trusted dieting companion or group who is focusing on the same activity. Fill out each survey or question with great care and thought. The more you write or journal, the more you will learn about yourself.

3. Be organized. Go in order and don't skip. This book is designed to be used in chronological order. After you have read Chapters 2 and 3, which walk you through the initial evaluation material and introduce the Love Hunger Diet, you will begin one of the twelve-week diets. Each week is divided into five days, with a Body, Mind, and Soul section for each day. We suggest that you do not skip days, since each day (and each week) builds on the preceding one. If you wish to do more than one day at a time, you may do so.

4. Be bold. Try new things. Your past lifestyle has not been working for you or you would not be reading this workbook now. You must be prepared to try some new foods, new attitudes, new beliefs, and new activities. In fact, new patterns can become firmly established in a two- or three-month period of time. By the end of this twelve-week course, you should be well on your way.

5. Be committed. Prioritize. It may sound selfish, but concentrate on yourself for the next eighty-four days. Make time for your workbook exercises, new recipes, and physical activity.

An overburdened person is someone who cannot take on new commitments. Give this diet plan your greatest effort. This can only be accomplished when it is near the top of your priority list.

6. Be realistic. Set reasonable goals. You may have dealt with extra pounds for a number of years. Don't expect an overnight cure, and, in fact, you should suspect any program that claims otherwise. You will lose weight as fast on this program as you would on any other isocaloric regimen. You can expect to lose anywhere from three to five pounds the first week and from one and one-half to three and one-half pounds every week thereafter. Weight loss that occurs at a faster rate than this can cause sagging of the skin and a decrease in skin elasticity.

PERSONAL NOTES

Personal journaling and expression of feelings is a hallmark of most recovery programs. Throughout this manual are pages with blank lines for you to express your new ideas, discoveries, and impressions. Begin your journaling now by thinking about all the reasons you want this weight loss program to be the last one you ever go on. List all the reasons you would like to lose weight.

1. _to look good_
2. _feel good_
3. _healthy_
4. _nice clothes_
5. _respect for self_
6. _love self_
7. _control over life & food_
8. _disipline_

more energy
do more activities
prepare for africa
live longer fuller life

CHAPTER 2

THE LOVE HUNGER DIET PLAN

Valerie and Todd were looking forward to their meeting with the nutritionist, Dr. Sneed. Some of their friends had graduated from the Love Hunger program and had said, "It's the easiest diet to follow and stick with. You can eat out, you can eat at home, you can have fast-food hamburgers with your kids, you can go to social functions, and as long as you adhere to the rules, the weight loss continues."

At their first meeting, Dr. Sneed told them that the other diet plans they may have followed probably led them down the path of a traditional food exchange program based on major food groups. This type of diet originated as a treatment program for diabetics and is now widely accepted among the medical profession for its healthful benefits, including simplifying the idea of a "balanced diet."

Dr. Sneed continued to explain that the Love Hunger diet plan was different from the more traditional exchange plan. Instead of exchanging foods, they would be able to exchange entire menus. "I will provide you with an entire list of breakfast, lunch, dinner, and snack menus. You may then choose whichever menu suits you from an array of about twenty others. All of the menus on the same list, such as the breakfast menus, are interchangeable with each other. Any of the menus may be used on any given day."

Valerie was pleased with this approach. "Unfortunately I often take the easy road, repeating the same old recipes over and over again—*particularly* when I'm on a diet. Then I just burn out because I get tired of what I'm eating."

Dr. Sneed assured Valerie that this was quite typical and one of the primary reasons she had developed a program of this nature. "You see, Valerie," explained Dr. Sneed, "you will be able to make instantaneous decisions using this type of system. This menu exchange idea will allow you to zero in on the menus that please you the most so that preplanning for the day or even the entire week will be very easy. You will find at-home choices, restaurant foods, and even quick food-fixes from your local fast food establishments on your menu exchange lists. As the weeks roll by, you will also find yourself committing these menus to memory so that no matter how many things you have to think about or how fast you are running, you will be able to make a wise and palatable food decision."

LOVE HUNGER DIET PLAN
(a menu exchange system)

INSTRUCTIONS FOR THE LOVE HUNGER DIET PLAN

Dr. Sneed then went over her written instructions for the diet plan with both Valerie and Todd.

Step 1. Understanding the Love Hunger Diet Plan

Briefly look at all of the menus beginning on page 343 to acquaint yourself with this system. You will choose one menu from each list at the appropriate eating time. For example, you may choose one entire menu from among the breakfast menus each morning, one menu from the lunch and supper menus at both the noontime and evening meals, and snack choices from among the snack menus as allowed by the calorie level you have chosen for yourself. (Calorie levels will be explained in Step 3.)

Both men and women will choose menus from the same lists. In other words, everyone on the Love Hunger Diet Plan will choose a breakfast, lunch, and dinner choice every day. The number of snack choices you are allowed per day depends on the daily calorie intake you choose for yourself.

Step 2. Understanding Specific and Basic Menus

Note that most of the menus are very specific and tell you exactly what you should eat. However, some general food choices have been included in a more basic menu plan on page 349 to help you achieve a greater variety of foods in your diet. This easy-to-follow format allows you an infinite selection of food choices. When using any of the menus that call for a basic food exchange selection (a fruit selection, a starchy vegetable selection, a meat selection), you then refer to the exchange lists to determine portion sizes allowable for individual foods. The page number of the particular food item is listed on the menu.

Step 3. Choosing a Calorie Level

You must now choose the calorie level at which you prefer to begin your Love Hunger Diet Plan. In the table on page 9, three daily calorie plans are offered. To lose weight most rapidly, the 800 calorie plan would be the best choice. However, the 800 calorie diet plan is only recommended for sedentary women or those who find weight loss very difficult to accomplish. It is inadvisable to consume less than 800 calories per day unless you are directly under a physician's supervision. More active or very young women should use the 1200 calorie plan.

If you find that the first calorie level you chose is too difficult, then you should choose a higher calorie level. The trick is to find a regimen with rules by which you can abide. To pretend you are having a 1000 calorie per day diet and then consume about 1200 to 1400 calories per day only teaches you to break rules.

On the other hand, because of the very large amount of bulk in the diet plans as well as careful planning and new recipes, many of you will find the diet quite filling and perhaps feel that you want to decrease your caloric intake even further. If you are losing weight at the rate of one and one-half to three pounds per week, resist the urge to further decrease your calories. In fact, dermatologists prefer that a maximum of one and one-half pounds per week be lost so that the skin will have ample opportunity to shrink as the underlying tissue decreases in size. This helps reduce sagging in the skin as weight loss continues.

Use the Daily Eating Plan chart to determine when and how much food you will eat at the calorie level you have chosen. You may use the same calorie level throughout the entire diet plan, or you may change to more or fewer calories per day depending on your comfort level with your initial choice.

DAILY EATING PLAN

Menu Choice	Time of Day	Calorie Levels		
		800	1000	1200
BREAKFAST (menus on p. 343)	6–9 A.M.	yes	yes	yes
MORNING SNACK (menus on p. 351)	10–11 A.M.	none	none	yes
LUNCH (menus on p. 348)	12–1 P.M.	yes	yes	yes
AFTERNOON SNACK* (menus on p. 351)	2–5 P.M.	none	yes	yes (2 snacks)
DINNER (menus on p. 348)	6–7 P.M.	yes	yes	yes
EVENING SNACK (menus on p. 351)	8–9 P.M.	none	yes	yes

*For those on a 1200 calorie diet plan, 2 choices from the snack list are allowed each afternoon.

Step 4. Understanding the Nutritional Values of the Menus

Even though all of the menu choices within the 300 calories lunch and dinner menu list roughly have the same caloric content, they are not all of equal nutritional value; a few are admittedly higher in sodium and fat than we ideally prefer. The healthier menu selections are listed first, followed by less healthy choices as each list of menus progresses. It is unreasonable to assume that you will always be in a place where it is possible to make the perfect food choice. So, instead of ignoring the whole issue, we have provided you with the best alternatives in less than optimal situations (such as, when fast food is a must). All menus were analyzed for nutritional value at the Nutritional Sciences Department of the University of Texas, using the most up-to-date information. The nutritional value of each suggested menu is shown under each menu. If you require a special low-fat or low-cholesterol diet because of medical restrictions, you will be able to choose your menus accordingly.

Step 5. Achieving Nutritional Balance

Using a menu exchange system allows you to make quick and easy dietary decisions whatever the circumstances. The down side of that coin is that nutritional imbalance or nutrient deficits are a possibility, depending on which foods and menus you consistently choose. This factor is easily corrected by selecting a diverse diet while keeping an underlying tally of major food choices throughout the day. Specifically, every adult needs a minimum of two dairy choices per day. Also, you should consume at least two cups of fresh vegetables per day and have enough high protein sources to prevent muscles from being broken down just to fuel the body. Having a minimum of three servings of starch per day is essential to keep your body from becoming ketotic during the weight loss process. The body produces ketones as it breaks down fat for energy, instead of burning glucose. By choosing your menus according to these guidelines (most of the time), your nutritional status will not suffer as the fat tissue disappears.

Step 6. Exploring Special Menus and Recipes

We want you to try new recipes and cooking techniques from the very beginning. Check into some new cookbooks at your local bookstore or supermarket. During Week 9, in the Body section of this workbook, a smattering of recipes has been included to show you how to take a normal recipe and make it healthy and weight loss promoting.

FLEXIBILITY AND THE "WHAT IFS"

Valerie and Todd were thrilled to find out how easy this was going to be. However, they both wondered about occasions that would dictate different timing or food selections and how they might cope with a situation which was sure to promote diet failure.

Dr. Sneed laughed as she told Valerie, "Every serious dieter has those identical questions. I call them the 'what ifs.' The Daily Eating Plan is meant to be a guide for you on most days. It is not meant to add stress to your life in any way. The schedule is set up to make you feel as full of energy as possible while still losing weight. Spreading out your calories throughout the day is all part of fulfilling that plan. If you must break training on occasion by adding extras or clumping more than one meal together, don't let it get you down. Now, let's design your first daily menu."

Just as Dr. Sneed's patients design menus for themselves, we want you to do this for yourself by filling in the following blanks.

What calorie level did you choose for yourself to begin the diet program? _____

At this calorie level, each day you will be eating:

Breakfast   Lunch   Dinner
0, 1, 2, or 4 snacks
(circle one)

Remember: All calorie levels except the 800 calorie plan contain daily snacks.

Look at the breakfast menus. What will you have for breakfast tomorrow? (menus on page 343)

_____

_____

Now, look at the lunch and dinner menus. What will you have for lunch tomorrow? (menus on page 348) _____

for dinner? (menus on page 348) _____

_____

What will you have for your snacks tomorrow? (selections on page 351)

800 calorie plan—no snacks
1000 calorie plan—2 snacks per day
1200 calorie plan—4 snacks per day

1. _____
2. _____
3. _____
4. _____

WRAPPING IT UP

The Hendersons were pleased to find a diet program that could meet all of their nutritional, social, and recreational needs. Valerie decided that the 1000 calorie plan would be most appropriate for herself. Her first menu looked like this:

BREAKFAST
2 slices light bread and
2 slices cheese, Borden's Lite Line
(made into cheese toast)
1¼ cup fresh strawberries
Hot herbal tea

LUNCH
Large Chef Salad (see page 350 for recipe)
¼ cup light Italian dressing
Diet soda

AFTERNOON SNACK
10 ounces skim milk

DINNER
1 cup spaghetti pasta
½ cup spaghetti sauce with meat
Steamed vegetables
Coffee

EVENING SNACK
½ cup light chocolate ice cream
(100 calorie serving)

Planning became consistently easier for Valerie. In fact, the concise information about the actual meals began to stick in her mind to the point that she no longer required the manual to help her make food choices. She thought she had found a miracle—weight loss and chocolate ice cream, too!

PART TWO

THE TWELVE WEEK
LOVE HUNGER
WEIGHT-LOSS PLAN

DAY 1

PREPARING FOR SUCCESS

*The more careful, advanced planning you do
for your new eating program, the greater your
chances are for successful weight loss.*

GETTING STARTED

TODD Henderson had never done well on a diet program before. Actually, he had never thought much about a diet until his family physician told him that his blood levels of cholesterol and triglycerides were elevated but would normalize if he lost about forty pounds. He had tried to lose the weight on his own, with very little success, when he decided to join Valerie at the clinic to be a part of the Love Hunger diet program.

Seeing the progress that other patients were making was a real encouragement to Todd and Valerie. They were starting to feel the momentum as they waited for their first appointment with the check-in personnel. Just to Todd's left sat a slender, middle-aged man who gave the appearance of one of those natural athletes who makes commercials for athletic gear or sunglasses. Right after Todd had decided that this man was at the clinic for some other reason than weight loss, he noticed the well-worn copy of *Love Hunger* in the man's lap. Todd couldn't resist asking, "Have you been through the diet program here?"

"Sure have," replied the sandy-haired gentleman. "I've lost sixty-five pounds and maintained it for more than eighteen months. I'm just here today for a quick maintenance check."

The material in this week's portion of the Body section is meant to prepare you for the diet just as it did for Todd and Valerie. If you would like to begin the diet, you certainly may do so. However, the assignments we will be making this week will more fully equip you for success. Above all, *do not skip this part.* We realize that you are excited and perhaps anxious to begin the diet program, but take time to complete this chapter for maximal, lifelong changes.

CONTRACTS ARE BINDING

The first thing you must do, at the risk of sounding trendy, is to "think positive." You really are going to make it this time. You can succeed and lose that unwanted weight that has hampered your lifestyle or impaired your health. But don't approach this plan loosely as you may have with other diets in the past, thinking, *Sure, I'll try this for a while, until something comes up or until I get tired of it.* Any good weight loss program is preparation for new and enjoyable, lifelong eating habits rather than a quick fix or even healthy but unreasonably strict guidelines that always make you feel a little bit unsatisfied. In fact, this program is a twelve-week partnership. In eighty-four days, you will know yourself better, understand what motivates and drives you, and be anywhere from twelve to thirty-five pounds lighter than you are today.

We suggest you seal your determination to succeed by signing an official contract with yourself. We use the following contract with our patients.

CONTRACT

I, _____, have wanted to be successful on a weight loss program for a long time. Sustained weight loss and weight maintenance is not always easy, but in the past I may have only focused on one aspect of weight loss, such as calorie control or increased exercise. I now understand that being overweight has many causes, including psychological factors which I may or may not have even considered in the past.

I will begin the Love Hunger diet on _____ (date) and will try hard to commit to that program for 84 consecutive days (twelve weeks). The authors of *Love Hunger* do not expect me to be perfect every day, and I understand that an occasional mishap should not discourage me to the point of quitting the program.

The ending date of the 84-day program will be on _____ (date). If I have not reached my weight loss goal by this date, I realize that I can continue on the eating program as long as I care to, since it is nutritionally balanced and will not harm me physically. I also understand that the Love Hunger eating program is just what I need for weight maintenance (except that I will be able to eat in larger quantities). The concepts presented here will help me maintain my weight for the rest of my life.

Signed _____

Date _____

DAY 1

YOUR RELATIONSHIPS

DURING Dr. Robert Hemfelt's first meeting with Valerie Henderson, he realized that her relationship with food began years ago in her childhood, which is typical of many patients. Dr. Hemfelt suggested that Valerie try to imagine what it was like eating dinner with her mom and dad and her sisters and brothers.

"What was a normal dinnertime like at your childhood home?" the doctor asked Valerie.

"Quite hectic," Valerie replied, "really very hectic, in fact. There were seven of us kids, and we never wanted to eat at the same time—because of all our different activities. Joe had football practice, Keith worked part-time, and I was a cheerleader. The little kids usually ate with Mom and Dad, and the rest of us got our own meals, except on Sunday. That was the command performance."

"Let's start on Sunday, then," said Dr. Hemfelt. "Imagine that you are at the Sunday dinner table. How do you feel?"

"Rushed. We were all there, but the older kids were trying to eat quickly so we could go somewhere. And you can imagine the noise level with seven kids all talking at once and all asking for the mashed potatoes or roast. I often just wanted to go back to my room where there was peace and quiet."

"Sounds as if you were pretty lonely at that dinner table, Valerie," said Dr. Hemfelt, who often uses "startle" questions to make patients see something they never realized.

"Lonely! You've got to be kidding. With seven kids at that table, no one would be lonely."

"Think back with me, Valerie. Weren't there some things you'd have liked to tell your mom or dad at that dinner table?"

"Well, of course," Valerie agreed. "Once I was nominated for class secretary, but that night at dinner I couldn't get a word in edgewise."

"Didn't that make you feel lonely? As if no one cared about you or what happened to you?"

"Well, maybe you're right."

"And could you have used food to fill that hunger for love and attention?"

Tears came to Valerie's eyes as she realized, as many other patients have, that her compulsion for food was much deeper than her craving for chocolate.

Many of our patients are like Valerie; their eating compulsion began years ago at the family dinner table. During Week 1, we'd like you to look back at your childhood. Let's begin with an exercise like the one Valerie just tried.

REMEMBER DINNERTIME DURING YOUR CHILDHOOD

Sit back, relax, and think about your childhood. Walk up to the house that you lived in and go through the front door. It's dinnertime, and everyone is beginning to gather around the table. Sit down with them.

Who is sitting at the table? Mom and Dad? Sisters and brothers?

Sitting around the table in my childhood were:

_____

_____

_____

Was someone often missing? _____ yes _____ no

_____ was often missing.

How did this make you feel? (For instance, if Dad was never there, were you angry?)
I felt _____

_____

_____

Now think about the conversation at dinnertime. Check the statement that best describes this conversation.

_____ My family enjoyed talking about the day's activities.

_____ My mom and dad were interested in me and what I had to say.

_____ My brothers and/or sisters and I enjoyed talking together about our activities.

_____ My brothers and/or sisters and I often bickered and argued at the dinner table.

_____ Mom often told Dad all that went wrong during the day at dinnertime, especially what
I and/or my brother(s) and/or sister(s) had done wrong.

Now think about how you are feeling. (Could you be feeling lonely, for example, as Valerie did? Why?)

I feel _____ because _____

_____

_____

Finally ask yourself, "How could this environment have affected my relationship to food today?"

DAY 1

♥

STEP 1: WE ADMITTED WE WERE POWERLESS OVER OUR DEPENDENCIES—THAT OUR LIVES HAD BECOME UNMANAGEABLE

BILL Wilson is a man known to millions of people who have been caught in one of the most common addictions—alcoholism. Bill Wilson's fame comes from his response to this addiction. Bill was an alcoholic who sank deeper and deeper into his addiction until doctors told his weary and despairing wife that his life would end shortly; he would either have heart failure during periods of withdrawal or he would develop a wet brain and have to be committed to an asylum.

Like millions of others, Wilson tried to overcome his addiction many times during its progression. He vowed to quit. He did so for a month or so then began drinking again.

Then one day an old school friend of his, Ebby Thatcher, asked to talk to him. Bill had heard a rumor that Ebby had been committed for alcoholic insanity. Yet Ebby told Bill that he had been sober for two months.

"Two men appeared in court and persuaded the judge to suspend my commitment," Ebby said. "They told me of a simple religious idea and a practical program of action."

The practical program was the Oxford group, founded in the early 1900s and popularized in America by the Episcopal minister Sam Shoemaker. The Oxford group was the forerunner of Alcoholics Anonymous.

"My friend sat before me," Wilson says in *Alcoholics Anonymous: The Story of How Many Thousands of Men and Women Have Recovered from Alcoholism* (also known as the *Big Book of Alcoholics Anonymous*), "and he made the point-blank declaration that God had done for him what he could not do for himself. His human will had failed. Doctors had pronounced him incurable. Society was about to lock him up. Like myself, he had admitted complete defeat. Then he had, in effect, been raised from the dead, suddenly taken from the scrap heap to a level of life better than the best he had ever known!"[1]

In the next days, Bill Wilson began a spiritual search that ended one night in the hospital when he humbly offered himself to God as he then understood Him. After that night Bill never had another drink.

In the next years, he founded Alcoholics Anonymous® (AA) and began the Twelve-Step Program which is used by AA today. In the last decade, counselors and lay people alike have realized that overeating and other obsessive/compulsive behaviors are addictions like alcoholism and can be effectively treated by the AA Twelve-Step Program. Groups like Overeaters Anonymous®, Emotions Anonymous®, the Adult Children of Alcoholics®, and Gamblers Anonymous have been founded on the same principles throughout the country.

The twelve-step program of Overeaters Anonymous® has helped millions of addicted people recover from obsessive/compulsive behavior. Each week we will look at one of these steps in the spiritual section. This week we will explore step 1: "We admitted we were powerless over our food compulsion—that our lives had become unmanageable."

Step 1 is a paradox. It says, "If I admit that I am powerless, I will win. If I surrender control, I will get control of my addiction."

As difficult as this paradox is to understand, it is not new. Over a thousand years ago Jesus told His disciples, "He who finds his life will lose it, and he who loses his life for My sake will find it" (Matt. 10:39).

As you begin the Love Hunger Diet Plan, you may be gritting your teeth and vowing, "This time I'm going to control my overeating. This time I'm going to win."

Instead we are going to ask you to let go of control. We are going to ask you to let go emotionally and spiritually, and admit, "I can't do it alone. I need help from someone or something."

Maybe you, too, will find that "If I admit that I am powerless, I will win. If I surrender control, I will get control of my addiction."

DAY 2

MEDICAL READINESS

To begin your new lifestyle and new eating patterns, you should first make sure that you are physically prepared for this or any other weight loss program. If you have not had a medical check-up and concurrent blood work in the last twelve months, we suggest that you do so as you begin this program. If you take hypertensive, thyroid, or diabetic medications, keep your doctor informed of your weight loss progress, as this may lessen your need for these medications. If you are diabetic or sensitive to sugar in any way, please check with your doctor before trying any of the recipes in this book. You should also find out about any exercise restrictions you may have.

A MEDICAL INVENTORY

Answer the following questions as you free your mind of any concerns you have about your current physical condition.

I have had a medical check-up and lab work within the last twelve months.

_____ yes _____ no

If I need a check-up and lab work, I will call my physician,

Dr. _____ this week. The office number is _____

The appointment time for my check-up is _____

My medical results indicate that a weight loss diet would be a very healthy choice for me to make. _____ yes _____ no

My specific medication problems include:

1. _____
2. _____
3. _____
4. _____
5. _____

Many medical problems can be corrected by weight loss alone. These include high blood levels of cholesterol and/or triglycerides, some forms of diabetes, high blood pressure, low back pain, fatigue, premenstrual syndrome, gout, and the symptoms of some orthopedic problems, to name a few. If any of these are listed among your medical problems, circle the ones which will improve as your new eating style becomes part of your lifestyle.

MEDICAL RESTRICTIONS FOR THIS EATING PROGRAM

You have chosen a very safe and effective method of weight loss by using this workbook. However, if you have a medical complication, additional factors should be considered. If you have *elevated serum cholesterol,* review page 355 and make a mental note of low-fat, low-cho-lesterol alternatives you can include in your diet.

_____

_____

_____

If you are a *non-insulin dependent diabetic,* you may use many of the meals outlined in the fol-lowing program that do not contain any sugar, syrup, molasses, or brown sugar. (If you have questions about whether to use any recipe in this book, consult your doctor.) For many matu-rity-onset diabetics who are non-insulin dependent, weight loss and diet modification will cure their problems with diabetes as long as they maintain their weight loss and healthful diets.

DAY 2

ANOTHER DAY AT THE FAMILY DINNER TABLE

Let's go back to your family dinner table for a moment. Look around that table and think about how the different family members related to food. Complete each section by writ-ing down your thoughts.

MOM

Think about your mom. (Did she enjoy eating? Or did she seem to use food for another purpose? For instance, did she tend to eat when she was upset or nervous? If so, she might have used food as a tranquilizer.)

My mom seemed to think of food as _____

_____

_____

DAD

Now think about your dad. (Did he ever say, "I just eat to survive. I really don't enjoy food"? Did he gulp his food down as quickly as possible so he could get back to the football game or outside to mow the grass?)

My dad seemed to think of food as _____

_____

_____

SISTERS AND BROTHERS

What relationship did your sister or brother have with food?

My sister or brother thought of food as _____

_____

_____

Now think about yourself. Could these family members' attitudes toward food have affected you? How?

My family's relationship with food caused me to think of food as _____

_____

_____

DAY 2

Step 1. We admitted we were powerless over our dependencies—that our lives had become unmanageable.

RECOGNIZING DENIAL

In order for Bill Wilson to overcome his addiction to alcohol, he had to "break out of denial," as counselors say today. He had to say, "I am an alcoholic. I am powerless over my compulsion to drink. My life has become unmanageable."

We tell our patients that in order to overcome their compulsion to overeat, they must be willing to admit that food has become an addiction. They must admit to themselves, "I am powerless over my food compulsion—my life has become unmanageable."

Our patients often say, "But my life hasn't become unmanageable. If I really want to lose this weight, I can."

Overeaters often deny their compulsion to overeat, just as alcoholics deny their addiction. Unfortunately, we all tend to lie to ourselves. One of the major steps in recovery from any addiction is to break through this denial by replacing these self-lies with truth.

Read over the typical statements our patients often make to deny their food compulsion. If you can hear yourself saying some of these things, replace these lies with the truth by filling in the blanks.

I eat just like everyone else. My metabolism is just slow, and my family is large-boned.

The truth is _____

_____

_____

My weight doesn't bother me. People don't really notice. They judge me by what's on the inside.

The truth is _____

_____

_____

My doctor says I have to lose this weight, but what do doctors know? If weight doesn't get me, it'll be cancer or a heart attack. I'd rather go out happy.

The truth is _____

_____

_____

When my life settles down a little (or when I close this big account or when summer is over and the kids go back to school), I'll stop overeating.

The truth is _____

_____

_____

Replacing these lies with the truth is a major part of working through Step 1 of the Twelve Step program. Every time you are tempted to accept one of these rationalizations, remember the truths that you yourself have written on this page.

DAY 3

GET RID OF THE BOOBY TRAPS

Your own worst dieting enemies may be right in your own home. One of Valerie Henderson's dieting problems revolved around the frequency with which she was exposed to food and the fact that some of the kids' snacks (homemade chocolate chip cookies, cakes, candy) were too tempting to resist. When these foods are served several times per day to an expectant and hungry group, that mother may decide to have some of those foods herself.

Remember: If you don't need those kinds of foods, chances are no one else in your house needs them either. Or maybe they can enjoy them with less frequency. Westerners have been led down the primrose path into believing that high-fat/high-calorie snacks are okay every day, especially if you are a child or are maintaining your weight. Any snack is all right sometimes, but if you consistently have foods in your house (ostensibly for other members of the family) that seem to call your name from the pantry, get rid of them. Let your family (or roommates) keep those items in their own rooms if it is necessary for them to be in the house at all. The following questions and action steps can be an aid to ridding your house of these dietary booby-traps.

What food items am I unable to resist when they are in the pantry or refrigerator?

_____ _____ _____

_____ _____ _____

I agree with and can comply with the following statements:

I can get rid of tempting "junk foods" or other very high-calorie or high-fat foods which are hard for me to resist when dieting. ____ yes ____ no

If junk foods are not in my house (my desk or my office) then I won't be tempted to eat them in a moment of fatigue or increased anxiety. ____ yes ____ no

Once I break these long-standing habits, I may be able to reintroduce some of these food items back into my house and have total control over whether or not I consume them. ____ yes ____ no

If there are not people in my house to eat these items now, I can throw these items away or give them to someone *before I begin the diet plan.* _____ yes _____ no

Valerie and Todd found it necessary to give several food items to their neighbors when they began the diet program. The value of these food items was cumulatively not more than twenty dollars' worth of groceries. They were not concerned about this loss because they knew (a) that this would help them succeed on the program, (b) that they had spent much, much more than twenty dollars on diet programs in the past, and (c) that this was also the right thing for them to do for their children.

Look at the list you made of pantry and refrigerator items. Circle the items on this list which you can eliminate on a routine basis from your kitchen and home. Look at what is not circled on your list. Will it be possible to ask the persons in your family who want these food items to do without them temporarily, even for a few weeks to help you get off to a good start on your new eating plan? Write the names of the persons concerned and think about what you will say to them.

NAME	FOOD ITEM	WHAT WILL I SAY TO THEM?
_____	_____	_____
_____	_____	_____
_____	_____	_____
_____	_____	_____

DAY 3

WHAT IS YOUR RELATIONSHIP WITH FOOD?

Now that you've thought about your family's attitudes toward food and how they might have affected you, it's time to think about your own relationship with food. How do you feel about food? Has it been a friend? Or a foe? Think back to your childhood. What was your relationship with food then?

As a child I thought of food as a _____ friend _____ foe
because _____

_____

Did that relationship change as you grew up? (For instance, did your mom or dad tease you about weight? Did one of them hound you to lose weight? Did you sometimes eat a pizza just to show them, "I'll do as I please"?) If your attitude did change, how did it change? And why?

_____

_____

_____

As a teen, I thought of food as a _____ friend _____ foe
because _____

_____

_____

_____

Did your relationship with food change when you moved out of your parents' home? How?

_____

_____

_____

Once I left home I thought of food as a _____ friend _____ foe
because _____

_____

_____

_____

Now think about your relationship with food today. (Check the statements that apply to you.)

_____ Food has become increasingly important in my life.

_____ I eat when I am nervous or angry.

_____ I crave food and think about it more than I'd like.

_____ I might eat to keep people from getting close to me.

_____ I could be addicted to food.

DAY 3

Step 1. We admitted we were powerless over our dependencies—that our lives had become unmanageable.

HIDDEN ADDICTIONS

Some say, "Bad luck always comes in threes." We don't know about bad luck, but we do know that obsessive/compulsive behaviors often come in threes and fours and fives because one addiction often leads to another.

Most of our patients who have overeating problems also have other "hidden" addictions or "approved addictions," like workaholism or shopaholism or compulsive cleaning. Todd Henderson, for instance, was a workaholic as well as an overeater. He also was addicted to risk taking. Although he didn't realize it, his passion for "playing the stock market" and especially for buying new stocks and junk bonds was another addiction. He felt a real high when he was sitting out on a limb, dangling between success and failure.

When we counsel these patients, we always ask them to look at the other areas of their lives that seem to be unmanageable or "out of control." We ask them to think of an area of their lives in which they feel like the dog in the old adage, "Instead of the dog wagging the tail, the tail is wagging the dog."

Are there areas of your life that seem to be controlling you rather than your controlling them? As part of the first step in the Twelve-Step program, you need to admit, "I am powerless over these areas of my life also."

Today we would like you to think about a few of these hidden addictions. Check the statements that apply to you and then decide if you suffer from one of these approved addictions.

MONEY

_____ It seems as if there is never enough money to meet my needs or the needs of my family.

_____ I am always paying on—but never paying off—my credit card(s).

_____ I have a false sense of power when I'm investing my money.

_____ I think about the stock market or a real estate deal when I'm at work or on my vacation or involved in another activity.

_____ It's almost as if I'm trying to buy other people's love.

Money may be one of my hidden addictions because _____

_____

_____

_____

WORK

_____ I am a perfectionist about my work (my job or my housework).

_____ Everything in our house must be just so. I feel guilty if anything is out of place.

_____ The hours I spend at work seem to continually escalate.

_____ I work so hard that I sometimes burn out.

_____ I catch myself swinging between extremes—periods of working long hours and times of accomplishing nothing.

_____ Sometimes I seem to sabotage my own success at the last minute.

_____ My friends have said that I should "take it easy" or I will burn out.

_____ Instead of working to provide for my family, I seem to live to go to work.

_____ Home just seems to be a pit stop between the rat race at work.

Workaholism may be one of my hidden addictions because _____

_____

_____

_____

SHOPPING

_____ I often go shopping when I'm feeling depressed or sad.

_____ Buying a new pair of slacks or a new suit makes me feel better.

_____ I feel more "in control" of my life as I select a new outfit or a new car or a new piece of furniture.

_____ Yet after a shopping spree I feel guilty or remorseful.

_____ I sometimes shop to express anger at my husband, particularly when he is too busy at work to spend time with me.

_____ Sometimes I know that I am spending money that my family needs for other things.

Shopaholism may be one of my hidden addictions because _____

_____

_____

_____

DAY 4

ENLIST YOUR SUPPORTERS

Valerie and Todd Henderson were fortunate to start a weight loss program as a couple and as a family. We have had many of our patients who were literally unable to remove all of the booby traps due to noncompliance in the removal of tempting foods by other family members, roommates, parents, friends, workmates, and other acquaintances. Some of our patients have even felt uncomfortable about their latest dieting attempt. The fear of failing in front of these significant others can be so great, they actually compromise their chances of success.

Don't let that happen to you. We think that the added support you will receive from others' encouragement will be to your benefit.

Answer the following questions and think about what you will say to others about your involvement in this program.

Are you able to talk with your spouse (or significant other) about weight loss?
_____ yes _____ no

What about a roommate or friend? _____ yes _____ no

Has extra poundage been a source of friction in the past between you and your spouse or significant other? _____ yes _____ no

What can your spouse do to help you succeed with this program? (Suggestions: Keep all tempting, high-calorie foods out of the house; help you cook healthful meals according to your meal plans; begin a walking or other exercise program with you; be kind and supportive as you work through some difficult issues.) Other:

_____

_____

_____

Now let's tell the nondieting family members about your good news and your new decisions. Give the letter below to your spouse, significant other, or even a roommate or parent to help them understand how they can be of the greatest support to you.

A MESSAGE TO ALL SIGNIFICANT OTHERS

Dear _____,

I have been asked to give you this letter by the group of doctors who are helping me with a new and innovative weight loss program I am currently learning about through the *Love Hunger Weight-Loss Workbook*. It is not just another diet. It is a food addiction recovery program, which deals with the emotional reasons people overeat.

The doctors have told me that you can be a very important part of my success. You can support me in the following ways.

1. Help me remove food items from the house that do not follow my food plan and might be tempting for me to eat at a tense, fatigued, or anxious moment.

2. Be supportive of me in these efforts. Breaking long-standing and frequent emotionally based habits such as overeating or eating inappropriately, is very difficult to accomplish. The doctors are asking you to simply be my friend and to be loving instead of judgmental. They don't expect me to be perfect on my eighty-four-day diet, and they hope you will be supportive when I need a boost to return to the program regimen.

3. If there is some way you can participate with me in my new lifestyle, you would be welcomed company. Maybe you could walk with me. Or perhaps we could enjoy cooking in the kitchen together. There are many new recipes that you will enjoy yourself.

4. Please be open-minded about possibly changing your own eating habits. A lower fat, higher fiber diet, which is balanced with foods from all of the groups, can help prevent cancer, heart disease, high blood pressure and diabetes. And even if you don't live long with all of this preventive health, you will live better!

If you can agree with these simple but important requests, please commit to it by signing your name below.

Signed _____

Date _____

DAY 4

TAKING INVENTORY

This week has been a preparation for your Love Hunger diet. In the Body section you've been taking stock of your weight and your physical health. Now we want you to take an inventory of your relationships, since your emotional health is often affected by your relationships with your family members, both now and in your childhood. And your emotional health is definitely related to your overeating.

We would like you to complete the relationship survey that we give our patients.

MY RELATIONSHIP SURVEY

MY CHILDHOOD FAMILY

During my growing-up years my relationship with my biological family was:
_____ Good _____ Bad _____ Indifferent

Describe your childhood relationship with your mom and dad, your sisters and brothers:

My relationship with my mom was _____ because _____

_____

_____

My relationship with my dad was _____ because _____

_____

_____

My relationship with my sisters and brothers was _____ because _____

_____

_____

Now think about other adults who influenced you, like your grandparents and your uncles and aunts.

My relationship with my grandparents was _____because _____

_____

_____

My relationship with my uncles and aunts was _____ because _____

_____

_____

MEMBERS OF THE OPPOSITE SEX

Beginning with your junior high years or earlier, who were your close friends of the opposite sex? List two or three below. What do you remember about each relationship? Was the relationship enjoyable? (If so, why?) Was it painful? (If so, why?) Place a star by any relationships that seem to be similar.

Relationship one (Name): _____

_____

_____

Relationship two (Name): _____

_____

_____

Relationship three (Name): _____

_____

_____

MY CURRENT FAMILY

Now think about your relationship with your current family if you are married. What is your relationship with your spouse? With your children? Is anyone else living in your home, a parent or friend? What is your relationship with this person? Is your current home a warm safe, nurturing place? _____

_____

_____

AUTHORITY FIGURES

What were your relationships with authority figures in your childhood, with teachers and coaches? Did these people seem to be all too ready to criticize you? Or were they supportive? Did they (and your parents) tend to yell at you when you made a mistake?

_____

_____

_____

Now think about your relationship with the authority figures in your life today. How about your boss? Do you have the feeling that he or she is just waiting for you to make a mistake? How do you feel when your boss criticizes you? Do you ever feel as if your boss or your doctor or your minister is out to get you?

_____

_____

_____

YOURSELF

Now think about yourself. When someone gives you a compliment, do you think, He or she really didn't mean that. He was just being nice? _____ yes _____ no

Do you really like yourself? Or do you sometimes think, If so-and-so really knew me, he or she wouldn't like me?

If I'm honest with myself, I _____

_____

_____

What kind of friend are you to yourself? Would you pick yourself as your best friend? (Have you ever realized that you must have a good relationship with yourself before you can build a good relationship with others?) _____

_____

_____

These relationships have a lot more to do with your hunger for food than you might realize. In the weeks ahead we will look at these relationships with people again and how they contribute to your love hunger.

DAY 4

Step 1. We admitted we were powerless over our dependencies—that our lives had become unmanageable.

OTHER OBSESSIVE-COMPULSIVE BEHAVIORS

Yesterday you looked at some of the hidden addictions that are common to our patients. Today we'd like you to look at the many other obsessive-compulsive behaviors that might be driving you. Read through the following statements and check off the ones that seem to apply to you.

ALCOHOL AND/OR DRUGS

_____ At times in my life it seems necessary to drink more than I would like.

_____ I do things when I'm drinking I normally would not do when I'm sober.

_____ My husband (or wife) or parents are concerned about my drinking.

_____ I go to a party and end up drinking more than I had planned to drink.

_____ I'm usually quiet, but when I drink (or take drugs), I'm the life of the party.

_____ At times I recreationally use drugs even though I know they're illegal and in some-ways they violate my moral values.

_____ I need more drugs to get the same high.

OBSESSION WITH ILLNESS (HYPOCHONDRIA)

_____ I've had vague, physical problems for years, but the doctors don't seem to be able to identify my illness.

_____ If I am fully honest with myself, I will notice that my physical symptoms escalate during times of stress.

_____ Medical doctors have suggested that I get a psychological (or psychiatric) assessment of my symptoms.

_____ I am often worried that I have some serious illness the doctors haven't diagnosed.

EXERCISE AND PHYSICAL CONDITIONING

_____ I engage in vigorous aerobic exercise more than three times a week. (Could you be doing this for reasons other than your health?)

_____ I look forward to getting that runner's or exerciser's high.

_____ I've had some recurrent joint pain (or injuries).

_____ If I don't get my full regimen of exercise, I am irritable or depressed.

_____ I exercise vigorously more than six hours per week.

_____ I continue to exercise even though I have bone and joint pain caused by overuse.

_____ I am such a fanatic about exercise, I cannot tolerate getting off my program even one time.

RELIGIOUS LEGALISM

_____ I'm constantly judging myself (and others) about whether or not we are conforming to the doctrines of our faith.

_____ I seem to be moving farther away from my friends at church since I became so concerned about doctrine.

_____ The more I work at adhering to the doctrine of my faith, the more distant God seems.

_____ Sometimes I catch myself arguing with myself about what to do. I'm almost afraid to make a decision because there are verses to support each side.

SMOKING

_____ I've tried to quit smoking, but I just can't.

_____ When I'm upset, I need a cigarette.

_____ I smoke every day. (If you do, you are probably addicted.)

BULIMIA

_____ I sometimes eat everything in sight and then use laxatives to purge the food from my system.

_____ When I know I've overeaten, I sometimes vomit to get rid of that food.

If you've added a few of these hidden addictions to the ones you identified yesterday, you might be feeling as if you're hopelessly out of control. In fact, you might be so depressed you're ready to give up.

Let us assure you, you are not alone. Many people who think they're A-OK actually have multiple addictions. And this feeling of being unable to do what you want to do is far from new. The apostle Paul, a man who spread God's Word throughout the Roman Empire, sometimes felt as if he was out of control. In a letter to the Christians in Rome, he admitted, "The good that I will to do, I do not do; but the evil I will not to do, that I practice (Rom. 7:19).

Paul, like Bill Wilson, found the only answer was for God to help him overcome his weakness. "The Spirit," he says, "also helps in our weaknesses (Rom. 8:26).

DAY 5

PRIORITIES AND TIMING—A KEY ISSUE

Valerie and Todd never seemed to put lifestyles and dieting high enough on their priority list to stick with a program for longer than a week. Something always seemed to come up. Learning to deal with crises, holidays, recreational events, extensive work schedules, and any number of other stressful situations *without* overeating was one of their biggest goals. It was explained to them that the whole Love Hunger concept was that they should eat to fill an empty stomach and not an empty heart. And even though they would eventually learn to resist poor eating habits during those times of crisis, they should optimize their chances for success by beginning this program at a time when they could turn full attention toward the formation of new habits.

SETTING YOUR OWN PRIORITIES

One should never begin a weight loss program without serious thought about how it interfaces with the rest of the person's life. (The only exception to this is a diet which must begin due to a medical emergency, like a heart attack.) We have talked to literally hundreds of downtrodden dieters who have had their enthusiasm and momentum snuffed out by failing on yet another ill-conceived diet. In many circumstances the rules were so restrictive, the time was so wrong, or the lifestyle was so hectic that it was a no-win situation from the onset. We must give ourselves every opportunity to succeed on these programs. The following guidelines will help accomplish this goal.

1. Never start a weight-loss program just before a holiday season or a planned vacation. Give yourself a month before any of these events occur to lose a few pounds and then to resume the diet after you return to your normal routine. Our greatest hope, however, is that you will be able to take this eighty-four-day program and work straight through without interruption.

2. Make sure you have ample time for food preparation and physical activity. This diet is realistic. It will not require hours of time spent in the kitchen, nor will it demand buckets of money to be spent on specialty food items. However, if you are overcommitted or anxious and are using food to anesthetize this stressful lifestyle, your chances of success are not as great. Take this opportunity to determine if you have one hour per day to commit collectively to new methods of food planning and to exercise, which will be discussed later.

I have one hour per day that I can commit to this program. _____ yes _____ no

If I answered no, how can I change my schedule to carve out the time I need to take care of my body and enact this diet program?

Check the ones you are willing to try:

_____ I can decrease my work schedule.

_____ I can get help in the house or get other family members to help with various chores.

_____ I can curtail my activities, such as volunteer work and save enough time for exercise.

_____ I can decrease my spending so that I can work less and have more free time.

Other possibilities include:

_____

_____

_____

3. Make the Love Hunger diet program a top priority. Being closer to your ideal body weight can make you healthier and more productive. But, sometimes we are reluctant, if not flippant, about new methods and ideas. This reluctance can lead us into the trap of not giving it all we have.

Think of it this way. You may have struggled your entire life with being overweight and with the emotional desire which can accompany poor eating habits. Think of the hurt and absolute anguish that have arisen out of this. Eighty-four days from today, you could be free from these old memories and habits that want to chain your potential. Give this program all you have! Be excited and remain focused!

TOOLS THAT HELP

A few items will help you as you change your patterns and track your progress through this program. Check off the things to which you already have access.

_____ **Bathroom scales.** You should weigh yourself only one time per week. *Do not weigh every day.* Record your weight at the beginning of each week on the Summary Weight Loss Graph on page 356 and on the Weekly Food and Exercise Journal, the first of which is on page 42. Begin doing this next week.

_____ **Pocket spiral notebook.** This may be used if you object to carrying around this manual to journal what you are eating, day by day, meal by meal, hour by hour.

_____ **Measuring cups.** If you do not have an easy-to-use set of measuring cups, get some. Many times what we think is a ½ cup serving can really by ⅔ or even ¾ of a cup.

_____ **Food scales.** Small food scales can usually be purchased for less than five dollars and can be quite revealing when it comes to measuring ounces of meat, cheese, etc.

_____ *Love Hunger.* The best-selling *Love Hunger* book may also be beneficial to you as the body, mind, and soul are explored in depth with regard to weight loss.

DAY 5

YOUR RELATIONSHIP WITH YOUR BODY

The final section of the relationship inventory we ask our patients to work through is their relationship with their bodies. Often their attitude toward their bodies influences their overeating. Work through this section carefully, being as honest with yourself as you can. If you suspect that something might be true, write it down.

YOUR APPEARANCE

How do you feel about your appearance? (For instance, do you often try to wear a bulky sweater to cover up those extra pounds?) Are you ashamed of your extra weight? _____

_____

_____

What did people say to you about your body as a child? (For instance, did Mom or Dad tease you about being overweight? Did either Mom or Dad suggest that you should lose weight or constantly prod you to stay on your diet?)

_____

_____

How did you feel when they teased or prodded you about your weight? (For instance, angry or sad?)

I felt _____ when people teased (or prodded) me about my weight because

_____

_____

_____

Did Mom or Dad compliment you about how you looked? (For instance, did they sometimes say, "You really look great today"? Or "That suit or dress really looks good on you"?)

_____ yes _____ no

Were these instances more frequent than the times they teased or prodded you?

_____ yes _____ no

Your Gender

Were you happy to be a boy or a girl? (Or did you feel, "Dad really wanted a boy" or "Mom really wanted a girl"?) _____ yes _____ no

Can you remember a specific time your dad or mom actually admitted this to you? If so, write it below. How did you feel? What did you do to make yourself feel better? (Or did you just feel that Mom or Dad felt this way? What did they do or say to make you think this way? How did that make you feel?)

_____

_____

_____

Did your parents talk to you about sex? Or did you learn most of what you know about sex from your friends at school? Or did you take a sex education course in school? How do you feel about sex now? _____

_____

_____

How do you feel about your body now? Are you happy with the way you look? Or do you often think, *If I could only lose weight, I would be happy*? Are you living comfortably in your own body? Or are you using food to wrap a protective layer of insulation about your body, especially to insulate yourself sexually?

We will talk about how your relationship with your body might be affecting your hunger during Week 9, Day 4. Just looking at this relationship, however, might cause you to make some associations now. If so, note them here.

DAY 5

Step 1. We admitted we were powerless over our dependencies—that our lives had become unmanageable.

TOTAL SURRENDER

Patients often wonder, *What happens at staff meetings of addiction treatment clinics?* When the staff meets to assess the progress of a patient who suffers from an eating disorder, all the formal data—the nursing notes, the psychological testing, the individual evaluations of therapists—are reviewed carefully.

After that, one question is always asked: "Has this person surrendered yet?"

The single, most important element of a successful recovery from food compulsion and any addiction is the answer to that one simple question.

You might want to ask yourself that now.

Have I surrendered? Have I admitted that I am powerless over my food compulsion—that my life has become unmanageable?

If not, are you willing to do so now? _____ yes _____ no

If your answer is yes, say Step 1 to yourself. Now tell a friend. We always suggest that our patients make this admission to their therapy group, which makes them more personally accountable because they have said it out loud and also makes them accountable to the group. The person you tell should be someone you trust; this person could become one of your supporters during the weeks of the Love Hunger diet.

WEEKLY FOOD AND EXERCISE JOURNAL

Date _____
Weight (First day of week only) _____

	Breakfast/ A.M. Snack	Lunch P.M. Snack	Dinner Nite Snack	Exercise	Feelings and Major Events of the Day
Day One					
Day Two					
Day Three					
Day Four					
Day Five					
Day Six					
Day Seven					

DAY 1

ANALYZING YOUR EATING AND BUYING PATTERNS

This week you will learn how to record your food intake with a daily journal that is provided with this workbook. Then you will learn what foods to purchase in the supermarket to give you your greatest weight loss advantage.

JOURNALING MAKES THE DIFFERENCE

Coming to terms with those small tidbits of cookies, candies, popcorn, cheese, or the notorious "slivers" of "this and that" is a crucial first step for many would-be dieters. So are our suggestions about meal preparation. (For instance, how many times must the potatoes be tasted in order to determine that the salt and pepper are just right?) Our goal in this section is definitely not that you should feel guilty but that you simply learn to recognize that all foods (even bite-sized snacks) have calories and cannot be eaten frivolously when weight loss or perhaps weight maintenance is the goal. We have had many patients fill out food records that revealed a 1200-calorie-a-day intake (or less) with very few snacks, and yet the patient is grossly overweight. This usually means that the patient is not yet ready to admit his true eating habits either to the therapist or to himself.

For the next eighty-four days, we want you to keep a food record of everything that goes into your mouth with the exception of water. This means that you not only keep the diary on the days you stay on your diet program but also on the days when you "blow it." Let us admit that if you get through all twelve weeks with a perfect food diary, you will be the first to accomplish such a feat. This diary is not meant to be a watchdog over you: it's a tool to develop a sense of responsible eating. Often you can learn more from analyzing the days you "blew" your diet, than by feeling good about the days you adhered to the plan.

In order to help you develop your journaling skills, consider the following hints.

1. Write down what you have eaten or drunk immediately. You could even write it down before the food is consumed. Don't wait until the following day or even the end of the same day since tomorrow you won't be able to remember what it is that you have eaten today. To convince yourself of this, try to remember exactly what you ate and drank yesterday and write it here:

Week 2

Breakfast _____

_____

Snack _____

Lunch _____

_____

Snack _____

Dinner _____

Snack _____

Are you sure that's all?

2. Make your journaling easy and convenient. The pages at the end of each weekly lesson are provided for your food and exercise journals. There is one journal page for each week and it includes space for journaling your results for seven separate days. Even though you have lessons for only five days per week, you should keep making entries in your journal every day.

If you do not want to carry around the notebook, you have two options. Detach the workbook pages from the book and use them separately. Or purchase a small, pocket-sized notebook to record daily eating and then transfer the information to your workbook at a more convenient time. The key is this—keep something with you at all times (preferably in your pocket) that will serve as a physical reminder that when food goes in your mouth, it must then be written down in your book. A one-hour lapse in time between these two events will destroy the results you are looking for. Start being honest about your true food intake, not just the food that you remember eating. No one will see this journal unless you want them to.

3. Be accountable to a group or dieting partner. Although we have just stated that the journal is personal and private, you can benefit from having an accountability group or even a dieting partner. Show each other your food diaries on a weekly basis and look for eating patterns. Discuss times of the day that give you the most problems with dieting and talk about alternative activities that might lead to solutions. Try to think of a group or an individual that you might trust with this information and list below. (We do not recommend that spouses take on this role as many times body image and sexuality make it difficult for patients to be honest with their husbands or wives about their food diaries.)

HOW TO USE THE WEEKLY FOOD AND EXERCISE LOG

1. Record your weight. This should be done only on the first day of each week. Do not weigh at any other time. This is difficult for many dieters who are literally addicted to weighing a minimum of one time per day. If necessary, put your scales in another room so they do not cue you in to checking your weight on a daily basis. The rationale for this is that water retention can occur at almost any time. If this is the case for you, then the discouragement of not having lost weight during a particular period of time, or possibly even gaining a few pounds, may cause you to give up and go off the diet.

After you record your weight on the first day of each Weekly Food and Exercise Journal, also record it on the Summary Weight Loss Graph found on page 356. This will help you see your results on a monthly basis.

2. Record all foods eaten—not just the foods that should have been eaten. Honesty is critical when it comes to journaling. Otherwise, nothing at all will be accomplished by this exercise. Be specific as to quantities and methods of food preparation. Everything counts!

3. Record your daily exercise. Write down the number of minutes, miles, or any other definition point that is meaningful to you. This will allow you to recheck your habits and see if you are getting as much exercise as you think you are.

4. Record general impressions of the day. Events can make a difference in how you feel, respond to others, and especially how much you eat. Make a brief notation of the day's most major events. Did you feel happy, sad, stressed? What were you generally feeling that day? This information can serve as a reaffirmation that emotions can drive improper eating habits. It may prove most useful when used retrospectively.

ANALYZING YOUR EATING PATTERNS

The Weekly Food and Exercise Journal will help you pinpoint where your problem areas are. In fact, the analysis of your food journal is probably the crux of the Love Hunger concept. *Why do I eat? Why do I eat in response to certain events? Why does seeing certain people cause me to eat more than I normally would? Why is maintaining a diet so easy on some days?* These complex questions are all part of the analysis of your food journal. As we go through the lessons on family relationships, cue eliminations, behavior modification, the Twelve Step program, and many other crucial issues, your food journal will make more sense. For now, it suffices to say that the more information you record, the more you will find out about your true motivations.

DAY 1

PAIN ON THE OLD HOME FRONT

Few of us realize that babies are born with preconceived notions. The truth is, we are all born with an innate or even God-given need for love from a parent, and if we don't receive that love, we know something is wrong. Psychologists call this need *narcissistic neediness* or *love hunger.*

The physical needs of infants are always obvious. Everyone is scurrying in the delivery room to make sure the all-important first breath is as it should be and on schedule. Then pulse and heart rates are checked and rechecked. Within hours after birth, food hunger pangs will cause that child to verbalize his or her own needs. Beyond these primordial beginnings, all children have a profound need to be connected and involved with a loving parent. That need is so great that it usually requires fifteen to twenty years of sustained, uninterrupted nurturance from a mother and a father to meet this need within a child.

Five components are necessary in satisfying this inborn love hunger of filling the child's love tank.

NEED FOR: THE CHILD INITIALLY ASKS:

Affection	Am I touched? Am I loved? Am I hugged?
Attention	Do I have Mom and Dad's attention or are they always preoccupied with thinking about something else? Am I a priority in my parents' lives or am I a burden?
Time	Are my parents willing or able to slow down enough to take care of me?
Security	Am I safe? Will Mom and Dad be here tomorrow? Are my physical needs being met? Will there be food and shelter tomorrow? Will tomorrow be the same? Does anyone abuse me?
Identity	Do my parents know who they are? Do they feel good about themselves? Can I grow up and use some of these qualities as a pattern in my own life? How should I respond to a member of the opposite sex based on the patterns established by my parents?

WHAT'S EATING YOU?

We've been asking you to think back about some of the components that might have been missing in your childhood. Now think about your current food hunger. When do you get hungry and under what circumstances?

I get hungry in (the afternoon, evening) _____

I get hungry when (I'm working) _____

Now think about that time of day and/or that activity. Could this be related to one of the five components that fill your natural need for love: affection, attention, time, security, or identity? _____ yes _____ no

TIME OF DAY

Do you tend to overeat right before bedtime? How are you feeling when you reach for that snack? Bored? Neglected? Could it be that you are wanting time and affection from your spouse and he or she is not there or not willing to give it to you? So you turn to food.

Now think back to the time of day when you get hungry. How were you feeling? Does that have something to do with your desire for food? _____ yes _____ no

I might be overeating at this time of day because _____

_____

(For instance, you are a businessman or woman and you realize that you are frequently starving at lunchtime. You have to order a complete meal to satisfy your hunger, even though you know you should only eat a salad. Is your hunger during work hours really coincidental? Or could you be driven by the challenges you are facing at work, which make you feel insecure?)

I might be overeating when I am (working) _____ because _____

_____

DAY 1

STEP 2: WE CAME TO BELIEVE THAT A POWER GREATER THAN OURSELVES COULD RESTORE US TO SANITY.

The phrase "came to believe" in Step 2 suggests a progression of faith that evolves over time. Members of AA say it this way:

First, we came. We physically showed up and stumbled through the door.
Second, we came to. We sobered up and came to our senses. We began to
experience emotional sobriety.
Third, we came to believe.

When Ebby Thatcher went to see Bill Wilson seventy years ago, Bill saw images of his childhood in his mind as Ebby talked about his newfound faith. "I could almost hear the sound
of the preacher's voice as I sat on Sundays," Wilson says in the *Big Book,* "way over there on
the hillside; there was that proffered temperance pledge I never signed; my grandfather's good-
natured contempt of some church folk and their doings; his denial of the preacher's right to
tell him how he must listen; his fearlessness as he spoke of these things just before he died."[1]

All of us have been affected by our relatives' beliefs about God and events that happened
in our childhoods. As you begin to work through Step 2, look at your relationship with God
by answering the following questions in a relationship inventory.

YOUR RELATIONSHIP WITH GOD

Check or circle your answers to the following questions.

My family (did, did not) attend church.

_____ Instead I went by myself.

_____ I did not attend church.

_____ I went to church with one parent while one stayed home or attended another denomi-
nation.

_____ My family alternated between two denominations.

What were you taught about God as a child (in Sunday school or by what your parents and
relatives said)?

I was taught that God was _____

_____

_____

Have you ever become disillusioned about God? If so, when? Why?

I became disillusioned about God when _____

because _____

_____

_____

Do you ever feel that the faith of your childhood has failed you? Sometimes our patients will say to us, "God allowed me to become addicted to food" or "God allowed me to become addicted to work, and my life has spiraled downhill ever since. Therefore, I will have nothing to do with God." When patients feel this way, we often remind them that God did not create us as puppets under His full control; instead we can make decisions throughout our lives. "God did not cause you to become addicted," we tell them. "He gave us free will, and sometimes the inappropriate exercise of our will by us or our parents has planted the seeds of addiction."

I feel as if my faith has failed me because _____

_____

_____

_____

Laying aside your past bitterness against God and the church is such an important part of your spiritual recovery, that the "Big Book" of *Alcoholics Anonymous* says, "We who have traveled this dubious path, beg you to lay aside prejudice, even against organized religion. We have learned that whatever the human frailties of various faiths may be, those faiths have given purpose and direction to millions."[2]

DAY 2

THE REWARD SYSTEM

It has been said that positive reinforcement is the most effective teacher. We want you to set up your own reinforcement and reward system in the chart below. Reward yourself for every ten pounds that you lose, starting from your initial weight that you just recorded.

Rewards for a ten-pound weight loss might include a new record or tape, new clothes, the golf club you've always wanted, makeup, or a new haircut. *The only thing we do not want you to reward yourself with is food.* Also, do not lighten your standards, thinking you can get away with more eating and continue to lose weight—it usually doesn't work that way.

Now fill out the chart and decide what you will reward yourself with for each ten-pound loss.

SUMMARY WEIGHT LOSS GRAPH

I have now lost	Date accomplished	My reward will be
10 pounds		
20 pounds		
30 pounds		
40 pounds*		

*Although 40 pounds is the most that anyone could expect to lose during the course of this program, don't stop here if you need to go further with your weight control. Make up a new chart and start fresh with a new set of goals and rewards.

A note about weight loss: Men tend to lose weight faster and in greater quantities than do women. Men will lose between twenty-two and even forty pounds during the twelve-week period of instruction provided by this workbook. Women will lose between ten and thirty pounds during this same period of time. Your rate of loss will depend on:

1. Your starting weight. The more weight there is to lose, the faster it will be lost. That last ten pounds, on the other hand, will be the most difficult to lose.

2 Your calorie intake. Fewer calories eaten mean quicker weight loss. Also, a low-fat diet will increase the rate of weight loss.

3. Your exercise level. A steady exercise program will increase your rate of weight loss by at least 30 percent.

DAY 2

THE COMMON THREAD

Today we would like you to apply the Love Hunger concept to your own life. Think back to your childhood. You had a natural need to satisfy your inborn hunger for love by feeling your parents' affection, by receiving their attention, by spending time with them, by feeling the security of their love, and by observing their identity as a way to establish your own identity.

Is there a time when you turned to food as a substitute for affection or attention or time or security or identity?

As a child, I first turned to food as a substitute for affection or time or security or identity when

_____

_____

Later, in high school, I turned to food as a substitute for affection or attention or time or security or identity when _____

_____

_____

Once I left home, I turned to food as a substitute for affection or attention or time or security or identity when _____

_____

_____

A "TRIGGER EVENT"

Looking back over these events, is there something in common? A feeling you might have had? A type of event, such as a new or uncertain situation? We call this a "trigger event," one that you need to recognize so you will know when you are likely to overeat and so you can identify the underlying emotional need that you are filling.

If one event or feeling was present all of these times, write it here. _____

_____

_____

Next time you find yourself in such an event, beware. Try some truthful self-talk, like "I don't have to overeat when I feel insecure. Instead I can devote that energy to _____
(if you overeat at work, you might devote that energy to a strategic plan to meet the challenge you are facing).

DAY 2

Step 2. We came to believe that a Power greater than ourselves could restore us to sanity.

RENOUNCING FALSE GODS

An important part of Step 2 is to renounce all the false gods that have been keeping you from the one true God. To be addicted means to "devote or give (oneself) habitually"; to worship means "to love or pursue devotedly." An addiction becomes a god to the addict.

During the first step you admitted that you were powerless over your overeating and that your life was out of control. Look back at those hidden addictions you identified in that first week. These hidden addictions need to be renounced or they will remain your gods.

I renounce the false gods of _____

_____

_____

_____

There are three other major false gods—intellectualism, self, and other people or human institutions.

INTELLECTUALISM

Bill Wilson was caught by this false god. "I had always believed in a Power greater than myself," he says. "I was not an atheist. Few people really are, for that means blind faith in the strange proposition that this universe originated in a cipher and aimlessly rushes nowhere. My intellectual heroes, the chemists, the astronomers, even the evolutionists, suggested vast laws and forces at work. Despite contrary indications, I had little doubt that a mighty purpose and rhythm underlay all. How could there be so much of precise and immutable law, and no intelligence? I simply had to believe in a Spirit of the Universe, who knew neither time nor limitation. But that was as far as I had gone.

"With ministers, and the world's religions, I parted right there. When they talked of a God personal to me, who was love, superhuman strength and direction, I became irritated and my mind snapped shut against such a theory."[3]

Ebby Thatcher, "a man who had been taken from the scrap heap to a level of life better than the best he had ever known,"[4] challenged Wilson to reconsider. During the next days and months, Bill opened his mind to the thought of a personal God.

SELF

Most of us tend to put ourselves in the role of God. We want control over other people, and we want what is best for us. To walk through Step 2, we have to be willing to renounce selfishness and narcissism.

OTHER HUMAN BEINGS AND INSTITUTIONS

We also have to be willing to knock a few human false gods off their pedestals. Sometimes a spouse becomes a god. We expect them to love and care for us as only God can. Then we are disappointed when they turn out to be human. Other times we have joined a movement or worshiped a guru whom we considered to be perfect.

Are you caught in worshiping any of these other gods? A spouse who enables you to continue overeating? A selfish desire to please your hunger for food? Why not renounce these false gods as you did your hidden addictions?

Now that you've renounced the false gods in your life, consider looking for the real God, a personal Friend to walk with you through your recovery process.

DAY 3

SUPERMARKET SMARTS

The rest of this week in the Body portion of your workbook is designed to help you make it through the grocery store without falling for old favorites that may be calling your name. Many of the products we recommend may be unfamiliar to you. Try them. You will find most of them to be wonderful alternatives to their higher-fat, higher-calorie counterparts. As you go through the food lists that follow, check off the foods that appeal to you so you won't forget to purchase them.

Note that these lists are intended to be a guide to help you with selection of food items both during the weight loss period and afterward, when you are maintaining your weight. Special nutritional information is listed below some of the products we are recommending to help you determine when these products might be appropriate to use.

SUPERMARKET SMARTS SHOPPING GUIDE

General Information. The shopping guide is meant to give you some new ideas about what might end up in your shopping cart. Although there won't be many interactive questions in this portion of the workbook, the practical applications will occur with the list you work from on your next trip to the supermarket. Mark items you intend to investigate or purchase as you go through each food group.

BREADS

In general, yeast breads are extremely low in fat, cholesterol, and even sodium. Fast breads, including muffins, cornbread, biscuits, pancakes, and waffles, inherently contain a higher percentage of fat, and are not recommended unless made at home where the ingredients can be controlled. Although we always recommend natural or whole-grain products first, be aware that some grain-packed, heavy health breads are also packed with fat (though usually polyunsaturated) and calories. You don't get overweight just on junk food.

Light or lite breads containing 40 calories per slice (look for local brands by your regional bakers). These are used throughout the menu exchanges and offer good fiber and carbohydrate sources for the dieter. Two slices are the same as one slice of regular sandwich bread.

Very thin-sliced breads usually contain 35 calories per slice. They offer a low-calorie choice for those who want an all-natural product with the same calories as the light breads. However, they crumble easily and are often dry tasting.

100 percent whole wheat bread or other whole-grain alternatives are your best bet after your weight has been lost and more calories can be added to your daily diet plan. Unless it specifically says "100 percent" then chances are you are getting a product that is mostly made from white flour with enough whole wheat flour to call it by that name.

Pita bread is a low-fat, flat bread. Generally, one-half a pita pocket contains the same nutritional value as one or two slices of regular bread.

English muffins and bagels average about 150 calories per whole muffin (two sides). These should be used as an alternative to higher fat biscuits, which contain large amounts of shortening. Both bagels and English muffins contain less than 10 percent fat.

Corn tortillas usually average 65 calories each with about 15 percent of the calories coming from fat. They can be cut into julienne strips for interesting salad toppings, can be used as part of Southwestern recipe cuisine, or may simply be used as a bread substitute. Flour tortillas almost always contain lard, and more calories (100–200 calories per tortilla).

DAY 3

FILLING LOVE TANKS

The filling of love tanks within new human beings is a huge commitment. Think of it this way—when babies are born, they may be cuddly and cute, but their ability to love and be selfless is at zero, and their love tanks are registering empty as is shown in the heart diagram below. In order for a child's love tank to be filled, not only must the five love tank components be present, but the child should have two parents who are sane, sober, and relatively at peace with themselves and each other. By sane, we mean that there is no significant emotional illness in either of the parents. By sober, we mean that the parents are not chemically addicted and also that they are not addicted to something else, like power, money, materialism, beauty, success. By peace with each other, we mean that both parents should feel good about themselves and with each other. Parents are unable to give away what they do not possess. How can the child learn about happiness from parents who have poor self-esteem or are basically unhappy with themselves?

Anything that interrupts or aborts that love flow from parent to child will result in the child's having an incompletely filled love tank. If this is the case, that child can emerge into adolescence or adulthood with unmet emotional needs or emotional codependency. This is, in essence, "love hunger" and forms the emotional and mental foundation of adult food codependency or food addiction.

LOVE TANKS

Look at the set of love tanks below; think about your childhood and then write about the experiences that flowed positively from your parents' love tanks into your own. List some positive memories, moments when your mother and father were helpful in filling your own childhood love tank. Be general, like, "My mom was always interested in my activities," and specific, like "I remember the day the guys made fun of me on the bus, mom talked to me about what happened, and then we went to the Dairy Queen® for a cone." Write whatever comes to mind. Even small things can be very significant in a child's mind.

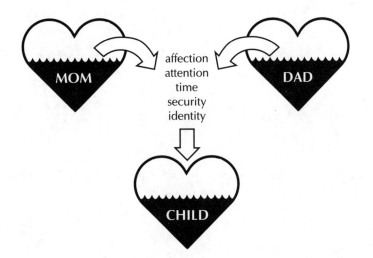

POSITIVE EXPERIENCES

AFFECTION

I remember a time when I felt that mom and/or dad really loved me. They (he or she)

_____

_____

_____

ATTENTION

I remember a time when I felt as if I had my mom's and/or dad's full attention. They (he or she)

_____

_____

_____

TIME

I remember a time when I felt as if I had lots of my mom's and/or dad's time. They (he or she)

_____

_____

_____

SECURITY

I remember a time when I felt very secure as a child. I was _____

_____

_____

IDENTITY

I remember a time when I really felt as if my mom and dad knew who they were and what they wanted out of life. I saw their goal in life as _____

_____

_____

I determined to model that goal in my life. ____ yes ____ no

DAY 3

Step 2. We came to believe that a Power greater than ourselves could restore us to sanity.

HUNGRY FOR HIS LOVE

Some patients' love hunger does not come from their childhood families. Instead their love hunger is spiritual, a yearning for God's unconditional love. There is a God-shaped vacuum inside all humans.

We would like you to look further into your relationship with God to see if you might, in fact, be hungry for His love. Read through the following ten statements and write yes if they apply to you, no if they don't.

____ 1. I see God as someone who cares personally and intimately for me and my welfare.

____ 2. I view God as a source of unconditional love.

____ 3. God is someone with whom I can dialogue openly and freely about my problems and my needs.

____ 4. I trust that God hears and responds to my deepest needs and concerns.

____ 5. I question whether or not God genuinely loves me and accepts me.

____ 6. I see God as a harsh, stern disciplinarian, and I fear His punishment and wrath.

____ 7. I am angry and bitter at God about past failures, illnesses, and disappointments. I wonder why God has not spared me from these.

____ 8. God seems distant and remote from me.

____ 9. I imagine God's agenda is filled with people and things far more important than me. Surely He doesn't notice me.

____ 10. Some part of me feels so unworthy, I question if I could ever win God's love and approval.

DAY 4

CEREALS AND CRACKERS

HIGH FIBER CEREALS (WHEAT BRAN VARIETIES)

The consumption of wheat bran or insoluble fibers in a calorie-restricted diet may speed your weight loss, because it pushes the food bolus (mass) along at a faster rate through the intestine. When 25 or more grams of dietary fiber per day are consumed, then less fat may be absorbed from the digesting foods and more calories are excreted.

Miller's Bran or unprocessed wheat bran contains only 60 calories per ½ cup. This size portion will provide you with about 13 grams of dietary fiber. When you add this to a diet containing fresh vegetables, fruits, and whole grains, the recommended 25 to 30 grams of daily fiber is attainable. Without this supplement, you will not be able to reach 25 grams of dietary fiber per day, especially on a calorie-restricted diet program. Companies offering unprocessed wheat bran include Hodgson Mill, Arrowhead Mills, and other local or regional brands. Miller's Bran is so low in calories that you may use it anytime, up to ⅓ cup per day, over other cereals or in mixed foods such as meatloaf and other casseroles.

Fiber One® cereal is a cold, ready-to-eat, breakfast cereal that contains NutraSweet®. It also provides about 12 grams of dietary fiber per ½ cup serving (60 calories worth). Other similar products include Bran Buds™ and All-Bran Extra™.

MEDIUM FIBER CEREALS (WHEAT BRAN)

These cereals contain about one-third as much fiber as the ones previously listed and about twice as many calories. For example, you would have to eat over 300 calories' worth of 40 percent bran flakes and over 400 calories of Fruit n' Fiber to give you the same amount of fiber as only 60 calories' worth of Miller's Bran or Fiber One®.

Fruit & Fibre® provides roughly 4 grams of fiber and 140 calories per ⅔ cup serving.

Raisin Bran in most brands is 120 calories per serving and provides 4 grams of fiber.

Multi-Bran Chex® or Post Bran Flakes® are both 110 calories per serving. Bran Chex are especially good snack items when made into a seasoned, low-fat snack mix with pretzels and other cereals. (See the *Love Hunger* book for details of this recipe.)

OAT BRAN CEREALS

Note: Oat bran and other soluble fibers have been touted as the cholesterol cure across the country. The truth is, they can make a difference for the person who has an elevated serum cholesterol level. The rule of thumb is that if you consume 5 grams of soluble fiber per day, the serum cholesterol level may drop by 5 percent. Five grams is roughly equivalent to two oat bran muffins (not a good choice for calorie counters) or one serving of a cooked or dry oat bran cereal.

Arrowhead Mills Oat Bran Cereal is intended to be a cooked, hot cereal. It contains 6 grams of dietary fiber and 110 calories per 1 cup of cooked cereal.

Oatmeal by Quaker® and other companies provides about 120 calories per serving and contains about 2 to 3 grams of dietary fiber.

CRACKERS AND CRISPIES

Hain Mini Rice Cakes (Teriyaki cheese, apple cinnamon, barbeque, plain, honey nut) are a nice alternative to crackers. Five cakes contain 50 to 70 calories depending on the flavor.

Large Rice Cakes made by Quaker®, Chico San, Crispy Cakes, and Hain, usually contain 100 calories per 2 or 3 cakes.

Fattorie and Pandea Whole Wheat (or sesame) breadsticks are wonderful alternatives to garlic bread when you are having salad or an Italian dinner. This brand contains only 57 calories for a package of three 10- to 12-inch sticks. An added advantage is that you don't feel the need to add butter as you do with bread.

Pretzels can be your chip alternative. They come in plain, whole wheat, soft, hard, and unsalted. Something for everyone. In general, 1 ounce is about 100 calories. For example, 22 Mr. Salty® sticks are about 100 calories.

Popcorn is about 100 calories for 3 cups of popped corn if made in the following manner. Pop the corn in a microwave or air popper. Then spray with butter-flavored Pam® and sprinkle with a butter substitute.

DAY 4

NEGATIVE EXPERIENCES

Yesterday you thought about the positive experiences in your childhood, those times that were really special. Yet, since no one is perfect, your childhood couldn't have been perfect. (Your parents weren't perfect, and believe it or not, you weren't perfect either.)

Now we'd like you to think about what was missing in your childhood. This is not easy to remember, since we all want to imagine that we had the perfect family. Finding fault in our parents is not easy. Be assured that this will help you along your road to food addiction recovery. (Next week we will talk about specific abuses, but right now just list negative experiences.) Categorize your answers within the same five love tank categories.

AFFECTION

I remember times when I felt that Mom and Dad didn't love me. _____

_____

_____

_____

Did I sometimes fill this love hunger with food? ____ yes ____ no

I would _____

_____

_____

_____

ATTENTION

I remember times when I felt that Mom and Dad were not interested in what I was doing. They were preoccupied with _____

_____

I sometimes filled this love hunger with food. I would _____

_____

TIME

I remember times when I felt that Mom and Dad never had any time for me. Their agenda was filled with _____

_____

I sometimes filled this love hunger with food. I would _____

_____

SECURITY

I remember times when I felt very insecure. We, in the family, felt threatened by _____

_____

I sometimes filled this love hunger with food. I would_____

_____

IDENTITY

I remember times when I felt very uncertain of who I was and where I was going. Mom or Dad's own identities seemed fragmented by _____

_____

I sometimes filled this love hunger with food. I would _____

_____

DAY 4

Step 2. We came to believe that a Power greater than ourselves could restore us to sanity.

LOOKING THROUGH NEW GLASSES

Today we'd like you to think about those earlier statements about God. Now think about your mother and father or another person who raised you. Put that person's name (instead of God's) in the blanks below.

1. I see (Dad or Mom or another person) _____ as someone who cares personally and intimately for me and my welfare.

2. I view (Dad or Mom or another person) _____ as a source of nonjudgmental and unconditional love.

3. (Dad or Mom or another person) _____ is someone with whom I can dialogue openly and freely about my problems and my needs.

4. I trust that (Dad or Mom or another person) _____hears and responds to my deepest needs and concerns.

5. I question whether or not (Dad or Mom or another person) _____ genuinely loves me and accepts me.

6. I see (Dad or Mom or another person _____ as a harsh, stern disciplinarian, and I fear his or her disapproval, punishment, and wrath.

7. I am angry and bitter at (Dad or Mom or another person) _____ about past failures, illnesses, and disappointments. I wonder why _____ has not spared me from these.

8. (Dad or Mom or another person) _____ seems distant and remote from me.

9. I imagine (Dad or Mom or another person) _____'s agenda is filled with people and things far more important than I. Surely (Dad or Mom or another person) _____ doesn't notice me.

10. Some part of me feels so unworthy. I question if I could ever win (Dad or Mom or another person) _____'s love and approval.

Now go back to page 57 and refer to the ten statements about God. Which statements are similar to your statements about God? The statements you associated with your mom? Your dad? Another person who raised you?

My description of God is similar to my description of _____

Many of our patients who have completed these questionnaires find a striking similarity between their description of God and their description of their fathers.

If you are currently having difficulty accepting God's love and help, you may never have felt that your dad loved you or helped you. Parents are your earliest representation of God. In fact, parents *are* gods in the lives of their children. If you were emotionally or physically abused by a parent, this may severely taint your perspective or emotional relationship with God.

It's almost as if you are seeing God through a distorted set of glasses. In fact, a major recovery writer, Chuck C, wrote a book called *A New Pair of Glasses,* in which he said his own spiritual conversion and rebirth were like taking off one old pair of glasses, through which he had been seeing God, and putting on a different set.[5] God was not the one who changed. This man's perspective of God changed during his Twelve Step recovery process. What pair of glasses are you using to see God?

DAY 5

DAIRY, DESSERTS, AND CONVENIENCE FOODS

LOW-FAT CHEESES

Most low-fat cheeses are from 4 to 7 grams of fat per 1-ounce serving. Cheeses made from skim or part-skim milk should be your only choices. Never consider the whole milk cheese. Regular "rat" cheese is as much as 85% fat. Just look through your dairy case, and you will see many new low-fat products.

Alpine Lace® Cheeses are good-tasting Swiss, provolone, mozzarella, American, and cheddar that are from 70 to 100 calories per 1-ounce serving. The sodium content ranges from 35 to 200 milligrams per serving.

Weight Watchers® cheese selection includes sharp cheddar, Monterey Jack, Swiss, mild cheddar, and colby. A 1-ounce serving is approximately 80 calories and contains 5 grams of fat.

Kraft™, like most of the large food producers, has paid attention to the growing number of people who are watching their fat intake. Their Light Naturals, which include mild cheddar, sharp cheddar, Swiss, and Monterey Jack, average 80 calories and 5 grams of fat per 1-ounce serving.

Borden's Lite-Line,® or similar alternatives, has 35 calories per slice and only 2 grams of fat. It comes in American, Swiss, and cheddar flavors.

Frigo Lite® from Frigo Cheese Corporation is shredded mozzarella. For a 1-ounce serving there are 60 calories and 2 grams of fat.

DAIRY PRODUCTS

Skim Milk. Later in the nutritional section, the reasons for purchasing skim milk are fully explained.

Dannon Light 'n Fit® yogurt makes a nutritional snack at about 100 calories for the 8-ounce serving with no fat at all.

Yoplait® yogurt cartons contain 6 ounces with no fat and 90 calories.

Daisy® Light sour cream has 40 calories per 2 tablespoons and contains 3 grams of fat.

Cottage cheese. Buy the light products.

Carnation® Skimmed Milk, evaporated. This is a good product to keep in your kitchen for cooking and baking. For ½ cup (prepared), there are 100 calories and less than 1 gram of fat.

Egg Beaters® by Nabisco™ can be very helpful as an egg substitute in recipes or prepared according to directions on the carton for breakfast. The equivalent of one egg is 25 calories with no fat and no cholesterol.

MARGARINES

Smart Beat® margarine has only 25 calories per tablespoon and 3 grams of fat.

Promise® Extra Light margarine by Lever Brothers has 50 calories per tablespoon with 6 grams of fat.

Diet Mazola® margarine has 50 calories and 6 grams of fat per tablespoon.

Whipped Butter (any brand) usually has only 60 calories per tablespoon.

DESSERTS AND FROZEN TREATS

Jell-O® Pudding Mix, regular, cook 'n' serve made with skim milk has about 130 calories per ½ cup. When you mix it with fruit you can dilute the calories to meet your 100-calorie dessert limit.

Jell-O® Pudding Mix, sugar-free, cook 'n' serve is the diabetic's alternative to the regular pudding. (We suggest that you use the regular one unless you have a sugar restriction in your diet.) It contains only 60 calories per ½ cup serving if it is made with skim milk.

Non-fat Frozen Yogurt by Wells Dairy. Try frozen yogurt for a light dessert: 3 ounces contain 50 calories, no fat.

Blue Bell® Light is one of the many low-calorie ice creams or ice milks in the freezer case. Most varieties contain approximately 100 calories for a ½ cup serving, and they are very low in fat, usually 20 percent.

Cool Whip® Lite by General Foods makes a nice garnish for some of the desserts in *Love Hunger,* or your own low-calorie desserts, puddings (above), or fresh fruits. One tablespoon contains less than 1 gram of fat and 8 calories.

Fresh Lites® by Dole are a refreshing snack. At 25 calories per bar (with no fat), enjoy them frequently.

Popsicle Lick'em Lights™ are a fun snack at only 18 calories.

CONDIMENTS AND DRESSINGS

Molly McButter® is a wonderful diet aid. It comes in natural butter, cheese, and sour cream flavors. Add this product to vegetables, popcorn, or baked potatoes for added flavor. One-half teaspoon contains 4 calories and no fat. There are other similar brands of this type of product. Try them all.

Kraft™ (Oil) Free dressings range from 4 to 20 calories per tablespoon.

Hidden Valley® Take Heart dressings, blue cheese, Italian, and thousand island, range from 12 to 20 calories per tablespoon.

Hellman's® Light Mayonnaise and similar dressings are approximately 50 calories per tablespoon.

Mustards are generally your best sandwich condiment choice. They contain only 6 calories per tablespoon and no fat.

DAY 5

FACING NEGATIVE FEELINGS

Now that you've taken a look at a few of the positive and negative experiences in your childhood, we want you to take another visit to your childhood home. Imagine yourself walking up to the front door of the house you grew up in. Notice the trees, the walkway, the front door.

What is the feeling in the pit of your stomach as you approach that door?

I feel _____

Who will greet you? _____

This is a weekday, and you have just returned from school. What do you think about as you approach that door after school? (Some of our patients, who were raised in alcoholic homes, would wonder, *Has Mom or Dad been drinking? What will I find when I open that door?* One patient frequently phoned home ahead to see what was going on so he would be prepared.)

As I open the door I am wondering _____

_____

Are you happy to be home? (Was your home a refuge where you could be honest about your personal needs and feelings?)

I am/am not happy to be home because _____

_____

As you walk through that door, do you feel afraid? Or tense? Or angry?

As I walk through that door, I am feeling _____ because _____

_____

_____

Is there any association between your feelings now and the trigger event you identified earlier this week? _____ yes _____ no

If not, could this experience be another trigger event _____ yes _____ no

Another trigger event for me is _____

_____

_____

DAY 5

Step 2. We came to believe that a Power greater than ourselves could restore us to sanity.

OPENING THE DOOR

Bill Wilson says in the "Big Book," "It was only a matter of being willing to believe in a Power greater than myself. Nothing more was required of me to make my beginning. I saw that growth could start from that point. . . . Thus was I convinced that God is concerned with us humans when we want Him enough. At long last, I saw, I felt, I believed."[6]

The importance of renewal, rebirth, and regeneration in the spiritual aspects of recovery cannot be stressed enough. Perhaps you are an agnostic who has never known God, and therefore in the recovery process you must discover who God is and allow Him to enter your life in order that the recovery process can work. Or perhaps you are a long-term church member and have had the knowledge of God and the belief in God for many years but recognize the absence of a close feeling toward God. Perhaps you have never let God enter into your recovery process from food addiction.

Do your old feelings tell you that God is mean, remote, and inaccessible? Lay aside these feelings and write down what you wish or imagine God to be like. In order to complete this exercise successfully, you must discount all biases and be creative with your character sketch.

If I could make a job description for God and list characteristics I would want to have in the God I believe in, they would include _____

_____

_____

If the God you want to be with you during the recovery process from food addiction is a loving, caring, merciful, just, omnipotent God, then you're in luck! There is good news! There is a God in the universe that meets all of those requirements. He is the one true God and is all of the wonderful things that you would hope and expect Him to be. Break out of the old biases and chains that bind you and read more about this marvelous and beneficent God in the Bible.

Often patients say to us, "Okay, maybe I do need to grow closer to God, but how do I do that? What are the mechanics of it?"

We answer, "Willingness. If you can just crack the door a little bit, then God will begin to direct you in that process."

Sam Shoemaker, Bill Wilson's minister, wrote a book called *I Stand by the Door*. In it he pictured Christ by the door of each of our hearts, knocking on that door to enter in. All we have to do is open the door—just a crack.

WEEKLY FOOD AND EXERCISE JOURNAL

Date _____
Weight (First day of week only) _____

	Breakfast/ A.M. Snack	Lunch P.M. Snack	Dinner Nite Snack	Exercise	Feelings and Major Events of the Day
Day One					
Day Two					
Day Three					
Day Four					
Day Five					
Day Six					
Day Seven					

DAY 1

EXERCISE AND METABOLISM

It is impossible to talk about weight loss and weight maintenance without giving equal time to the topic of physical activity and exercise. Many experts agree that it is very difficult for some persons to lose weight or to keep that weight off once it has been lost unless an exercise program is in place. And it's not just any exercise that counts—specifically, it is aerobic exercise that will aid you in accomplishing your goals. Too many times aerobic exercise is simply thought of as an activity which demands that you wear hot pink tights and join in with a "Jane Fonda-like" dance class comprised primarily of young women who already appear to be in great shape. Yet aerobic exercise includes a wide variety of activities, many of which you can enjoy in your own home.

DEFINITION OF AEROBIC EXERCISE

Aerobic simply means "with air" and refers to activities of moderate, sustained intensity, which utilize some or all of the major muscle groups, including the leg, thigh, buttock, and arm muscles. Examples include fast walking, jogging, cycling, swimming, cross-country skiing, rowing, aerobic dancing, and any other activity that can keep your heart at a quickened pace for at least twenty nonstop minutes.

WEIGHT CONTROL, GOOD HEALTH, AND EXERCISE

Many weight control researchers have gone so far as to say that anyone who has been significantly overweight cannot successfully lose weight and expect to retain that weight loss without a consistent exercise program for the rest of the person's life. It is no less important than a proper diet is when trying to lose weight. Now wait! Before you panic because this prescription just doesn't sound like you, consider these added benefits of establishing an exercise program in your life.

1. Exercise increases your metabolic rate. The natural survival tendency of the human body is to cut back on calorie expenditures when faced with energy deprivation (or a calorie-restricted diet). The body will also preferentially burn muscle as its energy source and save fat for the last fuel to be used before starvation begins. When this happens, the person may experience a weakness within the muscles that begins to make activities more tiresome and difficult. The general appearance in this case might be what we would term "flabby" since that person is no longer losing as much fat tissue. Exercise helps offset these basic physiological responses. Somehow exercise seems to send a message to the body that we are not suffering from deprivation in the seven-year drought but are intentionally causing this calorie restriction.

In summary, exercise will cause your muscles to burn calories while you are exercising and also continue burning them at an increased rate for an additional five to eight hours after your exercise session has ceased. It will also cause you to retain your muscle mass during a dieting program. All of these things increase your Basal Metabolic Rate (BMR) so that you can lose weight more quickly; in fact up to 30 percent more quickly than someone who just diets and does not exercise.

2. Exercise burns fat. During the first thirty to forty minutes of a moderately strenuous workout (such as walking two miles in thirty minutes) you will deplete your muscles of their carbohydrate energy reserves which are stored right inside the muscles. After this fuel source is gone, the muscles will begin burning fat stored as their immediate energy source. Exercising for sixty-minute intervals therefore provides a great benefit in the actual reduction of fat tissue since the exerted muscles use this as a direct fuel source.

3. Moderate exercise will reduce your appetite. Moderate aerobic exercise such as the programs suggested in this workbook will affect the hunger-control center in your brain and make you less hungry. Though some questions exist as to how this happens it does seem clear that the increased exercise helps insulin get glucose into the cells more efficiently.

4. Exercise helps reduce stress and depression. Depression and stress often cause overeating. When moderate exercise has occurred, the body secretes what are known as endogenous opiates, or endorphins. These chemicals are naturally occurring narcotics made by the body and can help relieve depression and promote a feeling of euphoria.

5. Exercise will help with weight maintenance. Since exercise increases your muscle mass, your body will be functioning at a higher metabolic level than before. Muscles are never "off." Instead, they are either working hard or are constantly burning calories while idling. This round-the-clock usage of calories will help you maintain your new weight loss.

6. Exercise will decrease your risk of developing heart disease by lowering blood pressure and serum cholesterol.

7. Physical activity helps prevent constipation. This can be a side-effect of any weight loss program. A daily walk will alleviate this problem in combination with an adequate fiber and fluid intake.

Look at the following chart and begin thinking about establishing your exercise routine.

YOUR EXERCISE Rx

Duration: 30 to 60 minutes of aerobic activity per session. An additional 5-minute warm-up and 5-minute cool-down is also needed.

Frequency: 5 to 7 times per week for weight loss 3 to 4 times per week for weight maintenance

Intensity: 65 to 85 percent of your maximum heart rate or a level that allows you to talk (between heavier breaths) while exercising (Use the formula given above to determine your own exercising pulse rate range.)

Activities: Fast walking, swimming, rowing, jogging, water aerobics, aerobic dancing, skiing, circuit training

---

DAY 1

PASSIVE ABUSE

Passive abuse, while not as readily apparent as active or physical abuse, can be just as devastating. Passive abuse is typically manifested when parents are preoccupied with any of the "isms" (workaholism, alcoholism, or even perfectionism to the extent that it consumes most of their being) and are thus incapable of being there for their children when they are needed. Passive abuse can also occur when there is a chronic emotional or physical illness on the part of a parent or another sibling: time and energy demands can be such that a child may feel neglected.

These "sins of omission" may be denied by both parent and child, but it is important for you, as you pursue recovery, to recognize abuse of this sort in your life. The following list is designed to help you acknowledge past hurts and voids.

Abuse	Check for Yes	Name of the Abuse
Abandonment (physical or emotional)	____	_____
Divorce	____	_____
Death	____	_____
Separation	____	_____
Parents gone much of the time	____	_____
Parents unable to give attention to children	____	_____
One or both parents were depressed	____	_____
An emotionally guarded parent	____	_____
An emotionally hysterical or overly expressive parent	____	_____
A parent with obsessive-compulsive behavior:		
____ excessive worrying	____	_____
____ excessive guilt	____	_____
____ cleaning/organization compulsions	____	_____
____ money hoarding	____	_____
____ sexual or relationship addictions	____	_____
____ perfectionism	____	_____
____ shopaholism	____	_____
____ busyaholism	____	_____
____ foodaholism	____	_____
Failure to provide adequate affection	____	_____
Failure to model appropriate intimacy with spouse	____	_____
Failure to honor the sexual fidelity boundaries of their marriage	____	_____
Rigid imposition of parental perspectives of God onto the child	____	_____
Transmission to the child of a harsh, overly judgmental picture of God (often based on the parent's own insecurity)	____	_____
Parent attempted to function as a "god" in the child's life	____	_____

DAY 1

♥

STEP 3: WE MADE A DECISION TO TURN OUR WILL AND OUR LIVES OVER TO THE CARE OF GOD, AS WE UNDERSTAND HIM.

It is interesting that the statement "There is one who has all power—that One is God. May you find Him now!"[1] is found in the paragraph that introduces all of the Twelve Steps, a strong indication of the emphasis on finding God as the source to recovery for your food addiction. Although the language in Step 2 is phrased "Power greater than . . . ," it is quite evident that the Power is God and that He is the One God. This is the unmistakable message from Bill Wilson regarding the exact nature of the "Power greater than ourselves."

At the same time, Bill Wilson emphasizes the Twelve Steps as suggestions and invitations—and the word *suggestions* is double underlined. He is so afraid people may rebel against dogma that he offers Step 3—in the same manner he offers all the other steps—as an invitation instead of a demand or prerequisite for religious faith.

We cannot overemphasize the significance of the spiritual understanding in which Bill Wilson invites you and every person in addiction recovery. To get a better understanding of what God is like, let's go back to the list of ten statements about God which we examined last week and see if any of them agree with the God of the Bible.

UNDERSTANDING WHO GOD IS: DISPELLING COMMON MISCONCEPTIONS

The following statements are accompanied by Scripture verses that prove or disprove the statement as a valid characteristic of God. Write your response to these statements in the blanks that follow.

I QUESTION WHETHER GOD GENUINELY LOVES ME AND ACCEPTS ME

One reason I may doubt God's love for me is that _____

_____

_____

The thing I think He might have a hard time accepting about me is _____

_____

_____

My perception of God's love for me and His acceptance of me could be influenced by how much I love/accept myself because _____

_____

_____

Jesus Christ is a symbol of the bridge between you and God. God's love for you is not conditional—it's not even based on the condition that you ever love Him back.

God's love for you is there. It's already shaped and full and complete. If you are having a hard time locking into a sense of God's love for you, it might be because you have avoided any kind of relationship with God. God's love for you is already complete. Your *awareness* of that love is made complete only in the process of a growing relationship with Him.

I See God as a Harsh, Stern Disciplinarian and I Fear His Punishment and Wrath

According to John 3:17, God's primary goal for the world is not judgment, but reunion and salvation instead. If you were to personalize this verse, it would read something like: *"For God did not send Jesus into the world to condemn me, but that I might be reunited with His love."*

This verse promotes a concept of God that is different from the one I have typically held. My concept of God has tended to be _____

_____

_____

This verse, however, suggests that _____

_____

_____

Some Part of Me Feels So Unworthy I Question Whether I Could Ever Win God's Love and Approval

God could never love me in light of the fact that _____

_____

In my mind, to win God's love and approval I would probably have to _____

_____

From cover to cover, the Bible is filled with stories of Jesus interacting with—and loving—men and women who were, according to themselves or society, not worthy of His attention.

Zacchaeus was a man hated by society for his exploitation of the taxpayers. Yet Jesus ignored the grumblings of the masses in order to meet the heartfelt needs of this hurting man. (Read Luke 19.)

According to the Bible, salvation is a gift, which means I don't have to do a thing to earn it.

> For by grace you have been saved through faith, and that not of yourselves; it is the gift of God, not of works, lest anyone should boast (Eph. 2:8, 9).

DAY 2

TAKING YOUR PULSE

Taking your pulse is the most accurate way of determining if you are exercising at the right intensity. To exercise with too little intensity wastes your time and to overdo it can be physically damaging to your body. Measuring your wrist pulse or the pulse which can be found to either side of the Adam's apple (the carotid arteries) will be the most convenient areas. To measure your wrist pulse, use your second and third fingers (not the thumb) and place them gently on the inside of your wrist on the opposite hand just under the crease. Be patient—it takes a little practice to become skilled at doing this.

How many times did your heart beat during 60 seconds while at rest? _____
This is your resting pulse rate per minute.

EXERCISE PULSE RATE RANGE

Now that you know how to find your resting pulse rate, you easily will be able to assess an appropriate exercise intensity for yourself by determining your own exercise pulse rate range. Here's how:

1. Subtract your age from 220 to find your maximum heart rate.

2. Multiply your maximum heart rate by .65 and then by .85 to give your exercise pulse rate range at 65 and then 86 percent of your maximal cardiac output.

The formula for a forty-year-old man or woman would be:

$$220 - 40 = 180 \text{ (maximum heart rate)}$$
$$180 \times .65 = 111 \text{ (65\% of cardiac output)}$$
$$180 \times .85 = 153 \text{ (85\% of cardiac output)}$$

Thus, this person should not let his or her pulse fall below 111 beats per minute while exercising or exceed 153 beats per minute while exercising. What is your exercising pulse rate range? Do the same calculations as above, using your own age.

My exercising pulse rate range is from _____ to _____ beats per minute.

> **Quick Tip:** The easiest and most accurate way to check your pulse is to count your pulse for 10 seconds and multiply by 6.

My "quick-check" exercising pulse rate range is from _____ to _____ per 10 seconds.

DAY 2

PERFECTIONISM AS A FORM OF PASSIVE ABUSE

Perfectionism is a particularly insidious form of passive abuse, since many of the requirements placed on children by overly perfectionistic parents might be considered socially acceptable or even normal aspects of healthy child-rearing. Yet a parent's need for a totally ordered world, when imposed on a child, can translate into irrational and excessive demands, such as washing "dirty" hands fifty times a day, unrealistic and unrelenting high academic performance, or keeping a bedroom by adult standards of order and cleanliness.

Keep in mind that passive abuse—particularly through perfectionism—is often difficult to detect and may be accompanied by a high degree of denial. You may be thinking, *My family was fine. It was like living with Ozzie and Harriet or June and Ward Cleaver.* But keep in mind that if there was a significant preoccupation with things or procedure rather than people and relationships, you may have come away with unmet emotional needs that now hold you captive.

Describe some of the more prominent procedures and rules that played a significant part in your family of origin. _____

_____

_____

How flexible/inflexible were these standards? _____

Were the rules and regulations in your home created to serve the members of your family, or did you sometimes get the feeling that you were there to serve the rules and regulations?

_____

_____

Which carried greater weight in your home: policy or people? _____

Describe one incident from your childhood that illustrates your answer to the previous question:

_____

_____

_____

How did this impact your relationship with food? _____

_____

_____

Did eating ever seem like one way to break out of the perfectionism that may have ruled your home? _____ yes _____ no

Did food ever seem to provide a replacement for relationships? _____ yes _____ no

If so, which relationships from your childhood seemed most lacking in warmth and substance?

_____

_____

_____

How would you have liked these relationships to be different?

_____

_____

_____

DAY 2

Step 3. We made a decision to turn our will and our lives over to the care of God, as we understood Him.

UNDERSTANDING WHO GOD IS:
DISCOVERING ACCURATE CHARACTERISTICS

Yesterday you examined six negative statements you may have had about God and saw how Scripture had just the opposite to say about the God of the Bible. Now let's look at two of the positive statements from last week and see what the Bible has to say about these.

GOD IS SOMEONE WITH WHOM I CAN DIALOGUE OPENLY AND FREELY ABOUT MY PROBLEMS AND MY NEEDS

We often think that God doesn't know what it's like to be human. Yet, the Bible reminds us that Jesus lived on earth as a human being:

> We have a great High Priest who has passed through the heavens, Jesus the Son of God; let us hold fast our confession. For we do not have a High Priest who cannot sympathize with our weaknesses, but was in all points tempted as we are, yet without sin (Heb. 4:14, 15).

Jesus was tempted, so He knows what it's like for me when _____

_____

_____

Jesus was rejected, so He knows what it's like for me when _____

_____

_____

Jesus was criticized, so He knows what it's like for me when _____

_____

_____

Jesus was abandoned, so He knows what it's like for me when _____

_____

_____

I Trust That God Hears and Responds to My Deepest Needs and Concerns

All too often we think of God as too busy to care about us and our individual concerns. Yet, King David tells us in the psalms:

> The eyes of the LORD are on the righteous.
> And His ears are open to their cry.
>
> The righteous cry out, and the LORD hears,
> And delivers them out of all their troubles.
>
> The LORD is near to those who have a broken heart,
> And saves such as have a contrite spirit.
> Psalm 34:15, 17, 18

God will hear and respond if I tell Him about the things that hurt me, such as _____

_____

_____

God will hear and respond if I tell Him about my dreams for the future, such as _____

_____

_____

God will hear and respond if I tell Him about the disappointments I faced today, such as

_____

_____

God will hear and respond if I tell Him about the times I failed this week, such as _____

_____

_____

God will hear and respond if I tell Him about the rough spots in my relationships, such as

_____

_____

Displacing negative misperceptions about God with perceptions that are true and accurate is an integral part of understanding God as a Power you can trust. This kind of healthy, positive, and accurate perspective of God is critical if you are, indeed, going to "turn your will and your life" over to His care.

DAY 3

BENEFITS OF CROSS-TRAINING

Many of our patients have gotten stuck on just one form of exercise and have never ventured beyond an initial routine. Although this has its merits, we recommend enough cross-training to exercise all of your muscles adequately. As you lose weight, your skin will contract with your smaller form. Sagging of the skin will be less apparent if the underlying muscles are well-developed.

Circuit training is one method of exercise that ensures success in terms of whole body fitness. It also burns more calories in a given length of time and provides an excellent aerobic workout as you tone all muscles in the body. In general, circuit training begins with a short aerobic warm-up (possibly five minutes) and then alternatives between a muscle toning exercise and intermittent spurts of aerobics, lasting from one to five minutes each. The toning exercises might consist of calisthenic-type exercises including sit-ups, push-ups, and leg lifts as well as work with either Nautilus®-type equipment or free weights. The aerobics portion might be stationary biking, skipping rope, jogging in place, or using a mini-trampoline (least effective). The idea behind this type of program is that the heart rate will jump to aerobic pace in the first five minutes. It then stays at that rate by doing the toning exercises at a quickened pace and interspersing at least sixty seconds of aerobics between exercises.

You can design a complete circuit training program in your own home, patio, or backyard. It should take you about forty-five minutes by the time you do aerobics, free weights, and floor exercises. If you prefer, there are videotapes, cassette tapes, CDs, and DVDs that can help you with a similar workout. Also, since daily exercise is recommended for maximum weight loss, you might try walking three to four days per week and circuit training three times per week for balance. Whatever you do for exercise, do it joyfully and know that it is making a difference in your weight loss progress, your mental outlook, and your health.

PRIORITIZING—AN ESSENTIAL ELEMENT

A patient once told Dr. Sneed that exercise was never really a part of her life until she made it one of the top three priorities of the day. Before, any number of responsibilities or commitments precluded her from the exercise she so desperately needed.

What are your top priorities? Do you often find yourself saying, "I just can't find the time for this? My house isn't clean yet. The kids—need I say more?"

Realize today that you will be more effective at home and at work, you will be more vibrant and full of energy, and you will be a healthier and slimmer person if you begin a lifelong pursuit of consistent exercise.

DAY 3

EMOTIONAL INCEST

Emotional incest is created by an "upside-down" family in which children actually assume various parenting functions. Children in these families end up taking on parental leadership roles and even functioning as substitute spouses for one or both partners. Emotional incest tends to occur when the parents' emotional needs are not being met by their spouses or when mother or father is greatly lacking in parenting skills.

A classic example might be a young girl being raised in a household headed by a chronically depressed mother. By the time she is six, the youngster may be fixing her own breakfast, getting herself off to school, and coming home to fix dinner for the family. She has become her own mother. She will very likely become a parent to her incapacitated mother as well as a surrogate spouse to her father who may lean heavily on his children for the emotional support he is not receiving from his wife.

If emotional incest is carried to extremes, it may actually cross into physical incest where mothers or fathers with unmet sexual needs fulfill those needs through their own children.

As you look back on your time in your family of origin, were there any "parental" roles that you began to assume prematurely? Check as many of the following activities that apply.

_____ Housekeeping

_____ Financial management

_____ Provision of emotional stability

_____ Sexual or romantic gratification

_____ Provision of identity for one or both parents

_____ Functioning as marriage therapist to parents

_____ Mediating with the outside world

_____ Functioning as a confidante

_____ Functioning as confessor

Looking back, name any members of your family that you helped "raise":

1. _____ What placed you in this role? _____

_____

2. _____ What placed you in this role? _____

_____

3. _____ What placed you in this role? _____

_____

Were your boundaries as a child infringed upon in any way? _____ yes _____ no

If so, how? _____

By whom? _____

Did physical incest or molestation play any part in this infringement?
_____ yes _____ no

If so, by whom? _____

As a child, did you realize your boundaries were being violated?
_____ yes _____ no

If so, how did you reconcile that information with the fact that someone responsible for your well-being was the perpetrator of the violation? _____

_____

_____

Your assumption of roles and functions that were beyond your years may have met with praise and affirmation from the adults in your life; it may not be pleasant to recognize this kind of positive reinforcement for what it was: reinforcement of your emotional incest. After responding to the previous statements/questions with as much honesty as you can muster, take a break. In a day or two, reread your answers with a cold eye, or better yet, read them to a third party (with or without revealing yourself as the source of the answers) and ask them if the answers seem to describe an "upside-down family" in which children assumed roles more appropriately left to adults.

Taking the focus off you and your needs can be a threatening venture because it requires trusting that someone else will take over the responsibility of seeing that you are cared for. Yet that is exactly what God says will happen as you begin to live life by the principles He has set into motion instead of by taking everything into your own hands.

Can you trust God enough for this? Can you believe He knows what He's talking about as He asks you to begin thinking of God and others before thinking of yourself? If not, what are the doubts that stand between you and the trust in God that will enable this kind of adventurous living?

I can't shake the fear that _____

_____

My main reason for doubting God is that _____

_____

I might be able to trust God better if I knew for sure that _____

_____

If I live according to God's principles—focusing on God and on reaching out to other people rather than on myself—my one fear is that _____

It might help to discuss these doubts with someone; one person who might have some answers would be _____

DAY 3

Step 3. We made a decision to turn our will and our lives over to the care of God, as we understood Him.

THE SIGNIFICANCE OF A DECISION

We often think of addictions as a way to cope with painful or uncomfortable feelings. A more accurate definition of addictions is a way to control these feelings. Yet a paradox exists: The more you use your addiction to control your feelings, in reality, the more out of control your life will become. You have probably already experienced living a life that is controlled by the very substance—food—you have embraced in your effort to control.

The flip side of this paradox is that if you will yield, if you will surrender, if you will give up trying to control your feelings with your addiction, ironically, you will begin to find the power to control the addiction.

Step 1 began to take you in this direction when it instructed you to admit your powerlessness over food. Recognizing that you are out of control is key.

Step 2 introduced you to the idea of a Power greater than yourself that could help you in your powerlessness.

And Step 3 is pivotal—you have the opportunity to respond in your powerlessness to the benevolent leadership of a compassionate, caring, and trustworthy God. Step 3 involves the process of surrendering to God your failed efforts to control, efforts which have backfired and have begun to control you.

The surrender of control is never an easy process. It begins with some level of trust which you began to develop earlier this week as you examined the true characteristics of God and began to see the fallacy of some negative misconceptions of God. Complete trust is not necessary at this point—just enough trust to enable you to take the next step.

That next step is simply making the decision to surrender. It doesn't matter that at this point you aren't quite sure how you'll go about surrendering your will and your life "to the care of God, as you understand Him." There is tremendous power in the simple act of making a choice. After that decision is made, there will be time for you and God together to begin working out the details of the execution of that decision.

To help set your decision in your memory, sign and date the following statement. This serves as a record of the day and moment at which you made the decision to fully launch the process of surrendering your will and your life to One greater than you.

My efforts to control my life through eating have backfired, and I have become the controlled, rather than the controller. I am making a decision to turn my will and my life over to the care of God, as I understand Him. As of this moment, I will begin to trust God with the fears, pain, and feelings I have tried, unsuccessfully, to control with food. As my first step of trust, I will trust God to help me find the strength to relinquish control in these areas. I hereby confirm my decision and commitment orally, as well as in writing.

Signed _____

Date _____

DAY 4

TURNING AROUND THE INERTIA—IDEAS THAT HELP

1. Slow, but steady wins the race. If you haven't exercised in years, you will do the most good for yourself by starting out slowly with reasonable goals. The emphasis is also on consistency, however. If you have never exercised, you may want to begin with five minutes of walking *every day* and progress until you have the ability to reach thirty minutes and beyond.

How long has it been since you have had a consistent exercise program (three times per week or more?) _____

Are you prepared to start out slow? Can you resist the urge to do too much in the first week of exercise and then decide to quit because of aching muscles?

_____ yes _____ no

How many minutes of exercise per week do you feel would make a good start? _____

_____

2. Diversify your activities. Did you know that mowing the lawn can be aerobic? Move all of the hoses, toys, papers, and other items which would cause you to stop and break your pace. Then begin the mowing and don't stop until it's finished. Walking your baby can be equally aerobic if you are walking at a fast enough pace without stops. What about pumping a child (or just yourself) on a bike ride through the park or neighborhood? The more types of exercise you get, the more muscle groups you will exert and the more complete your body conditioning will be.

3. Activity in any form counts. Taking the stairs several times per day might equal the same amount of burned calories as walking a mile. These types of small calorie burners may be important to your overall weight maintenance program. Volunteer to do the leg work in your office. Do your own yard work. Protect your car's paint finish and burn more calories in the process by parking at the end of the lot.

What simple daily activities at home and at work can you include to help burn up more calories in the middle of the day? _____

_____

_____

4. Find an exercise partner. Having a special friend or a spouse who exercises with you is a distinct advantage for success. The encouragement you get on a day when you haven't quite decided that this is what you want to do is invaluable.

Name four persons you would be willing to contact that might be an exercise partner either at home or at the office.

_____   _____

_____   _____

5. Allow enough time for exercise. If your schedule is packed so tight that there are no breathing holes, you're cramming too much into twenty-four hours. Humans must have down time and time to exercise in order to function properly. If this is not realistic for you at the current time, reassess your current schedule and decide what you are going to drop. There is no other alternative.

Does your schedule permit a three-hour-per-week commitment to an exercise program at the present time? _____ yes _____ no

How can you change your schedule to allow for this necessary time?

_____

_____

6. Make it fun and have a good attitude. You won't keep up anything you don't enjoy—that is a simple truth of human nature. Find an activity you love and stick with it. The chart below can give you some new ideas about how each of these activities may be of help to you.

BENEFITS OF VARIOUS EXERCISES

	Developing Cardiovascular Fitness	Developing Strength	Developing Muscular Endurance	Controlling Body Fat
Backpacking	•••	•••	••••	••••
Basketball	•••	•	•••	••••
Bicycling	••••	••	•••	••••
Bowling	•	•	•	•
Circuit training	•••	•••	••••	••••
Cross-country skiing	••••	•••	••••	••••
Dance, ballet	•••	•••	•••	•••
Dance, exercise	••••	••	•••	••••
Dance, modern	•••	••	•••	•••
Dance, social	••	•	••	••
Football	••	•••	••	••
Golf (walking)	••	•	•	••
Gymnastics	••	••••	••••	••
Hiking	•••	••	••••	•••
Jogging	••••	•	•••	••••
Racquetball	•••	•	•••	•••
Roller skating	••	•	••	••
Skiing, downhill	•	••	••	•
Soccer	••••	••	•••	••••
Swimming	••••	••	•••	••••
Tennis	••	•	••	••
Walking, fast	•••	•	••	•••
Weight training	•	••••	•••	••

•••• = excellent   ••• = good   •• = fair   • = poor

Which activities could you begin? _____

_____

_____

The chart above clearly shows the benefits of cross training (participating in more than one activity). Do you feel that your exercise program is balanced and trains all parts of your body? _____ yes _____ no

DAY 4

UNFINISHED BUSINESS

Unfinished business is any significant task, need, or ambition which has not been resolved by a parent and has now been thrust onto a child. An example would be the father who dreamed of making the major leagues in sports, settled for coaching junior-high ball instead, and now relentlessly drives his ten-year-old son to fulfill his lost ambition. Or maybe it's the mother who is bitter at the outcome of her relationships with the men in her life and now exacts revenge by teaching her young daughters to hate and distrust the opposite sex.

While all of us have unmet needs or dreams that have never come to fruition, it's important for parents to have taken responsibility for what has happened in their lives and have grieved for the losses. If this has happened, their children are not at high risk of being emotionally coerced or even forced to carry the torch for the unrequited desires of a parent.

In the following segment you'll find an imaginary will as it might have been written by your parents. This will does not concern legal or financial matters as much as it focuses on issues of the heart: what emotional legacy have your parents left you? This exercise can be completed whether your parents are living or deceased. The key is for you to write this will in the voice of your parent, imagining that your parents could be honest enough to express what they really felt and thought about each statement or question.

MOTHER'S LAST WILL AND TESTAMENT

Presented by (your mother's name): _____

to (your name) _____

I submit myself to the following analysis of my life:

Have I made peace with myself?   As a result, I expect you to _____

Do I like myself? _____   _____

Have I been a business/financial   As a result, I expect you to _____
success? _____   _____

Have I had successful relationships with the opposite sex? _____

As a result, I expect you to _____
_____

Have I made peace with my parents (your grandparents)? _____

As a result, I expect you to _____
_____

Have I made peace with authority figures?
_____

As a result, I expect you to _____
_____

Have I made peace with my own sexuality? _____

As a result, I expect you to _____
_____

Have I made peace with God?
_____

As a result, I expect you to _____
_____

Have I made peace with my body?
_____

As a result, I expect you to _____
_____

Have I made peace with food?
_____

As a result, I expect you to _____
_____

Do I have unfulfilled dreams or ambitions? _____

As a result, I expect you to _____
_____

I hereby bequeath to you the following:
  dreams to fulfill: _____
  grudges to carry: _____
  addictions: _____
  unrealistic standards: _____
  choices I wish I'd made: _____

FATHER'S LAST WILL AND TESTAMENT

Presented by (your mother's name): _____
                    to (your name) _____

I submit myself to the following analysis of my life:

Have I made peace with myself?
Do I like myself? _____

As a result, I expect you to _____
_____

Have I been a business/financial success? _____

As a result, I expect you to _____ _____

Have I had successful relationships with the opposite sex? _____

As a result, I expect you to _____ _____

Have I made peace with my parents (your grandparents)? _____

As a result, I expect you to _____ _____

Have I made peace with authority figures?
_____

As a result, I expect you to _____ _____

Have I made peace with my own sexuality? _____

As a result, I expect you to _____ _____

Have I made peace with God?
_____

As a result, I expect you to _____ _____

Have I made peace with my body?
_____

As a result, I expect you to _____ _____

Have I made peace with food?
_____

As a result, I expect you to _____ _____

Do I have unfulfilled dreams or ambitions? _____

As a result, I expect you to _____ _____

I hereby bequeath to you the following:
     dreams to fulfill: _____
     grudges to carry: _____
     addictions: _____
     unrealistic standards: _____
     choices I wish I'd made: _____

DAY 4

Step 3. We made a decision to turn our will and our lives over to the care of God, as we understood Him.

RELINQUISHING CONTROL OF YOUR STRENGTHS

As you refocus off self, you are beginning the process of turning your will and your life over to God. Yet, granting God control of your life means more than giving Him control of your problems and needs; it also means giving Him control of the things you grasp the tightest. By retaining full control of your strengths, you are placing your faith in your own abilities rather than truly turning your life—*all* of your life—to the care of God.

You may feel that you have firm control—at least the majority of the time—of parts of your job, some relationships, certain hobbies or athletic skills, certain emotions. What are the things in which you excel? Have you placed great confidence in a person, skill, or personal characteristic? What about intangibles like pride in your work or a rich ethnic heritage? What are the cornerstones of your identity? What are the things that give you great pride? Are you in control of your time? Your money? Your children?

Take a moment to fill in the following statements.

I feel I am in control of _____

_____

_____

People have told me I'm really good at _____

_____

_____

If I could be known for just one thing, I would want it to be _____

_____

_____

Now is the time to turn these things over to the care of God. Remember, this is God you can trust—not an ogre who wants to hurt you. There is no need to feel threatened as you make a verbal commitment to God of these parts of your life.

Submit these elements to God's control with a prayer:

God, I have turned my will and my life over to Your care. As a part of that, I give You . . . (*read through the above list*). Please help me, in the coming days and months, when I face any of these things and am tempted to try to take control myself. I let go and let God.

DAY 5

EXERCISE AND METABOLISM

Many people are actually afraid to go on a weight reduction diet program because of information they have heard about drastic reductions in metabolism which may accompany a very low-calorie diet. Though this is a possibility when you are involved on a protein-sparing fast, this should not occur when using the menu plans in this workbook. You will probably experience a small decrease in your Basal Metabolic Rate (BMR) but not to a great extent.

One of the major factors is that when you reach your ideal weight, you will burn fewer calories because you are carrying less weight. At 160 pounds, Valerie Henderson was burning more energy when she walked, got dressed, did housework, and even when she was sleeping than she did after she had reached her goal of 120 pounds. To compensate for this and help her maintain control over her weight, she formed new habits which helped her burn small amounts of calories she didn't even have to think about. The following questions helped her understand all of these relationships and were an aid in showing her where she could burn more calories throughout the day without having to work at it too hard.

CALORIE VALUES FOR TEN MINUTES OF ACTIVITY

	Body Weight		
	125 Pounds	175 Pounds	250 Pounds
Personal and Housekeeping			
Sleeping	10	14	20
Sitting (watching TV)	10	14	18
Dressing or washing	26	37	53
Standing	12	16	53

Making beds	32	46	65
Washing floors	38	53	75
Shoveling snow	65	89	130
Light gardening	30	42	59
Weeding garden	49	68	98
Mowing grass (power)	34	47	67
Locomotion			
Walking downstairs	56	78	111
Walking upstairs	146	202	288
Walking (30 minutes/mile)	29	40	58
Walking (15 minutes/mile)	52	72	102
Running (11 minutes/mile)	90	125	178
Running at 7 mph (8.5 minutes/mile)	118	164	232
Cycling at 5.5. mph (11 minutes/mile)	42	58	83
Swimming (backstroke)	32	45	64
Swimming (crawl)	40	56	80
Light Work			
Assembly line	20	28	40
Auto repair	35	48	69
Carpentry	32	44	64
Bricklaying	28	40	57
House painting	29	40	58

Which activities will you be able to incorporate into your everyday lifestyle to help you get into a habit of burning more calories?

Activities I already participate in include _____

_____

_____

Activities that I can begin now in order to increase my overall activity levels include:

_____

_____

_____

I anticipate that by including these extra activities in my daily living, I can burn _____ calories per day that was not previously part of my daily routine.

DAY 5

SPLIT-OFF FEELINGS OR NEEDS

The split-off feeling or need dysfunction in your family of origin presents a particularly frustrating form of abuse because it involves parents' denying children the right to express feelings that are basic to human existence.

We have all witnessed—with friends or even within our own families—parents who insist that certain behaviors or feelings may not be expressed in their household. An easy-to-spot example might be the parents who never raise a word in anger, forbidding their children to express anger as well. A family such as this may be considered "anger-phobic." This kind of behavior—denying the very real existence of anger, much of which may be appropriate and justified—can be just as damaging as the overuse of anger and rage.

Yet the mere denial of split-off feelings cannot make them disappear. Split-off feelings typically surface in the following way: Often someone in the family will pick up the denied behavior and carry it to an extreme. For example, a family that denied expression of anger will typically produce one member who is very angry. A family that denied any expression of sexuality will typically produce someone who rebels through exaggerated expression of his or her sexuality.

Identify any split-off feelings or needs that were not allowed expression in your family:

_____

_____

_____

_____

Has any member of your family become the living expression of that feeling or need? If so, who are they and how have they carried the feeling or need to an extreme?

_____

_____

_____

_____

DAY 5

♥

Step 3. We made a decision to turn our will and our lives over to the care of God, as we understood Him.

PREPARING TO TURN THINGS OVER TO GOD:
FOCUSING AWAY FROM SELF

Shortly after Bill Wilson recognized God as the key to recovery from his addiction to alcohol, he discovered a principle that Bible authors wrote about centuries ago. They called it "dying to self," and what it really means is that, in order to experience God and life and even self in the fullest senses, we have to focus *off* ourselves and refocus *on to* God and the needs of others. In *Alcoholics Anonymous,* Wilson wrote about his newfound faith:

> I was to sit to quietly when in doubt, asking only for direction and strength to meet my problems as He would have me. Never was I to pray for myself, except as my requests bore on my usefulness to others. Then only might I expect to receive. But that would be in great measure.
>
> My friend promised that when these things were done I would enter upon a new relationship with my creator; that I would have the elements of a way of living which answered all my problems. Belief in the power of God, plus enough willingness, honesty and humility to establish and maintain the new order of things, were the essential requirements.
>
> Simple, but not easy; a price had to be paid. It meant destruction of self-centeredness. I must turn in all things to the Father of Light who presides over us all.
>
> These were revolutionary and drastic proposals, but the moment I fully accepted them, the effect was electric. There was a sense of victory, followed by such a peace and serenity as I had never known. There was utter confidence. I felt lifted up, as though the great clean wind of a mountain top blew through and through. God comes to most men gradually, but His impact on me was sudden and profound.[2]

One of the most ancient spiritual paradoxes is that we must surrender our illusions of "self" in order to be reborn to our more authentic "self."

WEEKLY FOOD AND EXERCISE JOURNAL

Date _____
Weight (First day of week only) _____

	Breakfast/ A.M. Snack	Lunch P.M. Snack	Dinner Nite Snack	Exercise	Feelings and Major Events of the Day
Day One					
Day Two					
Day Three					
Day Four					
Day Five					
Day Six					
Day Seven					

DAY 1

MODIFYING BEHAVIORS I

ESTABLISH GOOD HABITS

"Out of sight, out of mind" is an effective axiom with more than putting away problem toys you don't want children to play with. This concept and many others which will be expressed over the next two weeks will center around simple things you can do at home, at work, or while socializing which will make an impact on weight loss and weight maintenance. You will focus on these skills for the next two weeks in the Body section of your lessons.

From now on, make these behaviors actual rules that you at least try to follow on a daily basis. None of these concepts actually tells you what to eat or what not to eat—they merely tell you how to eat whatever you have chosen. With this in mind, consider that the perfect diet (always making the right food choices, every time, no matter what) is an unrealistic goal to achieve. However, it is possible to form new eating behaviors that will make it easier for you to choose appropriate foods with greater frequency.

BEHAVIOR 1: CHOOSE AN APPROPRIATE EATING PLACE

In the "old days," how many food wrappers, bags, napkins, and empty packages could you find in a crumpled heap in the backseat of your car on any given day? If the car wasn't a favorite stash spot, what about a purse, a nightstand by the bed, your pockets, or a briefcase? The point is, if you give yourself permission to eat anywhere, then most likely you will do just that. And, the food you eat on the run is forgotten quickly. (You will rarely make a mental notation of what you consumed.)

One technique which can help you with this "grazer's syndrome" is to eat only when you are actually sitting down in an *appropriate eating place*. Keep yourself from eating "on the run" or as you walk from place to place or as you are preparing a meal. An appropriate eating place might be a kitchen or dining room table, a table in a restaurant, or a picnic table in your back-yard. Your sofa, a coffee table in front of the television, or your car are off-limits and are not considered appropriate eating places. Establish this habit today. The more you use this new habit, the easier it will be to maintain this behavior for the rest of your life.

Journal your feelings about the following habits to help you decrease inappropriate cues to eat.

I usually eat breakfast at _____ (location).

I usually eat lunch at _____ (location).

I usually eat dinner at _____ (location).

If the places that I am currently eating most of my meals are deemed appropriate eating areas, I will be able to make the following changes: _____

_____

_____

Many of our patients have a history of rewarding themselves with small but frequent amounts of food which they may store in their desks to "keep them going." Don't fall into this trap. When you eat at work, avoid eating at your desk if at all possible. The association between food and working at your desk can destroy your dieting attempts if they are out of control. The desk then becomes a cue and you think of food every time you sit down in front of it. If there is no alternative but to eat at your desk, at least change the scenery by adding a color-ful placemat and perhaps a real cup for your coffee. Try to establish a different décor which separates your eating place from your desk.

Reflect on the following questions as they relate to you. If you do not eat at the work-place for lunch (or other meals), skip this section.

On the days you work, where do you eat most of your lunches? _____

Is it necessary for you to eat at your desk? _____ yes _____ no

Do you work through lunch at your desk? _____ yes _____ no

If you answered yes to the previous two questions, are there alternatives? Is there another place you may go to have a short break away from your desk? List them here:

_____

_____

Are you eating at your desk because of company policy or because you want to?

_____

Do you keep candies, crackers, or any other high-calorie food items in your desk to "keep you going"? _____ yes _____ no

If you answered yes to the previous question, do you like your job and feel confident about your position there? _____ yes _____ no

Do you have job security? _____ yes _____ no

Do you like your supervisor? _____ yes _____ no

Is it possible that you are eating at work in response to the pressures of your job? _____ yes _____ no

List some things that you plan to do differently concerning weekday lunches in the future:

_____

_____

_____

DAY 1

NEGATIVE MESSAGES

Negative existential messages occur when a parent bombards a child with emotionally charged, negative feedback about that child, the world in which he lives, God, people in general, or the nature of all existence.

A child subjected to this kind of abuse may be exposed to literally thousands of hours of negative messages—parental statements regarding that child such as, "How did I raise such a stupid kid?", "You never do anything right," "I wish you had never been born." Or the statements might focus away from the child, yet still relay a strong message about his or her future in this world in which that child lives: "All men are cheats and liars," "God's out to get us all," "You just can't trust anyone these days."

These kinds of messages, received frequently by a child, begin to form the matrix of his or her developing personality. Heard enough times, the phrase, "You'll never amount to anything," will begin to shape the identity and become, in effect, a self-fulfilling prophecy.

As you examine the messages you received from your parents and other members of your family of origin, remember that communication is nonverbal as well as verbal. Tone of voice, inflections, and body language are also powerful communicators.

What messages did you hear? What were frequent negative messages about you as a child, about God, people at large or the world in general? What specific messages did you hear about weight? About food? Size? Hunger? Check the statements below that apply to y you.

Week

4

_____ Mom often told me she would have been a great artist if she hadn't become saddled with kids.

_____ Dad always told me I was lazy and a slow learner.

_____ Mom always complained about her struggles with weight.

What messages did you experience, in spite of contrasting spoken messages? Even though your parents might have given you a positive verbal message, did reality send a different message? Check the statements below that apply to you.

_____ Dad would tell me how special I was and that he would play with me when he got back from a business trip in three weeks; the verbal message was positive, but I still felt abandoned.

_____ Mom and Dad always told me how much they loved me; but they were always too caught up in their careers to be there when I needed them.

What about felt messages? Often messages go unspoken, yet are nevertheless communicated through other means. Looking back at your childhood, can you name dynamics that were significant in your family, yet were never the topic of conversation? Specifically examine unspoken messages regarding mealtimes, food or weight. Check the statements below that apply to you.

_____ No one said anything at all about food, weight or size—yet whenever we were together my family rallied around food and heavy snacking.

_____ No one ever talked about sexuality, yet I never saw my parents hug or kiss.

_____ No one ever talked about alcohol, but Dad's drinking impacted us daily.

DAY 1

STEP 4: WE MADE A SEARCHING AND FEARLESS MORAL INVENTORY OF OURSELVES.

While a single member of the family may take the split-off feeling to an extreme, virtually every person in the family finds his or her own way to indirectly express that same forbidden feeling. Split-off feelings or needs are often expressed in camouflage. In the following examples, you'll see how split-off feelings can reappear incognito in an entirely unrelated realm. You also see how this subtle cause and effect can result in food dependence. Finally, you'll have the opportunity to examine the 1–5 split-off needs you identified in the previous exercise, and how they may be surfacing in unlikely arenas in your own life.

Examples:

Split-off feeling or need	How need resurfaced in my life	Relation to food
Raised voices weren't permitted at home.	With no legitimate expression for my anger, I developed a sarcastic, biting tone.	This further isolated me from relationships; I ate to numb the pain.
My dad never allowed himself to show tenderness; cut himself off from expressions of love.	Hungry for affection, I became sexually active at fifteen.	By my early twenties, guilt over sexual experiences drove me to punish myself and reduce sexuality through eating and weight gain.
Boundaries were not respected. No privacy; need for personal time was denied.	I craved boundaries; putting on pounds became my way of creating a protective barrier around myself.	Food was my way of gaining weight and isolating myself.

Go back to the one to five split-off feelings you identified in the Mind section and summarize three of them in the spaces below. Then, following the pattern established above, describe how the split-off feeling surfaced in your life, and how the process may have impacted your relationship to food.

1. _____ _____ _____
   _____ _____ _____
   _____ _____ _____
   _____ _____ _____
   _____ _____ _____
   _____ _____ _____

2. _____ _____ _____
   _____ _____ _____
   _____ _____ _____
   _____ _____ _____
   _____ _____ _____

3. _____ _____ _____
   _____ _____ _____
   _____ _____ _____
   _____ _____ _____
   _____ _____ _____

DAY 2

FOOD: A LOVE/HATE RELATIONSHIP

From today onward, eating should be a point of luxury in your life. Something to enjoy, not something to ignore or hide. Many overweight persons, like Valerie, have a true love/hate relationship with food. They "love" food because eating is a natural and human pleasure, something that should absolutely be enjoyed. But many also hate food. Valerie recognized her addiction and emotional dependence on food and resented its control over her life. She woke up in the morning thinking about food and its control over her life, wondering, *What would it be like to not worry about my weight? What am I going to wear today that will hide these extra pounds?* Because of this love/hate scenario, Valerie tried to ignore the whole issue of food. She didn't want to appear to herself or others as someone who imbibes in long and leisurely meals. She often ate very little at meals so she felt that she *was* watching her weight. In reality she was eating more high-calorie snacks than she realized because she was ignoring mealtimes and making up for it and then some with indiscriminate snacking habits.

BEHAVIOR 2: MAKING YOUR EATING PLACE SPECIAL

The lesson to be learned is to fully recognize mealtimes so your subconscious knows that you have already eaten. So go ahead and pull out the placemats, good dishes, and flowers for the table. It will only take a moment each day but, whether you live with a family or alone, the extra niceties will be noted and appreciated.

Think about ways in which you can make your eating place more special. And, remember, special does not necessarily mean expensive. Candles are cheap!

Now that I have established the fact that I should only eat in appropriate eating areas instead of giving myself permission to eat almost anywhere, I can improve the atmosphere of my eating area by _____

_____

_____

_____

I will make a promise to myself that I will enjoy food and mealtimes from this day forward. By learning what and how much to eat, I no longer need to fear mealtimes.

_____ yes _____ no

One other point may also be helpful as you reestablish eating in a special and appropriate eating area. If you have already been eating at a particular place at the table, you should change your traditional seating arrangement so that you sit at a different location. It is possible that you may be cued into overeating in your home at your own table. It is rightfully a place of sustenance, love, and security. Let's just make sure that all these "good vibes" are not coming from the act of overeating.

After you have uncoupled the urge or cue to overeat in your old location at the dining or kitchen table, feel free to return to your old place.

DAY 2

ACTIVE ABUSE

Active abuse occurs anytime the parents' displaced hurt and pain is vented on to their child. A classic example of this is the father who is unhappy with his work situation and upon arriving home releases that frustration on the nearest targets, which are usually his wife and child. This is frequently done in an irrational and rageaholic manner and is triggered by minor if not nonexistent infractions. This father might trip over a son's roller skate as he heads up the walk toward home, become angry, throw the skate against the garage door, and then proceed to yell and scream at his family. Physical abuse and battering might also be a part of this whole scenario.

Active abuse includes rage, anger, verbal and physical abuse, as well as the violation of sexual boundaries, including molestation and incest. We call these the "sins of commission."

The following checklist will help you identify specific active abuses that may have occurred in your childhood. Place a check by each abuse that played a significant role in your life, then identify which family member or care-giver was responsible for that infraction.

ACTIVE ABUSES

Abuse	Check if experienced	Name of the Abuse
Abusive anger or rage	____	_____
Physical violence	____	_____
Excessive corporal punishment	____	_____
Profanity	____	_____
Sarcasm	____	_____
Derogatory "pet" names	____	_____
Criticism	____	_____
Excessive yelling	____	_____
Conversation domination	____	_____
Exploiting guilt feelings	____	_____

Inappropriate touching or fondling	____	_____
Overt sexual molestation	____	_____
Rape	____	_____
Alcoholism	____	_____
Drug Addiction	____	_____

If you think you experienced sexual abuse, we feel you should consult a counselor as soon as possible. You might call your local church or synagogue for a referral, or ask your family doctor.

DAY 2

Step 4. We made a searching and fearless moral inventory of ourselves.

A LOOK AT THE BIG PICTURE

An important step in completing your "searching and fearless moral inventory" is to develop an appreciation of the magnitude of your addictions and the shame that fuels them. There is no aspect of Step 4 that is easy, and that includes today's exercise. Yet, taking a long, honest look at all your symptoms and addictions is critical for two reasons.

First, it is yet another step in peeling off the layers of denial that have made your addiction possible for so long.

Second, an honest inventory actually serves to *reduce* the shame that helps motivate your codependency.

As we've discussed in previous sections, addictions are shame-driven. The shame can come from many things—you may have felt shame about the dysfunction in your family, or you may feel shame today regarding your physical appearance or your bondage to food. There may be specific incidents in your past, the memories of which generate shame even today. Shame is a powerful emotion, one which—if not confronted and overcome—must be medicated in some way. Food accomplishes this medication—this control, this mechanism of coping—with the shame. Yet, your addiction to food does more than medicate shame—it *generates* shame, creating a downward spiral that can only be halted when the shame is thoroughly confronted and removed.

Begin by taking a look at the ways your addiction has hurt you and others. Then take a moment to examine the many good things to which you've had to say "good-bye" as a result of your addiction. Finally, imagine what your life would have been like if you hadn't sought help and recovery—if you were still entangled in the web of your addiction ten, fifteen, even twenty years from now.

It is possible that examining your addiction in this light may create guilt which can propel your addiction since addictions are shame based. That is why it's important to separate false guilt and authentic guilt, confessing authentic guilt to the One to whom you've given control of your life. Steps 5, 6, and 7 provide the opportunity to do just that, outlining the process by which you can begin to turn authentic guilt to God and release yourself from the burden of the shame.

Week
4

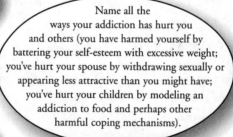

Name all the ways your addiction has hurt you and others (you have harmed yourself by battering your self-esteem with excessive weight; you've hurt your spouse by withdrawing sexually or appearing less attractive than you might have; you've hurt your children by modeling an addiction to food and perhaps other harmful coping mechanisms).

Name the many good things
you've lost as a result of your addiction
(well-balanced self-esteem; a healthy, active
lifestyle; intimacy in relationships; perhaps love
and marriage; enjoying sports or active hobbies
with friends and family).

Finally, imagine what
your life would have been like if you
hadn't sought help and recovery—if you were
still entangled in the web of your addiction ten,
fifteen, even twenty years from now. What might the
ramifications have been? (Divorce; adult children
caught up in the same addiction or other
addictions; early death from health factors
due to excess weight, bulimia,
anorexia)

DAY 3

CUE ELIMINATION

Leisurely relaxing mealtimes are no longer the norm for many Americans. There are more families now who have untraditional mealtimes than those who gather to enjoy each other's company as they eat. Many children are growing up with the distinct impression that dinner is not served until the television is blaring and the trays are set up. This is a tragic loss of communication with family or friends.

We find that many people will become addicted to the association of eating and whatever activity they do when they eat. For example, we have many patients who are TV-snackers. For them, it is an almost uncontrollable urge to watch nightly television and eat without restraint—TV becomes their cue to eat. Even if they are not hungry when the television goes on, they feel the need to eat out of subconscious habit. Or, what about the "newspaper nibbler"? Will you eat more because the Sunday paper is longer and you have become accustomed to eating while reading the paper?

BEHAVIOR 3: ELIMINATE ASSOCIATED EATING ACTIVITIES

FAMILY INVOLVEMENT

If other friends or family members need to help or participate with you as you change your eating habits, take time to show them this portion of the workbook. Think about the person(s) to whom you will need to talk and write down their names and a brief message concerning what you will say to them:

Name	Message
_____	_____
_____	_____
_____	_____

CHECKLIST FOR CUED-IN EATING

Journal your feelings about the following statements as a review of the action steps you can take to accomplish Behaviors 1, 2, and 3.

If I am currently eating in combination with any of the following activities, I am going to make a concentrated effort to quit. I realize that, because I am human, I will probably make some mistakes. When I "fall off the wagon," at the very least I promise not to lie there and let the wheels roll over me because I feel guilty about breaking the diet on an occasional basis. The associated eating activities and other cued-in eating habits I plan to quit include (check the ones that apply to you):

_____ Eating in the car.

_____ Eating while shopping or walking around the mall.

_____ Eating at work while at my desk.

_____ Eating from the snacks available in the break room or from someone else's desk.

_____ Eating while walking around the house.

_____ Eating while cooking.

_____ Eating while preparing food, meals, snacks for others.

_____ Eating while talking on the telephone.

_____ Eating while watching television.

_____ Eating while reading.

_____ Eating while at the movies.

_____ Eating while doing errands (such as candies at the check-out counter).

Note: Some of these habits may be very difficult to break because they are so ingrained in your subconscious. You may have to take drastic measures, such as not watching television for a few weeks, until you break that nighttime food/TV addiction.

Write down some additional measures you may have to take to fulfill the checklist or so that other inappropriate eating habits may be broken:

1. _____

2. _____

3. _____

4. _____

5. _____

Week
4

DAY 3

DISCIPLINE

The vast majority of abuse occurs under the pretense of discipline, yet even people who were overtly battered are often in denial about the experience. In their denial, they may reason: "All children are treated this way; all parents at one point or another lose control like this." These men and women have a clouded perception of the physical abuse to which they were subjected. For example, clients often tell us during counseling: "My father cut a switch off the tree and beat me, but I'm sure I deserved it." While these adults may veer away from using the actual term "abuse" to describe their punishment, the harsh realities of the treatment have nevertheless done damage. Whether the term "abuse" is used or whether violent incidents from childhood have been shrouded in denial, the fact remains that emotional pain may be springing from the past and driving a food addiction today.

How were you disciplined as a child? _____

_____

_____

_____

_____

Were you subjected to a combination of the abusive elements described above? If so, which elements?

_____ Punishment with a weapon

_____ Public humiliation

_____ A parent who disciplined out of rage

_____ Tissue damage

Do you realize that not all children were treated this way? _____ yes _____ no

Can you allow yourself to identify the treatment for what it was?

_____ yes _____ no

You may have been subjected to physical abuse if you experienced more than one of the following:

- Punishment with a weapon, such as a tree branch, belt or stick. (There is nothing wrong with gentle physical reinforcement of boundaries—in fact, the physical reinforcement of boundaries is actually reassuring to a small child. But corporal punishment in excess or in conjunction with any of the following very likely went beyond constructive discipline and into the realm of abuse.)

- The element of public humiliation (example: being physically disciplined in middle of shopping mall)

- If, as a child, you sensed that your parent was disciplining out of his own anger—raging at you—rather than out of the need to establish a boundary for you.

- Was there any tissue damage? Welting, bruising? Cut skin?

- Physical reinforcement can be helpful to young children with limited verbal or cognitive skills. Did your physical discipline from parents extend beyond the preschool years?

Both physical and sexual abuse represent violations of boundaries. A parent is literally transgressing physical boundaries, whether that parent beats a child with a hairbrush, pulls down his pants in public, or molests in him bed at 2 A.M.

A child subjected to these kinds of violations intuitively knows that something is wrong, yet at the same time may try to keep his or her parent up on a pedestal. He or she may rationalize that it's not as bad as it seems because it's coming from mommy and daddy, therefore all moms and dads must act this way.

Were your physical boundaries respected as a child? ＿＿＿ yes ＿＿＿ no

If not, how were they violated? ＿＿＿＿＿＿＿＿＿＿＿＿＿＿＿＿＿＿＿＿＿＿＿＿＿＿＿＿＿＿＿

＿＿

By whom? ＿＿＿

How often ＿＿

As a child, did you recognize that this treatment was abnormal, or did you assume that all children were subjected to like behavior? ＿＿＿＿＿＿＿＿＿＿＿＿＿＿＿＿＿＿＿＿＿＿＿＿＿＿＿

How have the boundaries violated in your childhood impacted the boundaries you were able to set and maintain for yourself today as an adult? _____

_____

DAY 3

♥

Step 4. We made a searching and fearless moral inventory of ourselves.

YOUR LIFE STORY

If you are like most people, you probably have never sat down and recorded on paper the major events in your life. Yet this is one of the best ways to get a good grasp on where you have been and where you may be headed in life.

Do that on a piece of blank paper. But first, a few suggestions.

1. *Feel free to record your life story in any fashion that feels most comfortable.* You might want to write the events as they occurred chronologically or group your comments around stages in your life or perhaps focus on events as they happened in relation to significant persons in your past and present.

2. *Try not to sound like an obituary.* More important than facts and dates are events and relationships and your memories and feelings about them.

3. *Include a representative sampling of the good and the bad.* Don't be afraid to admit on paper when you made mistakes or when others made mistakes with regard to you. Feel free to write about the moments you felt devastated by someone you trusted, as well as the times you practiced the craft of cruelty yourself.

Remember, no one needs to read this life history except you. So don't be afraid to be as searching and fearless as possible as you retrace your steps to your childhood and recreate, on paper, the events that have played a part in molding who you are today.

Do not hesitate to celebrate your strengths, virtues, and accomplishments. Also, give ample acknowledgment to the joyous, grace-filled events of your life and thanks to friends, family, teachers, and mentors who have protected, guided, and comforted you at so many junctures along the journey.

DAY 4

BEHAVIOR 4: OUT OF SIGHT WILL MEAN OUT OF MIND

If you have any foods sitting out (even good foods like fruits), put them away. You don't need anything to cue you to eat. Arrange both your refrigerator and your pantry in a way that higher calorie foods are hard to see. For example, when you open the pantry, do not put your crackers, vanilla wafers, or breadsticks at eye level. Put the cereal out front. You are much less likely to grab a quick handful of corn flakes than you are to reach for a handful of wheat crackers. In the refrigerator, place low-calorie vegetables, already cleaned and prepared, ready to eat, front row and center. Look for carrot and celery sticks in an attractive jar as you open that door, instead of leftovers that might easily be microwaved or instant food like cheese. Opaque food storage containers (rather than see-through ones) will also be a great help in keeping things out of sight and out of mind.

BEHAVIOR 5: ALTERED ROUTES

Have you ever known a bakery, convenience store, restaurant, fast food place, candy machine, coffee shop, teacher's lounge, break room at work, or even a particular grocery store aisle that was difficult to pass without falling prey to one of your old favorite security foods? In group sessions, many of our patients have described perfect food choices until they pass through an old haunt that had provided them with instant junk food on many stressful occasions. After you determine your emotional reasons for eating these items you might consider altering your routes for a short period of time in order to initiate your new habits. For example, don't get gas at the station where you are accustomed to purchasing a snack; go to another gas station instead. Don't even drive by your favorite bakery that seems irresistible on most occasions.

DAY 4

BREAKING THROUGH DENIAL

A key aspect in breaking through denial is to actually use the word *abuse*. Sometimes we have that word in our mouths, yet try to hedge its meaning as we relate it to our family of origin relationships. Completing the following statements may help you in the continuing process of acknowledging the full scope of abuses committed against you as a child:

I was abused by you, _____ (include the name of perpetrator: father, mother, brother, sister, uncle, aunt, grandparents, others), when you _____

_____

_____

I was abused by you, _____, when you _____

_____

_____

_____

_____

A second stage in this acknowledgment of abuse is the important step of recognizing any ways you are continuing the pattern of abuse. Abuse is perpetuating; victims often become violators as well, confirming their damaged self-esteem with added hurts. How have you been abused yourself? Think about non-food-related methods of self-abuse: maybe you are drawn toward abusive relationships because you think you don't deserve anything better; perhaps you sabotage your own successes on the job because you really believe what your folks said about never amounting to anything.

Non-Food-Related:

(I now abuse myself with relationships by being drawn to overcontrolling people who put me down.)

I now abuse myself with _____

by _____

_____

(I now abuse myself with isolation by withdrawing anytime someone wants to get too close.)

I now abuse myself with _____

by _____

_____

DAY 4

Step 4. We made a searching and fearless moral inventory of ourselves.

YOUR RIGHTS

Working through the past two weeks has probably not been easy. Regardless of the intensity of dysfunction in a family of origin, the dynamics from childhood, at some level, become the perceived "norm." Even family members who suffered extreme physical battering at the hands of their parents may have difficulty seeing the full scale of dysfunction involved.

Taking a new look at old pains isn't fun, but it's important for three reasons.

1. This kind of inventory can provide a reference point for what really happened to you in your childhood. When you wonder why you respond in certain ways or carry certain fears or doubts, it helps to mentally walk back to this point of reference—this awareness of past pains—and analyze the present in light of the past.

2. This kind of inventory can actually help promote healing for the emotional child that still lives inside you. Every adult, in some place deep inside, is still very much a child. This is the part of you that still feels and thinks like a child. Even though your emotional child is, at the most conscious levels, overridden by your adult self, if your child-within is racked with pain, that pain *will* impact your behavior and decisions today.

By going back and looking at past hurts, you are acknowledging, "There is a child-part of me today that still feels these hurts as if they were new," and you are in effect saying to that child-self, "I know you are hurting. And there are good reasons for that hurt. This is what happened, and it wasn't right; it shouldn't have happened." This kind of candid acknowledgment and pledge of ongoing self-care is critical in the process of healing past hurts, moving past the pain, and removing the influence of old wounds from present-day relationships.

3. Statistically, if you were subjected to any of these abuses as a child—even if you vowed to yourself that you would never subject your children to the same thing—you are actually at a high risk of inflicting the same abuse on your loved ones. If you don't fully acknowledge the abuse you suffered as a child, you will not be in a position to fully acknowledge or control the abuse you inflict on your own children. If you don't take steps to acknowledge the pain being experienced by your own emotional child, you can't fully recognize the same pain your own children are experiencing.

The following "Bill of Rights" allows you to make a statement to your emotional child-within: I as a child deserved protection from the abuses I suffered.

It also is a statement to yourself as an adult: Just as I deserved protection from abuses as a child, I deserve protection as an adult, as well. Often, abused children grow up with low self-esteem and the damaging belief that their abuse was, somehow, deserved. As adults, they may be drawn toward destructive relationships or self-destructive behaviors as a means of feeding their low self-esteem. Therefore, the following Bill of Rights has powerful implications for you as an adult and for your adult relationships.

Finally, the same rights you are claiming for your emotional child-within and for your adult-self apply to your family of procreation: your spouse and children. Let this Bill of Rights make a statement to them about the abuses from which they, too, deserve protection. This is an important step in stemming the damage that comes when dysfunctional and abusive behavior crosses the generations.

BILL OF RIGHTS

I, _____, have the right to be protected from active or passive abuses including physical incest, emotional incest, physical battering, verbal abuse and any other violation of physical or emotional boundaries.

I, _____, should not have been subjected as a child to the following abuses: _____

_____

_____

I, _____, give myself my assurance as an adult that I will never allow myself to be subjected to these abuses again, either at the hand of others or by my own hand.

I, _____, will never knowingly inflict upon any other child these or any other passive or active abuses. The children I come in contact with, by my procreation or the procreation of others, deserve, as I did, to be protected from boundary violations and other inflictions that will damage their self-image or otherwise hinder their development into confident, healthy adults capable of loving and being loved.

Another key component to healing pain from the past is extending forgiveness to those who harmed us. This topic of heartfelt forgiveness is so important that we will devote portions of future weeks to it.

DAY 5

TABLE MANNERS

Research has shown that the size of the plate that your food is served on has a large influence on how you perceive the amount of food you are eating, and consequently, how full you feel after the meal is finished. Even though you know that the size of the plate does not affect the portion of food that you are served, it at least appears like more food when served on a salad-sized plate rather than a dinner-sized plate. A psychology experiment demonstrated that 70 percent of the people in a weight loss program were more satisfied with less food when it was served on a smaller plate. Consider this also: the salad plate probably represents a more realistic portion of food for most adults age thirty-five and over, although this does depend on the calorie density of the particular foods chosen.

BEHAVIOR 6: USE SMALLER PLATES

Do you have salad-size plates? _____ yes _____ no

Have you ever used them before to serve a main meal? _____ yes _____ no

Are you willing to purchase some smaller-sized plates if you do not already have some?
_____ yes _____ no

Can you see that the same amount of food may look like more when served on a smaller plate?
_____ yes _____ no

BEHAVIOR 7: SET SOME ASIDE

Most of us have been strongly conditioned to be members of the "clean plate club" from a very early age. We have even been made to feel guilty if we leave unwanted food uneaten on our plates. Whether for economy, aesthetics, or because of the starving children in Third World countries, almost everyone has been taught this lesson. The implicit belief is that if I finish my meal completely, it will somehow benefit someone else and will certainly please my care-takers. The unfortunate corollary to that is that if I do not finish all the food on my plate, then I am bad.

Break those old bonds and know that you are not only free to leave food behind but you should actually do this as an exercise. From today on, leave something uneaten, even a bite of rice or a crust of bread, at every mealtime. Try this procedure all week and you will be amazed at how quickly you can feel totally free to leave food on your plate.

Did you consider yourself to be a bad girl or boy when you did not finish everything on your plate? _____ yes _____ no

Can you see the fallacy in this line of reasoning and why you must now make a concentrated effort to break this habit? How will you accomplish this goal?

_____

_____

_____

DAY 5

BREAKING THROUGH FOOD-RELATED DENIAL

You have considered the abuse which was part of your relationships in the past and the present. Now focus specifically on the ways you may be perpetuating abuse through your relationship with food.

FOOD-RELATED

(I now abuse myself with food, by chronically overeating to the point of endangering my health.)

I now abuse myself with _____
by _____

(I now abuse myself with diets, by putting myself through self-punishing fad diets and depriving myself of even basic nutrition.)

I now abuse myself with _____
by _____

(I now abuse myself with the way I look, by neglecting even simple things like makeup and appealing clothes that might make me feel better about my appearance.)

I now abuse myself with _____

by _____

You have just broken through a significant barrier of denial. It is not an easy task to accomplish, and we congratulate you.

DAY 5

Step 4. We made a searching and fearless moral inventory of ourselves.

HERE'S THE GOOD NEWS, FOLKS . . .

Sometimes a person can get discouraged in the recovery process—yet, while there is still much to do, it's important to keep at the forefront of your mind the positive steps and progress you have experienced thus far.

Begin by going down the following list and placing a check by the statements that apply to you (hint: every statement should apply).

_____ I recognized my problem and took action to get the help I needed.

_____ I have completed the fourth step in my recovery process.

_____ I am changing my life.

_____ I have asked God into my life.

_____ I am peeling back the layers of denial that have enabled my addiction.

_____ I am learning to confront guilt and shame—both false and authentic—and finding healthy ways of releasing myself from both.

If you didn't do it yesterday, this is a great time to begin to pursue a release from guilt, either false or authentic. This may be one of the most positive steps you can take in your recovery.

WEEKLY FOOD AND EXERCISE JOURNAL

Date _____
Weight (First day of week only) _____

	Breakfast/ A.M. Snack	Lunch P.M. Snack	Dinner Nite Snack	Exercise	Feelings and Major Events of the Day
Day One					
Day Two					
Day Three					
Day Four					
Day Five					
Day Six					
Day Seven					

DAY 1

MODIFYING BEHAVIORS II

A WAY OF LIFE

This week, in the Body portion of the workbook, we will continue discussions and exercises in the area of behavior modification. Act on as many of these desirable behaviors as possible. There will be interactive questions to help you determine how you might best accomplish these goals.

BEHAVIOR 8: MINIMIZE YOUR CONTACT WITH FOOD

Try to arrange your daily contacts with food in ways that minimize the chances for impulse eating. For example, prepare your evening meal early in the morning (or on the weekend), wrap it, refrigerate, and then reheat in time for supper. Many homemakers mistakenly prepare the family's meal at their most vulnerable, fatigued, and possibly their most hungry time of the day. The consequence can be snacking while cooking to the extent that weight gain occurs.

If you prepare food for young children, you must be especially vigilant in coping with your dieting days at home. Small children seem to require snacks every few hours since the volumes of food they eat are usually small. Make the snacks ahead of time and put them in a snack box. Train them to choose one item out of the snack box, and then the food doesn't even have to pass through your hands. Suggestions for the snack box might include juice boxes, packages of dried raisins or other fruits, small plastic bags filled with graham crackers, vanilla wafers, animal crackers, popcorn, pretzels, or cereal mixes.

In summary, try to do virtually all but last-minute food preparations in the morning hours when you are least likely to engage in impulse eating. You will save yourself hundreds of unintentionally eaten calories per day.

Now think about how all of this applies to your own life. When do you do most of your impulse eating? (at what time of the day) _____

Where are you (location) when this occurs? _____

Do you feel since you may be around food more (if you are the major food preparer of the family), that you do more snacking just because you are exposed to it so frequently?
_____ yes _____ no

How can you tangibly minimize your contact with food throughout the day? Check off the following goals that will fit into your lifestyle.

_____ I can cook dinner in the morning before fatigue and stress become a problem in the afternoon.

_____ I can cook foods ahead of time on the weekends and freeze them or store them for weekday meals.

_____ I can train my family to eat less often (3 meals and 3 snacks per day should be sufficient for anyone).

_____ I can provide a snack box, such as the one described above, for the rest of the family so that I will not have to touch foods that are meant for children's snacks.

_____ I can provide boxed or bottled juices for my children so that I will not have to pour juice for them several times per day (important only if you are a juiceaholic).

BEHAVIOR 9: A WORD ABOUT SECONDS

Many different people with many different needs will read this book. Some have not served family style meals, with all the food in the middle of the table, in years. And others serve family style every day. Our recommendation is that you do *not serve family style* as a routine. Leave the food on the stove, prepare the plates (you may reheat them in a microwave, if necessary), and put the plates on the table. If you have had an appropriate amount of food, it is difficult to then sit in front of a casserole without "picking at it" or "trimming an edge" while you wait for others to finish. You will be less likely to do this if the food is not on the table. "Food out of sight is food out of mind" also applies here.

For persons without children living at home, another option is to actually serve the plates, then clean the pans, package and store the leftovers, clean the kitchen thoroughly and then reheat your dinner and enjoy a leisurely meal. If your kitchen is already clean you will be much less likely to return for seconds or nibble as you clean later on.

DAY 1

CHILDHOOD FAMILY ROLES

Think back to your childhood. If you are like many adults, you may have memories of school plays or church pageants in which you played a part. You may remember a grand moment that launched the entire experience when a teacher gathered the pint-sized cast and handed out the pieces of paper that would alter everyone's life for the next six weeks: your roles.

In your family of origin, chances are no one came to the dinner table one evening and handed out slips of paper defining your role in the family. Yet in dysfunctional families, there is a very real sense of "roles" being played out in the family structure. These roles—first defined by Sharon Wegscheider-Cruse in her book *Another Chance: Hope and Health for the Alcoholic Family*—are a way for family members to cope with the pain that exists in the family as members drift into designated roles—sometimes by default—as a means of surviving the emotional pain.

There is typically a lot of denial surrounding these roles: for example, if you were the family hero, you may have convinced yourself that you really wanted to get straight A's, letter in six sports, or hold nine offices in your church youth group. You may have actually believed that you chose these high demands for yourself. But that's the denial talking. In reality, the four most widely recognized roles offer an illusion of escape from pain, yet each role is the source of its own special form of pain as well.

Throughout this week we will be examining the different roles that you or others in your family may have been "assigned." Remember that parents as well as siblings are candidates for each role, and that roles may even have shifted over the years. For example, a child who plays the hero for many years may get burned out and suddenly shift to a different role, such as the rebellious scapegoat.

But more than a simple examination of the various roles, this week will focus on the unique pain that each role tends to generate and how that special pain may have segued into a new coping mechanism such as food addiction.

Close your eyes and try to imagine yourself back in your family of origin. Imagine a master playwright stepping into the living room and assigning roles to you as well as to others in your family. Who would have gotten what role?

FOUR KEY FAMILY-OF-ORIGIN ROLES

Hero. This family member attempts to redeem the family pain through his or her own "perfection," "good behavior," or accomplishments.

Who in your family—parent or child—seemed to have the reputation of never doing anything wrong? _____

Scapegoat. Often the "troubled one" of the family, this member provides an expression of the family pain through his or her own behavior, often delinquent or rebellious.

Name any member(s) of your family who seemed to have a reputation for being irresponsible:

_____

_____

Was there a problem child? _____

Lost Child. This is the quiet member of the family. He or she literally tries to tune out the world, finding ways to fade into the background or otherwise maintain a sense that he or she is not a member of the family.

Who was the quietest member? _____

The loner? _____

Mascot. This member is the one who keeps the family laughing. The mascot focuses on being cute, lovable, or funny, functioning almost as a court jester who distracts everyone away from the pain. The mascot is often trapped in a role of perpetual immaturity or inadequacy.

Who was the cut-up? _____

Name anyone, parent or child, who seemed to rally the family with his or her performances.

_____

Can you think of any time when it felt "convenient" to think of a family member in terms of his or her "role" in the family? If so, when? _____

_____

Can you recall any family jokes or nicknames that seemed to pigeonhole or stereotype you or any other family member? (For example, there may have been friendly jokes about one member who was the family "klutz" or the "brain" or the "beauty" who never left the bedroom with a hair out of place.) If so, what were these jokes or nicknames, and to whom did they apply?

_____

_____

_____

Did you have a nickname or family "image"? What was it? _____

Did you ever feel stifled by that image? If yes, can you name an instance?

_____

DAY 1

STEP 5: WE ADMITTED TO GOD, TO OURSELVES, AND TO ANOTHER HUMAN BEING THE EXACT NATURE OF OUR WRONGS.

Bill Wilson cautions in his introduction to the Twelve Steps that the single, greatest barrier to recovery is the ability to be honest.

Sharing with another person is an extraordinary step of trust and honesty. All addictions tend to isolate and cut us off from other human beings. Yet Step 5 sharing is a crucial step toward breaking down the sense of isolation. Fifth step sharing is the process of saying, "For once in my life I'm going to open the deepest, darkest secrets of my life and the most sensitive pains in my life to another human being."

It is important to adhere to the three-way sharing endorsed in this step. The most hidden and hurtful aspects of your life must be acknowledged to yourself, to God, and to another human being. This other person might be a therapist, pastor, Twelve Step program sponsor, or a trusted friend.

Fifth step sharing is a two-fold process. There is a formal fifth step where you set a time and a place and make your confession to the third party you have selected. You will spend several hours together as you read through the inventory you've prepared in Step 4 as well as the inventories included in the following pages.

There is also a continual, daily process of what we call "mini-inventories" where you realize an issue is troubling you and you seek out another person, perhaps your sponsor or another friend, and discuss the matter for a few minutes by phone or in person. These innumerable, mini-fifth step confessions are another important part of breaking down the isolation that denial and addiction have built around you.

Tomorrow we will begin that process.

DAY 2

BEHAVIOR 10: DON'T BE AFRAID TO THROW IT AWAY

One alternative for leftovers is to begin a plastic container of "amounts too small to save and too big to throw away" in your freezer. Add small amounts of meat and vegetables on top of the already frozen leftovers for a future soup or goulash concoction.

It is also helpful to designate leftovers. This simply means that when you do put up the leftovers, package them in containers with a plan for when they will be eaten. Some of our patients package their own frozen dinners and keep a stash on hand for days when they choose not to cook. Others will package leftovers for someone's lunch the following day. You are much less likely to munch after hours on something that has been mentally designated as "John's lunch."

When patients come into our office, we may ask them to talk about some of the following issues in relation to this particular behavioral goal.

What is the normal method of serving meals at your home?

_____ Family style (all foods on the table)

_____ From the stove

_____ No regular plan

If you live with others, will they be willing to serve plates from the stove or counter instead of putting all of the food on the table? ____ yes ____ no

Can they understand how this type of activity might make any member of the family overeat? ____ yes ____ no

Are you willing to designate leftovers by placing them in microwavable containers for future quick and easy meals? ____ yes ____ no

BEHAVIOR 11: THE TWENTY-MINUTE RULE

Did you know that it takes at least twenty minutes for the food that you have eaten to be partially absorbed, enter the bloodstream and turn off the hunger center in the brain? *At least twenty minutes.* So where does that leave those who slam down a meal in ten minutes or less? It leaves them hungry with a desire to overeat to quell their appetites, even if they have already consumed enough calories to eventually suppress hunger.

We once had a patient who was unable to get out of a local fast food chain without ordering a large hamburger, fries, and a sugary soda. These foods were made fast and eaten fast—usually in about five minutes. Even though that patient had just consumed about 1,000 calories for lunch instead of the recommended 300-calorie lunch, he was still hungry at the end of the five-minute meal because there had not been ample time to turn off the hunger signal in his brain. Have you ever felt physically full but hungry at the same time? This is usually the result of eating too quickly.

Describe times when you have experienced the same feelings of physical fullness but hunger at the same time. _____

_____

_____

We recognize that a leisurely approach to eating is not always possible. But, when it is, take advantage and accustom yourself to a slower pace of eating. Another technique which is helpful is to have your salad or a bowl of clear soup prior to your meal. Not to mention cutting your appetite, it will also add elegance to your serving style.

BEHAVIOR 12: DON'T ACCEPT FOOD YOU DON'T WANT

As we have discussed in the Mind portion of this book, many people will try to nurture you with food. When that line is crossed from sustenance and good nutrition to insistence, it is time for you to politely set the record straight. Simply tell them that this is something you cannot indulge in at the present. This will usually be enough to deter them from attempting that again. In fact, you may put the blame on us if you like. Most hosts do understand when food or drink is turned down because of "doctor's orders." The other advantage to this system is that once you have made the announcement that you will not eat such and such a food, it is another source of accountability for you. You would probably be too embarrassed to go back later and change your mind.

Is there anyone in your current living situation that insists on your eating food? (Examples: mother, spouse, girlfriend, boyfriend.)

Names: _____

_____

If you have anyone listed above, can you commit to speak with them at your earliest opportunity about this issue? _____ yes _____ no

If yes, what will you say? _____

_____

If no, why not? _____

_____

Holiday time and large family gatherings can be one of the most difficult situations in terms of accomplishing this particular behavior goal. Some of our patients have told us that in the past they felt that they must even avoid these types of activities because of the foods which were passively or overtly foisted upon them, such as having a favorite bowl of candies placed in front of them during a vulnerable time of the day. Our suggestion is not that you should desert your family and friends, but that you might gently and lovingly educate them about your new eating habits and request that they abide by your new practices, at least for the duration of the visit. In most cases they will happily comply (especially if you blame it on your doctor) and then become interested in what it is that you are doing.

DAY 2

MEET THE HERO

The basic premise for the foundational role of hero is simply—if the hero can be good enough or perfect enough, it will somehow ease the pain in his or her family or help the members of the family who are in pain.

A prime example of the hero is the child in an alcoholic home who literally believes that she is somehow responsible for her parent's drinking. The outgrowth of that sense of responsibility is a misperception that says, "If I'm a 'good' girl, Daddy won't drink as much." In the child's mind, "good" may translate into beauty, perfect grades, athletic prowess, or congeniality at the expense of any negative emotion.

Another function of the hero is literally to save the family—if the hero denies himself enough pleasure, if she sacrifices enough—it will somehow redeem the shame or pain of that dysfunctional family. While not universal, it is common that a hero might be the firstborn or eldest in a series of children.

If this is beginning to sound familiar and you have indeed functioned as the hero in your family of origin, you need to know that even years after you've left home—even though you tell yourself intellectually that you weren't responsible for the pain in your family—at some deep emotional level that equation is still there. Heroes in their adult years typically manifest forms of perfectionism, workaholism, and/or overachievement, continuing to function under the misconception that setting and meeting unrealistically high demands can somehow compensate or "fix" pain, in their personal lives and in the lives of others as well.

While heroism feeds on the illusion of easing the pain of dysfunction, it creates its own special crises.

For starters, heroes may simply burn out. We see this at different points in life: it might occur in late grade school as the hero suddenly blossoms into a juvenile delinquent. Or it might occur at the end of high school or college. Another very common time for burnout is in mid-life crisis. Suddenly, in mid-life, a hero may find him- or herself seeking a divorce, negotiating the purchase of a red sports car and launching into full-fledged rebellion. After all, since years of sacrifice and meeting high demands ultimately failed to erase the existence of family and personal pain, the former hero may find him- or herself drawn to all the self-indulgences that were sacrificed, seemingly, in vain.

If the hero doesn't burn out, it's still not good news. The second liability for the family hero is the simple fact that the original equation was faulty: no matter *how* perfect, *how* good, *how* hardworking the hero is, he or she will never be good enough to save the family. Yet the hero doesn't know that. That's dangerous because if you, as a hero, are caught up in being a workaholic, there's no ceiling. You may start out at forty-five hours a week, then find yourself working sixty, then eighty hours a week.

As you consider the following questions, remember that in many families, members can shift roles over the course of the years together. Yet most people find themselves to be a composite of several roles—so you may be surprised at what you find. Feel free to acknowledge any experiences in which you played the hero, even if the experiences occurred over a seemingly insignificant period of time.

Did you at any point in childhood or adolescence feel that you had to earn your worth or lovability? If so, how did you attempt to earn these things? (Examples: through achievements in athletics, academics, social popularity, looks.)

As you strove to earn affirmation or prove your worth, did you ever feel resentment? If so, whom did you resent? (Examples: parents, siblings who didn't have to live up to the image, peers who seemed to have it easier than you did.)

_____

_____

Did you even feel "locked" into a role or image you didn't really want? Describe that role:

_____

_____

_____

Who expected you to fill that role? _____

At the time, what did you think would have happened if you had disappointed people by behaving outside these expectations? _____

_____

What things were "missing" from your life during your hero years with your family? (Name things you craved or dreamed about having.) _____

_____

_____

Did you ever turn to food as part of that compensation or coping mechanism?
____ yes ____ no

What about now? Are you still trying to "win" approval or "fix" the people you work and live with? If so, list some examples: _____

_____

_____

Are there new ways you can begin to be more compassionate and less demanding in terms of the day-to-day performance standards you set or you allow others to set for you?

_____

_____

THE HERO

If you are, indeed, a hero on the way to burnout or if you are still enslaved in rampant perfectionism, the link to food may be strongly forged.

- Food could be your pain killer, tranquilizer, or antidepressant. For example: If you are a dutiful, workaholic hero, you very likely are, at some level, experiencing pain as a result of your unbalanced life. Food becomes your way of medicating that pain. Every time you put in a long workday or close a big deal, you may celebrate with food, rewarding yourself for your sacrifice. Or every time your spouse nags you about neglecting your marriage and family, you may turn to food again.

- You might also use food as your one area of rebellion, the one area in which you can allow yourself to splurge. The more tightly you put yourself into a perfectionistic box, you can bet that somewhere exists another dimension where you are trying to compensate for that sacrifice.

- A third link between heroes and food addiction relates to bulimia and anorexia. Women heroes in particular may tend to be anorexic or bulimic. For example: If you are a woman who grew up with the feeling that you had to please people in order to feel loved, you might have come to the conclusion that the only way you could be lovable is if you have a perfect figure and size and body image. Jane Fonda is one example of a celebrity who has talked openly about a struggle with bulimia.

DAY 2

Step 5. We admitted to God, to ourselves, and to another human being the exact nature of our wrongs.

PREPARING TO TAKE STEP FIVE

To prepare for your formal fifth step confession, complete the following statements:

When someone I care about opens up to me about something hurtful in his or her life, I feel

_____

I (circle one:) (encourage, discourage) friends and family to trust me with their secrets or hurts, I think that probably makes them feel _____

_____

I've always wished I could talk to someone about feeling _____

_____ whenever _____

_____

My greatest fear in opening up to someone else about _____

_____ is that _____

_____

I know what it's like to feel better after talking about something that bothers you because there was the time I opened up to _____ about _____

_____

DAY 3

GET OFF THE CHAIN GANG

Behavior chains seem to envelop most of what is talked about in the book *Love Hunger* and also in this workbook. A general definition of this type of behavior chain is: *A frequent activity you pursue that always ends in overeating.*

Look at the following behavior chain and then write down thoughts about how this might apply in your own life. As an extension of this exercise, write down at least one new behavior chain that is specific for you.

BEHAVIOR CHAIN NO. 1

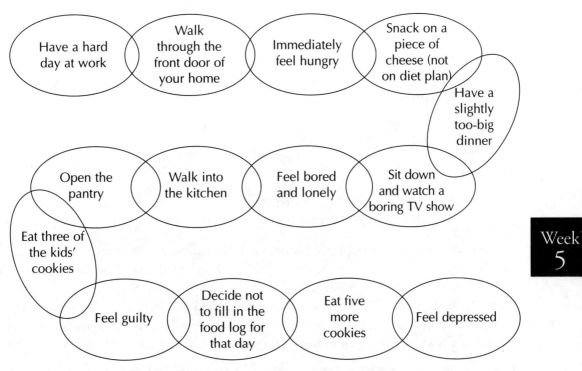

Does this series of events ever apply to you? To break behavior chains, you must catch them as high up the chain as possible. The closer you get to the open pantry, the less likely you will be able to control this situation.

Dr. Sneed advised Valerie and Todd. "You need to realize that when you have a tough day at work, you are susceptible to this series of events. Perhaps you should allow yourself to have an allowed snack, followed by a twenty-minute rest period, then a thirty-minute brisk walk to relieve your tension and anxiety before dinner is even begun, or if the association between television and nighttime snacking continues to be a prevalent problem, you may need to give up TV for a week or so. If you continue to have similar problems, Valerie, you should remove the children's cookies from the house. It won't take long to form those new habits."

My own behavior chain is: _____

_____

_____

If this behavior chain applies to you as it did to the Hendersons, journal how you might deal with it next time it occurs. _____

_____

_____

_____

_____

DAY 3

THE SCAPEGOAT

The term *scapegoat* comes from Old Testament biblical times when a tribe, village, or family would symbolically place the sins of the family on a goat, then drive the animal out of their presence and into the wilderness. Later they abbreviated the ceremony by killing the animal. In modern homes, animal sacrifice is not practiced, but in many families one member is nevertheless designated to serve as the scapegoat for the "sins" of the whole.

The family scapegoat functions in any of three ways:

1. The scapegoat can actually become a living sacrifice for the family, bringing pain on him- or herself as a way of "paying a price" for the family pain, which no one seems willing to acknowledge or "own."

2. The scapegoat can also serve as a living expression of the pain. While everyone else in the family is in denial, refusing to talk about their own pain or the collective pain, a teenager gets pregnant or arrested and suddenly the pain is screaming so loud that everyone has to hear it.

3. Finally, the scapegoat can also function as a diversion. We have worked with many couples who came to us saying they've spent the past so-many years bailing a child out, dealing with a drug problem or unwanted pregnancy or drunk driving or problems in school. Yet as much as these parents complain, it is apparent that their problem child has served a purpose in distracting the family away from the real pain. For example, the marriage might be in trouble, yet as long as these parents are unified over their child's troubles, it is possible for them to ignore their own crisis.

At any time in your growing-up years did you seem to consistently be in trouble? If so, when? _____ What kind of trouble? _____

_____

As you examine your family as a whole, what purpose might your "delinquency" have served? (Example: were you expressing family pain that no one else seemed willing to acknowledge?)

_____

_____

If you were not the scapegoat in your family, who was? (Note: children are not the only candidates for the role of scapegoat. Parents can also fulfill this role.)

_____

The family scapegoat faces two major liabilities resulting from the role he or she has been asked to fulfill. First, some men and women playing this role simply don't survive; they actually die through teen suicide or as the result of drinking and driving, gang warfare, and so on.

Even if they survive physically, often times they have lost much. By the time the man or woman who played the role of family scapegoat reaches adulthood, he or she may have dropped out of school, experienced the physical ramifications of substance abuse, or found herself facing the long-term challenges of being an unwed mother. Facing these kinds of self-inflicted strikes against them, the scapegoat as an adult may find it difficult to feel he or she has ever gotten "back on track" again.

Even if he or she gets back on track, the family scapegoat often has an extra measure of guilt and shame that is very difficult to shake. One woman grew up in a very conservative, religious, yet dysfunctional, home. As a teen she coped with that dysfunction by acting out sexually. As an adult she became obsessed with food, her subsequent excess weight becoming a way to protect herself from her own sexuality—a way of saying she shouldn't and couldn't be sexual as an adult—as well as punishment for how she'd acted out her role of family scapegoat.

If you at any time played the role of the family scapegoat, your addiction to food may be tied dramatically to the role you played.

Typically, both the family hero and the family scapegoat have low self-esteem. Yet as the hero tries to superachieve to feel better, societal values provide some level of affirmation for his or her efforts. For the scapegoat, there is no affirmation—just punishment and condemnation. As a result, the family scapegoat has a basement-level self-esteem. This frequently leads such a person to do something physically to his or her body to reflect his or her sense of worth. For example: If I feel I am worthless, as I put on seventy pounds I begin to look on the outside the way I feel on the inside.

All food addictions are, at some level, a form of self-destruction and slow suicide. This dynamic fits perfectly with the scapegoat's mandate to express, distract, or personally carry the family's pain and shame.

Is it possible that your food addiction is a way of coping with the pain caused by your "scape-goat-motivated" behavior? ____ yes ____ no

Could your addiction to food be integral to your role of scapegoat? (For example: A family, where looks and body shape are perceived to be highly important, may provide an environment where the scapegoat's obsession with food is one of his or her ways to "buck" the system.) If so, how did your weight or shape impact the dynamics of your family?

_____

_____

Think about other members of your family. Does anyone else struggle with excess weight or food compulsion, or are you the only one? _____

_____

Are you willing to lay down this scapegoat role? Can you begin to endorse and nurture yourself as a beloved child of God? What would be some tangible, practical steps toward this new self-love? _____

_____

DAY 3

Step 5. We admitted to God, to ourselves, and to another human being the exact nature of our wrongs.

CHOOSING A CONFIDANTE

When you choose the person with whom to do this fifth step, consider the following:

1. Find someone you can trust, preferably someone with whom you are not too close. A spouse or family member is not a good candidate. You may want to do what some people have done, contacting a pastor in a neighboring city with whom to complete this formal confession, pray and then say good-bye, knowing you will never cross paths again.

2. Find someone who is understanding and compassionate and not someone who will shame or condemn you for the things you are confessing. This is extremely important to your success.

In the following space, write down the name of the person with whom you will share, as well as your plans for contacting that person.

My fifth step confidante will be _____

I will contact him/her (how: by phone; at work; at church; during our Overeaters Anonymous meeting) _____ (when) _____
to arrange the date and place where we can meet for Step 5 of my recovery program.

DAY 4

MORE ON BEHAVIOR CHAINS

Valerie was particularly interested in this behavior chain idea. The second behavior chain that follows applied to her before she went back to work part-time. She shared with Dr. Sneed that she had gained a lot of weight with this one. See if it applies to you.

BEHAVIOR CHAIN NO. 2

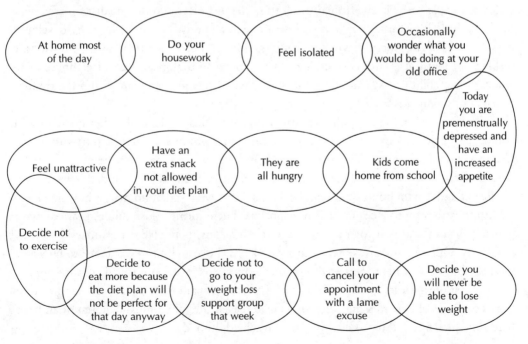

This scenario occurs in the lives of thousands of American housewives who feel isolated, lonely, and perhaps a little bored. We are definitely not minimizing the all-important job of a home-maker, care-giver, and mother. We are simply saying that it can be tough. In days of old, women frequently worked communally rather than in a single home. Or multiple generations lived under the same roof. Also, if you are lamenting a previous career, you must deal with that issue. Be satisfied to be a homemaker or perhaps you could find some type of part-time work that could fill your professional needs and allow you to pay for someone to clean your house one time per week. This would alleviate two of the problems listed above. Other problems with this behavior chain could have been avoided by use of a preprepared snack box for the children, treat-ment and preparation for premenstrual problems, and moderate exercise to decrease the appetite.

DAY 4

THE LOST CHILD

Family members often come in for counseling and explain how everyone in their family seems impaired except one person. A patient will say something like, "Thank heaven for little Susie—she hasn't been affected by all this. She just plays and doesn't disturb anyone."

In reality, "little Susie" has learned how to be in a family but *not* be in it. By developing whole realms of imaginary playmates, finding refuge in books or other "loner" activities, or seeking out physical locations where he or she can get to disappear, like a tree house or the woods, a lost child manages to keep a low profile and pretend the pain within the dysfunc-tional family simply isn't there.

It is a survival mechanism that appears to serve the lost child well in her quest to avoid conflict and pain. Yet that very mechanism is the source of much greater pain down the road, when the lost child, as an adult, wants to date and marry—and discovers he can't because he doesn't know how to bond. Many men and women in their twenties and thirties who are intelligent and dynamic and want relationships are discovering that no matter how much they date they can't get into a committed relationship. These former "lost children" are drawn to people who can't commit, or they sabotage relationships themselves as intimacy becomes a possibility. Other men and women who have played the lost child role manage to move into marriage but do so with a spouse who is equally incapable of an emotional commitment.

Because of the years spent equating the avoidance of pain with the avoidance of relation-ship, bonding skills are missing, and adults who played the roles of lost children often have a hard time picking up those skills when they reach adulthood.

For just a moment, think about the words *safety* and even *comfort*. As a child or adolescent, you probably had things, places, or behaviors that made you feel safe or comforted. Can you recall some of the things or places that made you feel safe? (Examples: a doll or toy; a particular parent or family member; a special place that was yours alone; having a boyfriend or girlfriend.)

_____

What did you turn to when you were in need of comfort? (Examples: a favorite book, behavior such as thumb-sucking or whining; a toy or blanket; a parent; relationships with playmates; or as an adolescent, with people you were dating.)

_____

_____

What about now, as an adult? What are the things, persons, places, or activities that evoke feelings of safety? _____

_____

What comforts you? _____

_____

Does food create a sense of safety for you? If so, why? (Is it the sense of eating—of filling a void inside—that makes you feel safe, or is it the presence of the resulting weight?)

_____

_____

If you have used food to create a sense of safety, from what are you being protected?

_____

_____

Does food create a sense of comfort for you? If so, how? _____

_____

When do you most often turn to food for comfort? Complete the sentences that apply to your situation. Check the statements below that apply to you.

_____ I turn to food when I feel *lonely*.

_____ I turn to food when I feel *bored*.

_____ I turn to food when I feel *abandoned*.

_____ I turn to food when I feel *rejected*.

_____ I turn to food when I feel *tense*.

_____ I turn to food when I feel *sexual*.

For the person experienced at the role of lost child, there are several ways in which food addictions can come into play.

Food may become a substitute. The lost child may find him- or herself turning to food as a source of nurturance. He or she may feel, at some level, unable to connect with people, lonely in a crowd, and riddled with emotional needs that are not being met through relationships. Food, then, becomes the means to somehow fill or numb those unmet needs.

A second common pattern is that lost children, especially teenage girls, will become anorexic. Many will tell you later, in recovery, that at some level they were trying to disappear. Often we hear comments like, "In my family I felt as though I didn't deserve to take up space and time." The expression of these feelings is evident in the anorexic's drive to physically reduce to a dangerous level.

Finally, if the lost child, at some deep level, believes she doesn't deserve intimacy, excess weight can become a safety buffer. She may think, "If I'm fat enough, I won't even have to deal with the issue of dating." Many adult lost children, especially women in their twenties and thirties, admit that as much as they hate their obesity, it's "safe." This same dynamic can apply to men and women who are married. Marriage suggests there should be a fair amount of physical and emotional intimacy. But if one partner can put on fifty or sixty pounds it may "push" the spouse away and inhibit the intimacy with which the lost child feels so uncomfortable. If you observe any number of newlywed couples, it's not at all uncommon for one or the other to experience a sudden weight gain over the first one to three years of marriage. For many of us, marriage is a scary venture into intimacy and, despite the jokes about the sudden access to good cooking, weight gain among the newly married—particularly among those of us who have played the role of lost children—has very little to do with recipes and a lot to do with fears about intimacy.

DAY 4

Step 5. We admitted to God, to ourselves, and to another human being the exact nature of our wrongs.

FIVE WRONGS YOU MAY WANT TO ADD TO YOUR LIST

As you embark on this fifth step, there are five types of wrongs that may need to be addressed as you share. Answering the following questions will help you think through these five areas and prepare to discuss them with a trusted confidante.

1. What are all of my addictions? (Again, this is the endless process of breaking out of denial.)

_____

_____

_____

2. What went wrong in my family of origin to initiate and fuel my codependent love hunger?

_____

_____

3. What multi-generational wrongs may have led to the situation in my family of origin? (Strive to understand and be compassionate toward the families your parents emerged from.)

_____

_____

_____

4. What are the wrongs that have occurred in all major relationships in my life? How have I been wronged, and how have I wronged others? _____

_____

_____

_____

5. What are all the ways I have wronged others or myself by the practice of my addictions?

_____

_____

_____

DAY 5

CHECKLIST OF GOOD EATING HABITS AND BEHAVIORAL GOALS

The following summarizes the behavioral goals we hope will become a part of your own lifestyle. Place a check mark by the things you either already do or are willing to improve.

_____ I will use smaller plates for breakfast and lunch.

_____ I will purchase some smaller plates if I do not already have some with my current set of dishes.

_____ I will prepare a snack box for other members of my household to avoid so much food passing through my hands.

_____ I will attempt to cook at times of the day when I am not hungry and fatigued.

_____ I will attempt to do more cooking and freezing on the weekend so that I am not around food so much on a daily basis.

_____ I will fight the urge to finish all the food on my plate even though that was a part of my upbringing.

_____ I will consciously make a decision to leave at least a scrap of food to be thrown away at the end of each meal for a period of one month.

_____ I will not serve family style meals anymore except when absolutely necessary.

_____ If seconds are a problem for me, I will clean my kitchen before sitting down to eat.

_____ I will designate leftovers so that they will not be haphazardly eaten.

_____ I will not be afraid to throw away food that has no purpose.

_____ I will slow down my pace of eating and now realize that at least twenty minutes is required for food to make me not hungry anymore.

_____ I will no longer accept food that I do not want which is foisted upon me by others.

_____ I will attempt to identify and keep in check any behavioral chain patterns which seem to always end in overeating.

DAY 5

THE MASCOT

The final family role we are going to examine is that of the mascot. This may be a family member, often a youngest child, who never quite received permission to grow up; it may be a person who functioned as the family court jester, who felt the need to be cute and funny; it may be a family member who earned a reputation as the class clown. It may be the family member who, like a family pet, is seemingly the one safe person on whom others can pour out repressed affection and attention. As children—and later as men and women—mascots have learned that one way to survive in a painful family is to laugh instead of cry or to stall their development and remain perpetually immature.

One problem with this role, however, might be described as the Peter Pan syndrome. The class clown who is cute in first grade may be an irritation by sixth grade and downright pathetic by college—yet family mascots often feel they are expected to continue functioning in that childlike role and have never received "permission" to grow up. Men who played the role of mascot in their families of origin may feel the need to "play" a lot as an adult: they may engage in a lot of playing sexually or may feel the need to buy themselves a lot of toys. Women may find themselves, in marriage, falling into a childish role with husbands, keeping themselves in an unrealistically dependent state.

Take just a moment to remember that for many people, identifying the role they played in their family of origin actually means identifying the composite roles they have played over the course of a lifetime. You may be able to immediately identify yourself or another family member as the dominant family mascot; but chances are that if you look a little deeper, you may rediscover periods of time in your history or the history of other family members when the role of mascot became a temporary coping mechanism and a brief shift from a different and more consistent role.

We all have memories of making people laugh; feeling like we were "on stage" and the center of attention. Describe your feelings at those moments. (Examples: anxious, filled with dread, excited, fulfilled, scared, intoxicated.)

Can you think of times you "hid" behind a performance of some kind? Perhaps it was telling funny stories or acting dumb or playing a gregarious role when you felt just the opposite inside. If so, when? _____

_____

_____

If you were not the family member who functioned primarily as the mascot, was there a person who played this role? If so, who? _____

An addiction to food can figure into the equation in a number of ways.

Because the mascot feels he has not received permission to grow up and have authentic, mature relationships, there is a lot of pain and loneliness on the inside. As a result, the mascot may turn to food as a substitute for mature relationships or as a means of medicating the pain. Often behind the cuteness and laughter and jokes, the mascot is an angry and sad person—it's a well-known fact that many professional comedians, if interviewed, will admit they grew up in painful backgrounds. For anyone fighting pain or anger, food can become a stuffing mechanism to push feelings back down.

Food addiction and resulting excess weight can also help perpetuate the illusion of being childlike. Think about famous comedy teams down through the years: The Three Stooges, Abbott and Costello, Laurel and Hardy. One member of the team was the funny fat person who also happened to be childlike and stupid. Elementary school teachers will tell you that overweight children often seem less mature than others and get a lot of teasing as a result. Fat can be a way of trying to say, "I'm not an adult; I'm not growing up. I'm keeping this chubby, childlike role around me."

Especially for women, eating disorders, resulting in chronic obesity or anorexia, can be ways of covering up sexual maturity. For example, a teen going through severe anorexia will almost appear to have reversed her biological clock: she will stop having periods, her breasts will reduce in size, body hair may drop off. Anorexia can, at some level, succeed in covering up the physical symbols that say a woman is moving into adulthood and growing up. Obesity hides developing sexuality as well, but in a different manner, smothering feelings as well as sexual attractiveness beneath excess pounds.

DAY 5

Step 5. We admitted to God, to ourselves, and to another human being the exact nature of our wrongs.

HEALING AND WHOLENESS THROUGH CONFESSION

One of the powerful dynamics of this verbal confession is that Step 5 actually works to reduce your shame through confession. There is something healing about speaking about the darkest parts of your soul to find that the world hasn't ground to a halt, you haven't been struck by lighting, and that the person you've chosen to hear your confession hasn't recoiled in repulsion. Hearing your challenges and hurts spoken aloud, in your own voice, also helps dispel the denial that has been both a cause and result of your addiction.

Confession is an ancient Christian tradition. There is healing and wholeness available through the admission of guilt and hurts.

First John 1:8, 9 has this to say about the power of confession:

If we say that we have no sin, we deceive ourselves, and the truth is not in us. If we confess our sins, He is faithful and just to forgive us our sins and to cleanse us from all unrighteousness.

And to whom should we confess? James 5:16 instructs:

Confess your trespasses to one another, and pray for one another, that you may be healed. The effective, fervent prayer of a righteous man avails much.

The fact is, we really do need each other. A significant aspect of your recovery process is rediscovering healthy relationships and thus bridging the isolation that your food addiction has both created and thrived on. Healing and wholeness are sparked with the heart-to-heart connection made when you become vulnerable before friends and before God.

By opening my darkest secrets to a confidante, I will be _____

_____

The thought of this kind of intimate sharing makes me feel _____

_____

Some of the risks of this kind of sharing might include _____

_____

Some of the advantages might include _____

_____

WEEKLY FOOD AND EXERCISE JOURNAL

Date _____
Weight (First day of week only) _____

	Breakfast/ A.M. Snack	Lunch P.M. Snack	Dinner Nite Snack	Exercise	Feelings and Major Events of the Day
Day One					
Day Two					
Day Three					
Day Four					
Day Five					
Day Six					
Day Seven					

DAY 1

GUIDES FOR EATING OUT

EATING OUT WITHOUT FEAR

Eating away from home has become a major part of the American lifestyle. Whether you are vacationing, going out with friends, attending a social, or just having a take-out lunch at the office, more calories are eaten outside the average home each year. Consequently, most of us cannot approach this part of our lives casually and expect to maintain our waistlines. The American Restaurant Association estimates that the average American buys and consumes 3.7 meals per week outside the home.

How many weekly meals do you have per week outside the home? _____

Does this make you above or below the national average? _____

The long and short of this subject is that when you are dining out, you have less control over what you are actually getting in your food stuffs. What about cooking methods or added butter and other fats? The minute you walk out of your kitchen and into a restaurant, you can no longer be sure of what is going on behind those closed kitchen doors. Therefore, dieting usually becomes more difficult for those who must eat outside the home either most or all of the time, even if you are continually searching out the most nutritious choices.

If you eat out more than three times per week, can you alter your lifestyle enough so that this does not occur? ____ yes ____ no

How? _____

_____

List two fast food or other restaurants that you anticipate going to within a week's period of time. Name a few of the items off the menu that you might have chosen in the past, as well as a menu choice that corresponds with your Love Hunger diet plan. (We recommend that you eat breakfast outside the home only when absolutely necessary because it is so difficult to stay within the 200-calorie limit. Follow the guidelines as closely as possible if you plan to eat breakfast out.)

Name of restaurant: _____

Old menu selections: _____

Name of restaurant: _____

Old menu selections: _____

Over the next week, we will discuss restaurant selection, menu selection at restaurants, fast foods, and other topics which should aid you in staying on your diet plan when eating out. By the end of the week, look to see whether the selections you have just made are ones that you still agree with.

DAY 1

YOUR PRESENT RELATIONSHIPS

Your relationships with people, past and present, have a great deal to do with your relationship with food. In fact, the premise of the whole Love Hunger approach to weight maintenance is that relationships have more to do with weight and food issues than with nutrition or calories.

In the past weeks, you've had the opportunity to examine many of your relationships and how they tie in to your addiction to food. This week you are going to take the issue of relationships a step further, starting with your parents or other significant parental figures in your life.

You will be looking at how these relationships have shaped your life and the choices you've made as well as any resulting emotional pain that may be fueling your addiction to food.

FEMALE PARENTING ROLE

Beginning with maternal influences, think about the woman who played a significant parenting role in your life. This might have been your biological mother or another woman such as a stepmother, grandmother, or aunt.

In what ways have I mimicked aspects or traits belonging to this parent? (If Mom was a rageaholic, despite my vows never to follow in her steps, am I as well?) _____

_____

Which of the four basic roles did this parent play in the home (hero, scapegoat, lost child, mascot)? _____

Does that role in any way foreshadow the roles I've been drawn toward in my life?
____ yes ____ no

If so, how? _____

_____

Do I, at any level, resent these similarities? ____ yes ____ no
If so, why? _____

_____

Do these similarities cause me any emotional pain? ____ yes ____ no

How might my addiction to food be related to my feelings about these similarities? (Examples: Could food be a means to block out, stuff down, or numb any negative feelings you have about similarities between yourself and this parent?) _____

_____

In what areas of my life am I living a stark contrast to this parent and what she believed in or stood for? _____

_____

Are these contrasts things I have chosen freely, or have I been driven to an extreme by my need to rebel and react? _____

_____

Week
6

How might my addiction to food be related to my reaction against aspects or traits belonging to this parent? _____

_____

Do I avoid or welcome contact with this parent? _____

If I avoid contact, why? _____

_____

(This is more extensive than other kinds of denial that deny the existence of pain or difficulty in the relationship. If a child has been severely embarrassed or wounded by a parent, he or she may try to pretend that parent never existed. You may have taken measures to reduce contact with this parent, such as working on holidays or avoiding phone contact.)

If I have, at any level, attempted to deny my relationship with this parent, how does that leave me feeling? _____

Do I ever wish things could be different? ____ yes ____ no

In light of this broken bond with this maternal parent figure, is there a void in my heart or life? ____ yes ____ no

If so, how do I experience this void? When and how does it make itself felt? _____

DAY 1

STEP 6: WE WERE ENTIRELY READY TO HAVE GOD REMOVE ALL THESE DEFECTS OF CHARACTER.

A major question arising at this point is whether or not you are ready to have God remove *all* of your addictions and dependencies. You may have come into recovery because of the pain of your food addiction—because of your weight or health or the increasing frequency of binges.

I came into recovery because _____

_____

Yet in the process of completing the first five steps, you have probably come into a greater understanding of yourself. Remember the section on hidden addictions? Since multiple addictions are the rule rather than the exception, you very likely discovered other addictions or dependencies that didn't seem to play a big role in driving you into recovery but nevertheless must be dealt with now that you're here.

If these "subtle" dependencies are not purged, your recovery from food addiction may send you deeper into perfectionism, controlism, alcoholism, or whatever the other self-abuses are with which you struggle.

So it is important to identify *specific* and *individual* defects of character and how you—in a very individual fashion—need to recover. There can be no blanket or universal recommendations at this point. The rageaholic, for example, may need to moderate and reduce his anger expression. Conversely, the anger-phobic person who has no permission to feel or express anger may need to mobilize anger expression and assertiveness.

To help you begin to fully identify all your dependencies, thumb back through the completed pages of this workbook to the section on hidden addictions (pages 28–30). The addictions examined were money, work, shopping, anger, and sexuality. There are also other addictions and dependencies.

The following list includes many of the persons or things which can become addictive agents in your life. Place a check by the ones you suspect may be problem areas for you.

_____ Control addictions, especially if they surface in personal, sexual, family, and business relationships

_____ The misuse of sexuality

_____ Approval dependency (the need to please people)

_____ Rescuing patterns (the need to rescue or fix other people)

_____ Toxic relationships which are damaging or hurtful

_____ Cosmetics, clothes, cosmetic surgery, or other excessive efforts to look good on the outside

_____ Academic pursuits and excessive intellectualizing

_____ Religiosity or religious legalism (preoccupation with the form and the rules and regulations of religion, rather than benefiting from the real spiritual message)

_____ General perfectionism

_____ Compulsive cleaning and avoiding contamination, and other obsessive-compulsive symptoms

_____ Compulsive organizing, structuring (the need always to have everything in its place)

_____ Excessive materialism

(I am, I am not) willing to ask God to remove all of these defects of character. (Circle one.)

DAY 2

BEHAVIORAL GUIDES FOR EATING OUT

Concentrate today on general eating-out attitudes, actions, and techniques that will save you hundreds of calories each time you use them.

1. Plan ahead. Try to find out where you are going and decide what you will order before you get there. If you need to lighten up your other meals and snacks, that is an acceptable compromise for anticipating a somewhat larger meal than those described in your menu exchanges. However, we advise that you not starve yourself or quit eating altogether before going to a restaurant. That usually backfires and causes you to eat more than you would have normally.

Whether going to a restaurant of which you have no previous information or one of your old favorite haunts, decide what you need to eat before you ever cross the threshold of the door. Keep in mind that if you have not done this, you may be influenced by the daily specials, what the rest of your dinner party is ordering, or a cavalier food decision made on the spur of the moment.

When Dr. Sneed talked about this issue with Todd, he admitted, "I was out with some office buddies one day at a local diner and after everyone else at the table had ordered the double cheeseburger and fries, I found myself doing the same thing, I had become accustomed to the lighter meal choices, and it kind of made me sick. I just didn't think long enough about what I was going to order before I went in and ended up ordering something like I would have in the old days. It was a reflex action."

Think back to the last time you were influenced by someone you were with to make a wrong decision at a restaurant. Describe what happened.

_____

_____

How could you better handle that situation next time? _____

_____

_____

2. Don't hesitate about making special requests. The waiters are in a restaurant to wait on you. Don't ever be embarrassed about asking for a special instruction that might save as much as 200 or 300 calories from the meal. Let's look at some examples of what this might entail. Check off the ones that you would be interested in using.

_____ 1. Place the salad dressing in a cup on the side.

_____ 2. Do not cook in butter.

_____ 3. Do not add butter to the top.

_____ 4. Place the sauce for the meat in a cup on the side.

_____ 5. Remove the skin from the poultry.

_____ 6. Bring only the leanest cuts of meat.

_____ 7. Ask the waiter not to leave a bread basket.

3. Dealing with restaurant portion sizes. Many restaurants serve about twice as much food as an adult watching his or her weight would need to eat. Here are a few options you might consider next time you are faced with this situation. Check the ones which you might be able to try and add some others yourself.

_____ 1. Ask if you can order a child's portion (or senior portion)

_____ 2. Ask for a take-home carton and designate half of the meal for your lunch or dinner the next day.

_____ 3. Take a friend with you who wants to split a dinner.

_____ 4. Don't return to that restaurant.

4. Avoid high-calorie drinks and desserts. There can be absolutely no negotiation on this point if you intend to stay with your diet program when you go out. Extra calories sneak into restaurant food so easily that an extra beverage (alcoholic or nonalcoholic) or even a portion of a dessert will push you over the edge on your calorie intake. Look forward to those extras on an occasional basis after the weight is gone. Substitutes for the beverages might include mineral water with a lime twist. Carry one peppermint candy in your purse or pocket for something to enjoy after the meal.

5. Don't fall for the extras. Many a good menu selection has been made only to languish before the indiscriminate eating of all those wonderful "extras." In the southwest, it is the tostada basket. In the north it might be a fabulous whole-grain bread, and in the South it will probably be homemade biscuits and cornbread. These things will not be restricted forever. Try asking the waiter not to bring them to the table if that is possible. Another thing that helps is keeping your food diary in hand, prepared to write down any infractions. Do your best. We know it's tough, but with practice, resisting these extra calories will become easier and easier.

DAY 2

MALE PARENTING ROLE

Now think about the man who played a significant parenting role in your life. This might have been your biological father or another man such as a stepfather, grandfather, or uncle.

In what ways have I mimicked aspects or traits belonging to this parent? _____

_____

_____

Which of the five basic roles did this parent play in the home? _____

_____

Does that role in any way foreshadow the roles I've been drawn toward in my life?
____ yes ____ no

If so, how? _____

_____

Do I, at any level, resent these similarities? ____ yes ____ no

If so, why? _____

_____

Do these similarities cause me any emotional pain? ____ yes ____ no

How might my addiction to food be related to my feelings about these similarities? _____

_____

In what areas of my life am I living a stark contrast to this parent and what he believed in or stood for? _____

_____

Are these contrasts things I have chosen freely, or have I been driven to an extreme by my need to rebel and react? _____

_____

How might my addiction to food be related to my reaction against aspects or traits belonging to this parent? _____

_____

Do I avoid or welcome contact with this parent? _____

If I avoid contact, why? _____

_____

If I have, at any level, attempted to deny my relationship with this parent, how does that leave me feeling? _____

Do I ever wish things could be different? ____ yes ____ no

In light of this broken bond with this paternal parent figure, is there a void in my heart of life? ____ yes ____ no

If so, how do I experience this void? When and how does it make itself felt? _____

_____

How might my addiction to food be tied into this lack of connection in my relationship with this parent? _____

Did this parent ever experience food compulsion such as overeating?
____ yes ____ no

How might my addiction to food be mimicking or reacting to the relationship this parent had with food? _____

DAY 2

Step 6. We were entirely ready to have God remove all these defects of character.

MAKING THE GRAND SWEEP:
PATTERNS IN YOUR RELATIONSHIPS

Look carefully at your relationship inventory from Week 1 and Week 4. Are there any patterns? Maybe you always need to be in control, or seem drawn toward needy or abusive people, or have always been unable to say no or otherwise set boundaries. Answering the following questions may help you evaluate your inventory.

I seem to be drawn repeatedly to the kind of person who _____

_____

This might have something to do with my fear that _____

_____, or my need to _____

_____

The one thing that really bothers me about a lot of my relationships is _____

_____

The fact that I am so bothered, or the fact that this is a recurring problem, may be a signal of a dependency in me. It might have something to do with my fear of _____

_____ or my need to _____

If I could change one thing about my relationships in general, it would be _____

_____

If I could change one single relationship, past or present, it would be my relationship with _____ and I would change it in this way: _____

_____

_____

DAY 3

FOOD SELECTION GUIDELINES FOR EATING OUT

Your menu exchanges will be your first and primary guide to what to eat when you eat out. This chart is provided as a quick reference and summary of what types of food you will find on the menu exchanges for both the breakfast and lunch/dinner entrees. For specific menus and portion sizes, review Part Three: The Menu and Food Exchanges.

Breakfast

Order These

Juices	Oatmeal or grits
Black coffee or tea	½ bagel or English muffin
Fresh fruits	Lean ham or Canadian bacon (best meat)
One egg *a la carte,* one toast	Whole grain muffins, pancakes
High fiber cereals, low-fat milk	

Avoid These

Sugary drinks	Hash brown potatoes
Cream or coffee creamers	Biscuits (usually very high in fat)
Jams, jellies, preserves	Sausage, bacon
Large omelets with all the extras	Waffles, other bakery items
Sugary cereals with whole milk	

Lunch

Order These

Sandwiches with mustard and lean meats and or low-fat cheese	Chef salads, including limited amounts of meat, cheese, egg, low-cal dressing
Regular-sized hamburgers, no mayo or butter (omit ½ bun if possible)	Ask for sliced tomatoes instead of extra side-dishes
Clear soups, salads with low-cal dressing	

Avoid These

Sandwiches made with mayo or other dressing and processed meats (bologna, salami, etc.)	Heavy creamed soups, salads with regular dressings
Hamburgers with mayo, salad dressing and/or cheese (they use high-fat cheeses)	Chef salads with unlimited amounts of toppings and/or high-fat salad dressing,
Chips, potato salad, cole slaw served with sandwiches	

Dinner will be discussed in detail tomorrow.

VACATION TIMES

When you are on vacation it is very important not to eat every meal out. Even if you are not staying in a place that has refrigeration capabilities (such as a kitchenette or condo situation), you can purchase items from any local grocery that will be suitable for breakfast or lunch. We recommend that you try to eat out at a full course restaurant only one time per day while on vacation.

Here are a few ideas for you. Fill in with a few more of your own.

Breakfast (Examples: bagels, boxed or canned individual servings of juice, low-fat yogurt, English muffins, low-fat cheese sticks.) _____

_____

Lunch (Examples: bread, mustard, lean meat purchased each day, canned tuna or chicken breast, graham crackers, baked chips, diet sodas or mineral water, fruit.)

_____

_____

One further point needs to be made. Vacation time can be one of those cues that causes us to deviate from good health habits, including food and fitness. How many times have you come back from a vacation or retreat and been absolutely exhausted? You may feel tired, drugged out, unhealthy, and even tense. Many times there are physiological reasons for this that go beyond burning your candle at both ends. At a time when you need your full physical armor to ease fatigue and give you energy, perhaps you have temporarily quit exercising and are eating foods that weigh you down.

**Week
6**

DAY 3

THE OPPOSITE SEX

How do you feel about members of the opposite sex? The inventory below will help you identify your feelings.

Who are the persons in my past and present who have most influenced my perceptions of the opposite sex? _____

_____

My feelings about the opposite sex might be described as:

___ angry	___ curious	___ confused	___ disillusioned	___ bitter
___ threatened	___ rejected	___ bored	___ fearful	___ desiring
___ disappointed	___ hungry	___ content	___ respectful	___ sad
___ satisfied	___ apathetic	___ isolated	___ excited	___ hateful

I feel wounded by the opposite sex in the following ways: _____

_____

I feel appreciation for the opposite sex because _____

_____

How have these feelings helped my relationships?_____

_____

How have these feelings harmed my relationships?_____

_____

In what areas might I need to make peace with the opposite sex?_____

_____

THE SAME GENDER

Now think about your gender. Go through the same questions to identify your feelings. Who are the persons in my past who have most influenced my perceptions of my gender?

_____

How am I similar to the traits I included on my list for my same gender? _____

_____

_____

How am I different? _____

When I compare both lists, are my characteristics more in line with those I listed for the opposite sex or for my gender? _____

My feelings about my gender in general might be described as:

____ angry	____ curious	____ confused	____ disillusioned	____ bitter
____ threatened	____ rejected	____ bored	____ fearful	____ desiring
____ disappointed	____ hungry	____ content	____ respectful	____ sad
____ satisfied	____ apathetic	____ isolated	____ excited	____ hateful

Does my list more accurately represent:

____ How I see myself

____ Things I'm not, but should be

____ Things I don't want to be

In what areas might I need to make peace with my gender? _____

_____

There are many men and women who have not given themselves permission to be the gender they are. They may see all others of the same sex possessing strengths they don't have or being riddled with weaknesses they are afraid to acknowledge in themselves. This kind of rift between a man and his identity with his same sex, or a woman and her identity with her same sex, can create the kind of emotional pain that any addiction, including food addiction, thrives on.

It can also create a setting in which a person might use food to further blur the connection to his or her sexuality. Just as the mascot from Week 5 may use excess weight or anorexic behavior to hide his or her sexuality, men or women who are not at peace with their own genders can rely on excess pounds to decrease sexuality and result in a more gender-neutral perception of themselves and their bodies.

Week
6

DAY 3

Step 6. We were entirely ready to have God remove all these defects of character.

MAKING THE GRAND SWEEP: HIDDEN FLAWS

It is possible that you, like the rest of us, are blind to some of your own flaws. Sometimes the best source of information can come from others. That's why it's important for you to be sensitive to what God and other people may be trying to tell you about yourself.

I've been told more than once that I _____

_____

One of the areas in my life that my family and/or friends have a hard time living with is
_____ because _____

_____

I wish (name of spouse, family member, friend, or coworker)_____

would stop nagging me about_____

I wish (name of spouse, family member, friend, or coworker)_____

would stop nagging me about_____

I wish (name of spouse, family member, friend, or coworker)_____

would stop nagging me about_____

Do you see any patterns emerging from the messages you're getting from other people? If so, write the patterns in the following space. You may also want to consider asking one or more of the significant persons in your life whether or not they have observed patterns that you may or may not be fully aware of. Write their answers here as well.

_____

_____

_____

_____

_____

I (am, am not) willing to ask God to remove all of these defects of character. (Circle one.)

DAY 4

ETHNIC EATING I

America is a wonderful melting pot of peoples from all over the world. And, luckily, they brought their family recipe with them. Learning to control calorie intake in various ethnic restaurants can be a real challenge. The following guidelines will help you accomplish this goal.

American Restaurants

Order These

Clear soups	Seafood or poultry salads
Green salads (low-cal dressing)	Pasta with marinara sauce
Lean meats (grilled, broiled,	Raw or steamed vegetables without or
served au jus)	butter or sauces
Fish or poultry (steamed; poached	Breadsticks, hard roll, melba toast
in wine, lemon, or lime juices;	or pocket bread
grilled; baked; or broiled)	Sandwiches, no mayo or high-fat
Lean beef (4 oz. maximum)	dressings or cheese

Avoid These

Buttered	Crispy
Creamed	Au gratin
Fried	Cheese sauced
Batter-fried	

Chinese Restaurants

Order These

Steamed vegetables	Fish and chicken dishes with vegetables
Steamed Rice	(Moo Goo Gai Pan, Chicken with
	Snow Peas, etc.)

Avoid These

Fried Foods	Sweet and sour chicken
Nuts	Lemon chicken
Fried rice	

Seafood Restaurants

Order These

Broiled, steamed, poached or grilled	Seafood cocktails
Lemon and cocktail sauce	Clear or tomato-based soups

Avoid These

Fried foods	Butter sauces
Cheese sauces	Hush puppies
Cream-based chowders	Tartar sauce
Crunchy coating mixes	

Mexican Restaurants

Order These	
Bean tostadas, no sour cream or guacamole	Chicken fajitas, one tortilla, meat, and pico de gallo, salsa, lettuce, and tomatoes
Lean meat tacos	Rice (if cooked with little fat)
Taco or fajita salads, with limited cheese, sour cream, and guacamole	Grilled meats

Avoid These	
Cheese	Chili con carne
Chili con queso	Enchiladas
Large dinners	Fried dishes
Tortilla chips	

DAY 4

THE FAMILIES OF YOUR PRESENT

Sometimes clients who have done an excellent job of recognizing and resolving the pain from their family of origin will come to us in the middle of the recovery process and say, "I've worked through this like you told me to, but I'm still eating as ferociously as ever."

Imagine for a moment someone rolling snowballs at you from the top of a powdery hill. To stop the process, you have to get the person at the top of the hill to stop the new snowballs from coming down. That's the process of eliminating the pain being generated from your years growing up in your family of origin. But there's another dynamic that needs your attention. You've prevented any new snowballs, yet the momentum of the existing snowballs can keep the problem rolling.

In your current family, if you are living with stress or fighting dysfunction, the momentum can create enough pain to keep you locked in your addiction even if you've adequately resolved the issues that launched the addiction to begin with. For example, if you are living in a marriage that leaves you feeling tormented, you can spend ten years dealing with pain from your family of origin, yet your current situation will create enough pain to keep you addictive.

Take a thorough look at the families in which you are currently involved. Can you detect dysfunctions in any of your relationships which might be working to feed the momentum of your food addiction?

WORK FAMILY

What is the quality of my relationships with the people I work with? _____

Five key people with whom I interact on the job are (include a phrase about the quality of that relationship—good, poor, difficult).

_____

_____

_____

_____

_____

Are the relationships within my "work family" healthy or is this family suffering from some dysfunction? _____

Who are the authority figures—the "parents"—in my work family, and do they promote a healthy work environment or one that is dysfunctional? (Is the setting dictatorial? Based on fear, guilt, or shame? Is workaholism the expected norm?) _____

_____

_____

Within my work family, is there the freedom to set appropriate boundaries?
_____ yes _____ no

Are these boundaries honored? _____ yes _____ no

If not, why and how are they dishonored? _____

Am I being passively or actively abused in this family? _____ yes _____ no

If so, how and by whom? _____

_____

At the end of a long workday everyone is relieved to go home. But on a deeper level, what is my emotional status when I leave the workplace and head home for the evening? Do I feel worn down? Angry? Relieved? Resentful? Anxious? Furious? _____

At whom are these feelings directed—myself, coworkers, or both? _____

_____

What is my emotional status when I head into work each morning? Am I filled with dread? Resignation? Anticipation? Apathy? Fear? _____

What is the basis for these feelings? _____

RELATIONSHIPS WITHIN FAMILY OF PROCREATION (SPOUSE AND CHILDREN) OR WITH DATING PARTNER

Do I have the freedom to set appropriate boundaries? _____ yes _____ no

Are these boundaries honored? _____ yes _____ no

If not, why and how are they dishonored? _____

_____

Am I being passively or actively abused in this relationship(s)? _____ yes _____ no

If so, how and by whom? _____

_____

Am I being subjected to someone else's unfinished business? (Example: A woman who is in a relationship with someone who is looking for a surrogate mother rather than a mate.) If so, what and from whom? _____

_____

How do I perceive the distribution of power in this relationship(s)? _____

_____

The distribution of affection? _____

The distribution of time? _____

The distribution of money and material resources? _____

_____

How are some of my most important needs being met (or not met) in this relationship?

_____

_____

DAY 4

♥

Step 6. We were entirely ready to have God remove all these defects of character.

MAKING THE GRAND SWEEP: THE PAIN BENEATH THE PEARL

It is a fact of nature that the beautiful pearl is a product of pain: it is the oyster's way of coping with an irritating grain of sand that has worked its way into the tender, fleshy part of the shellfish.

In your life, even positive patterns such as always being helpful, or never saying no to a favor, might be your way of coping with the pain of a hidden hunger. For instance, are you helpful because you truly want to be? Or because being helpful meets some hidden need in your life? It's important to look beneath the surface to whatever it is that motivates you to do the things you do—even if the things you do seem constructive. This is the time to focus on areas in your life you may think of as strengths yet mask a hidden dependency.

Without invalidating the good works that you do, it's important to acknowledge the pain that may underlie any of these "pearls." These dependencies, as well as the destructive addictions we've examined in the past few days, must be candidates for removal by God.

In the following exercise, think about the statements on the left. If any statement or statements in the second column seem to complete the sentence appropriately for you, draw a line between them. It's all right to have more than one statement in the right column connected to a single statement in the left column and vice versa. Write any additional phrases that come to mind in the blanks provided at the bottom of each list.

If I'm not happy . . .	people won't like me.
If I say no . . .	people will get angry.
If I don't appear strong . . .	I'll be alone.
If I lose my temper . . .	people will see the "real" me.
If I say how I really feel . . .	I won't be safe.
If I don't work overtime . . .	I'll be sinning.
If I'm not perfect . . .	people will laugh at me.
If I show that I'm displeased . . .	I'll be rejected.
If I gain a few pounds . . .	no one will love me.
If I don't look great . . .	I'll feel out of control.
If I'm not in control . . .	I'll be a bad person.

If I admit my mistakes . . .	God will judge me.
If I'm not the life of the party . . .	God won't love me anymore.
If I show that I'm afraid . . .	I'll be a failure.

_____   _____

_____   _____

_____   _____

_____   _____

The perfectionistic drivers, or "shoulds," listed in the left column are the "pearls" that eventually become dysfunctional ways of coping with old pains. These dysfunctional coping mechanisms become destructive defects of character.

I (am, am not) willing to ask God to remove all of these defects of character. (Circle one.)

DAY 5

ETHNIC EATING II

Here are guidelines for four more popular ethnic restaurants.

French Restaurants

Order These	
"Nouvelle cuisine" or	Chicken, seafood, or veal (without
"Cuisine minceur"	heavy sauces)
Poached dishes	Clear soups
Simple fresh fruits, vegetables	

Avoid These	
Cream sauces	Brown gravies
Béarnaise sauce	Butter enrichments
Mornay sauce	Pastries and crust
Béchamel sauce	

Italian Restaurants

Order These

Vegetable soups	Tomato sauce
Bean soups	Pasta
Clear soups	Veal, chicken, or fish dishes (without
Vegetable antipasto	heavy sauces or cheese)
Fresh fruit	
Bread	

Avoid These

Fried foods	Heavy use of oil
Italian sausage	Pastries
Cheese, to excess	

"Steakhouse" Restaurants

Order These

Salad bar (with low-fat dressing)	Baked potato (with low-cal dressing or 1 Tbsp. sour cream)
Best beef choices: sirloin, tenderloin (no more than 4 oz.)	

Avoid These

Marbled and fatty meats	Gravies
Cheese sauces	Fried breads
Butter	

Pizza Restaurants

Order These

Plain cheese pizza	Vegetable toppings (especially onions,
Salad (low-cal Italian dressing)	pepper, and mushrooms)
Best meat topping: Canadian bacon	

Avoid These

Salami	Sausage
Pepperoni	Extra cheese
Extra oil	

DAY 5

MARRIAGE RELATIONSHIP

Particularly within a marriage relationship, there are four key indicators of the health of the relationship. Regarding the interaction between you and your spouse, ask yourself the following questions.

1. How do we share sexuality? Does one partner use or withhold sex as a weapon or bargaining chip? Do both of you have "permission"—from yourselves and each other—to express sexuality? Have both of you established trust in the realm of your shared sexuality? Can you both be sexually vulnerable in the relationship?

2. How do we share decisions and authority? Does one partner feel controlled by the other? Can decisions be made jointly? Does one partner feel threatened by decisions or independence wielded by the other? Is there an imbalance of power? Does one partner feel a lack of control over everyday decisions? Are child-rearing decisions shared or dictated by one spouse? Are one or both of you consumed with trying to change the other?

3. How do we share time? How much time do you spend together? Do you have "permission" to spend quality time apart or with others? Is there time to spend on "self"? When you are together, how is that time spent—fighting, working, talking . . . ? Does one partner invest an unbalanced amount of time in child-rearing?

4. How do we share money? How do you determine who spends what? Does the partner who earns more money have a greater claim to power within the marriage? Is there shared accountability regarding spending, or is one partner expected to be more accountable than the other?

If you are currently in a marriage relationship that is dysfunctional and the source of emotional pain for you and/or your spouse, you may want to consider marriage counseling at this stage in conjunction with your food recovery program.

OTHER CLOSE-KNIT FAMILY SUCH AS PEER GROUP OR CHURCH

Are the relationships within this family healthy or is this family suffering from some dysfunction? _____

Who are the authority figures—the "parents"—in this family, and do they promote a healthy environment or one that is dysfunctional? (Examples: Are the relationships dictatorial, based on fear, guilt, or shame; is there an uneven distribution or abuse of power?)

_____

_____

Within this family, is there the freedom to set appropriate boundaries?
____ yes ____ no

Are these boundaries honored?   ____ yes ____ no

If not, why and how are they dishonored? _____

_____

Am I being passively or actively abused in this family?   ____ yes ____ no

If so, how and by whom? _____

_____

Am I being subjected to someone else's unfinished business? If so, what and from whom?

_____

_____

DAY 5

Step 6. We were entirely ready to have God remove all these defects of character.

POSITIONING YOUR WILL TO SAY YES TO GOD

The key in Step 6 is your *willingness* to have God remove from your life all of the unhealthy and destructive coping mechanisms and addictions you have been identifying in these past six steps. Notice that the step doesn't ask you to remove them from your life yourself—that's God's part. Neither does it ask you, at this point, to turn these defects over to Him.

It simply asks that you be ready and willing to do so.

The emphasis in step 6 is on the positioning of your will. (Step 7 will ask for an attitude of your heart and give you the opportunity to take action by making a request of God Himself.)

Just as coming to believe was a process that began with "coming" and progressed into belief, just as making a decision to turn will and life over to God involved making a decision and trusting God to show you how to turn that decision into reality, asking God to remove your shortcomings is a process that begins with your willingness and progresses into His response.

But first, in your heart of hearts, you have to be willing for it to happen.

Finally, don't become overwhelmed with the discoveries you are making about yourself. It's important to avoid self-shaming and self-condemnation. The goal, after all, is spiritual release and not spiritual self-punishment. You deserve to be free from these areas of struggle—not just the struggle of food addiction but all the areas in your life in which you are destructively dependent.

Photocopy the inventory worksheet pages from Steps 4, 5, and 6. On these photocopied pages you will find all the inventories representing the deepest hurts and fears and mistakes and addictions in your life.

Holding these pages, take a moment and, in prayer, express your willingness to have God remove these things—and all of their far-reaching side effects—from your life. Then keep these photocopied pages—you will need them again in Step 7.

Week
6

WEEKLY FOOD AND EXERCISE JOURNAL

Date _____
Weight (First day of week only) _____

	Breakfast/ A.M. Snack	Lunch P.M. Snack	Dinner Nite Snack	Exercise	Feelings and Major Events of the Day
Day One					
Day Two					
Day Three					
Day Four					
Day Five					
Day Six					
Day Seven					

DAY 1

NUTS ABOUT NUTRITION

A certain amount of basic nutrition information seems mandatory in any book concerning weight loss. In a strict sense, nutrition is the scientific study of that which nourishes the body; and thus, it is clear that understanding the workings of things like protein, carbohydrates, fat, vitamins, minerals, and fiber will give us an increased chance for success in long-term weight loss.

This week, in the Body sections of your workbook you will learn about a new facet of nutrition each day that will make an impact in your dieting process.

UNDERSTANDING CARBOHYDRATES

Carbohydrates comprise the largest portion of our food intake, both in America and throughout the world. Generally, these dominate at least 50 percent of the total daily calorie intake. One thing that can be confusing is that carbohydrates include both starches and sugars. When someone is referring to increasing your intake of complex carbohydrates, they are talking about starches and are not wanting you to increase your intake of sugars.

When Valerie and Todd discussed carbohydrates with Dr. Sneed at one of their weekly sessions, Valerie asked this common question, "But I thought carbohydrates would really make you fat. How do you know when enough is enough on this carbohydrate business?"

"Good question," replied Dr. Sneed. "One tangible piece of information we can hang our hats on is the fact that everyone needs at least fifty grams of carbohydrates per day while on a low-calorie diet so that muscles will not be broken down in the body and used as a fuel source. When muscles are diminished in this manner, one's lean body mass is decreased as well as the person's metabolism. The other side of that coin is that you certainly don't want too much carbohydrate in your diet while trying to lose weight. There is an increasing amount of impressive research data indicating that women over the age of thirty-five especially may be sensitive to excessive amounts of carbohydrate. The diet that you began about two months ago seems to be a happy medium. Even on the eight-hundred-calorie plan, you will have about fifty grams of carbohydrates per day in your diet. At the higher calorie levels, the carbohydrate intake may escalate to as much as one hundred grams of carbohydrate per day depending upon the snack choices."

Valerie found herself understanding the physical mechanics of the diet program for the first time. Dr. Sneed went on to recommend that when carbohydrate was eaten, the very best sources were whole grains.

"We will later find out that a higher fiber diet may help you lose weight a little bit faster as well," explained Dr. Sneed. "The best sources include very high fiber cereals such as those on page 58. Other sources of high-fiber carbohydrates include whole grain breads and the outside skins of vegetables and fruits."

Name your most common sources of carbohydrates while you have been on this diet program.

_____

_____

_____

Now circle the ones that you think are high-fiber sources of carbohydrates.

For all the foods which you listed that are not circled, please think of higher fiber alternatives that might meet your carbohydrate needs as well. List them here.

_____

_____

_____

_____

DAY 1

UNDERSTANDING THE CYCLE OF ADDICTION

Mary is twenty-five pounds overweight and has been for most of her adult life. Her repeated attempts at diets inevitably end in failure. At times, through sheer willpower, she has managed to shed some pounds. But without exception, Mary's hated weight returns.

Sometimes it's a significant event that spells the end to her diet: a fight with her husband or a stressful day at work. Other times it's just a slow, imperceptible shift from "dieting" to "not dieting." One small treat leads to the next, and soon the diet is abandoned. Regardless of how it happened, *it happened.* The diets went by the wayside, and she gained back the weight.

What Mary doesn't realize is that she's caught in a trap, an addictive cycle that hinders her from losing weight—no matter how hard she tries. In essence, by dieting Mary is trying to treat a symptom of her true, deeper issues. Because she has not gotten to the root problems, the pattern repeats itself continuously.

Perhaps you can identify with Mary's seemingly insurmountable cycle. The good news is that by understanding the nature of the addictive cycle, you can address the root issue and break unhealthy patterns.

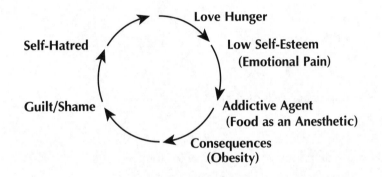

The cycle starts with *love hunger,* the trigger that sets off the addictive cycle. Next comes *low self-esteem* or emotional pain, which drives one to search for an anesthetic to numb the discomfort. That anesthetic comes in the form of the *addictive agent,* most often food, alcohol, drugs, sex, rage, work, or excessive sleep. The *consequences* naturally follow the addictive agent—weight gain or obesity for food abusers. The condition brought on by consequences—excess weight in this case—then produces deep feelings of *shame* and *guilt.* Unresolved and untreated, these feelings can lead to *self-hatred* which in turn can lead to more self-destructive decisions.

This sequence is not linear. That is, it does not begin with love hunger and end with self-hatred. It is a self-perpetuating cycle that continues spiraling as long as no intervention is initiated. Like a drill bit, the cycle travels in a circular motion and sinks deeper and deeper. The cycle also tends to be chronic; it doesn't just heal with time and go away by itself. Action must be taken to stop the pattern.

To break out of the cycle, it is not necessary to intervene at *all* the different points on the cycle. For instance, Mary's repeated attempts at dieting addressed only two points in the cycle—addictive agent and consequences. She recognized her addictive agent (food) and tried to rid herself of the consequences (extra pounds), but she failed to examine why she abused food, namely, low self-esteem. That's why she—and so many others—are mired in the addictive cycle.

Take a few moments to examine your own struggles with this cycle by answering the following questions.

How many times have you launched diet or exercise programs? _____

How often have your efforts met with success? _____

How long did each success last? _____

What happened then? _____

_____

Is there any pattern to the kinds of events that seem to trigger the end of your successful efforts toward weight loss? _____

_____

How do you feel after each diet failure? _____

_____

How do your failures impact your resolve for future efforts? _____

_____

DAY 1

STEP 7: WE HUMBLY ASKED HIM TO REMOVE OUR SHORTCOMINGS.

While at first glance Step 6 and Step 7 appear similar—one reason for their similarity being the resulting emphasis on the importance of God's intervention—they are different in that Step 7 builds on the preparation completed in Step 6. While Step 6 focused on the positioning of your will, Step 7 allows the opportunity to approach God with your request.

Step 7 emphasizes the humility required in approaching God—yet it's important that you don't confuse humility with humiliation. Especially in light of the fact that your addictions, codependencies, and compulsions are shame based to begin with. Step 7 is *not* an invitation toward further humiliation. Instead, it's a call to unpretention and honesty, Humility is vital for three reasons:

1. To recognize the severity of the character defects. Remember, one aspect of your addiction has been to deny and minimize the pain. Even now, as you are attempting to deal with these character defects, you may, unless you take a very humble approach, underestimate their severity.

2. To acknowledge the limits of human power. You can't do it on your own; you can't do it by sheer willpower; you can't do it by intellect and reasoning alone. Humility helps you to realize that you can't heal the hurts, or remove the defects, on your power alone. Humility allows you to reach deep within and mobilize the Spirit of God working within you.

3. To appreciate the enormity of God's power to transform lives. When we invite you to experience humility, it is not the same thing as asking you to have poor self-esteem or a negative self-image. In fact, quite the reverse. Let's imagine putting poor self-esteem on one end of a balance scale; it will be counterbalanced on the other side by a very heavy weight of false pride. In contrast, if you find the balance of healthy self-esteem, you can comfortably experience appropriate humility. So humility and self-esteem are not antagonists. Instead, they complement each other as a pair.

DAY 2

PROTEIN AND WEIGHT LOSS

Protein is that part of your diet that provides you with the necessary building blocks for muscles, blood proteins, and other essential elements of life. The smaller structural units from which protein is made are called amino acids. Of the twenty or more known amino acids, the essential amino acids include isoleucine, leucine, lysine, methionine, phenylalanine, threonine, tryptophan, and valine. Essential amino acids are those which must be consumed with the foods you eat and cannot be produced in the body. Without essential amino acids, growth, repair of body tissues, and even life are not possible.

Protein is a key factor in a weight loss program in that it takes your body more effort to metabolize (digest and assimilate) protein than either fat or carbohydrates. In other words, protein is less readily converted to fat than either of the other two major nutrients. The protein sources we have recommended in this workbook are those which are moderate to very low in fat content and, with the exception of eggs and shrimp, are also low in cholesterol.

The key is to incorporate the best protein sources available that contain the lowest amounts of fat. The foods recommended in this diet program do a good job of meeting this requirement. Fish is your best meat choice. Remember not to add extra fat to your recipes.

Skinned white meat of turkey is your next best choice to give you high-quality protein for the least amounts of fat. The skinned white portion of chicken is also a great choice followed by the dark meat portions which are a little higher in fat, even when skinned. Certain beef and pork cuts can also be very low in fat and are comparable to the nutritional content of dark meat of chicken except that they are slightly higher in saturated fat but not cholesterol.

After you have committed to choosing only the leanest sources of protein, the final step is understanding that there is no place in a healthy diet for the larger meat portions that most of us were accustomed to in our formative years. The eight-ounce sirloin and twelve-ounce T-bone (never a good choice at any size) should be things of the past. Current nutritional recommendations indicate that even on a weight reduction diet you don't really need more than four to seven ounces of lean meat per day for women and men, respectively. No matter which calorie level you choose, you get a more than adequate supply of protein in your diet by using the menu exchange system provided in this workbook.

List the types of meats you grew up with and include their method of preparation (such as "fried" chicken instead of chicken). _____

_____

_____

Now, circle the ones that fit in with the Love Hunger Diet Plan. Are there others still on the list—things which you would like to eat but know are not good choices for you? Circle these in red or another color of ink and then transfer them to the lines below.

_____

_____

Carefully consider the items above or any other foods which you don't think are good choices for your diet program at the present. For almost any recipe there is a lean or lower fat alternative.

Now let's talk about some new habits. Have you ever prepared fish in your home?
____ yes ____ no

What methods of preparation do you use and do these follow the *Love Hunger* guidelines?

_____

_____

Are you willing to buy a few new ingredients and try some new recipes even though these may not have been foods that you or perhaps the rest of your family grew up with?
____ yes ____ no

Pull out a favorite cookbook and list at least five new recipes you are willing to try that give you a very lean meat source without any added fat.

1. _____

2. _____

3. _____

4. _____

5. _____

We have spent a considerable amount of time today showing you what good nutrition can mean in your own kitchen. We purposefully talked about what protein is in relation to which foods you choose. That's the bottom line—food choices and portion size. Regardless of what your old habits once were, they can be changed, and you can feel satisfied and even joyful about a new way of life.

Week
7

DAY 2

RESIDUAL EFFECTS

When a person goes on a roller coaster of dieting and failing, dieting and failing, there are residual effects. With each failure come deeper and more pervasive feelings of guilt and self-condemnation. Each time a person loses weight and regains, he or she is psychologically even more prone to failure. We see this more readily with drug addiction: a habit may begin at $50 a day, then jump to $100, and quickly increase as the addict falls deeper and deeper into the mire of his or her addiction. The same thing can happen with food. Without proper intervention, the cycle tightens its grip on the compulsive overeater until there seems little chance for escape.

Examining the first two points on the addiction cycle will lead us in a review of much of what has been covered in the past weeks. Based on what you've already discovered about yourself in the process of completing this workbook, respond to the following statement:

I might use the following definition to explain "love hunger" to someone who had never heard the term: _____

_____

I think my love hunger may have started when _____

_____

It may also have been impacted by _____

_____

I most often seek to satisfy this love hunger with food, but also with _____

_____

Other emotional pain in my life includes: _____

_____

The factors that have helped contribute to my low self-esteem have been _____

_____

Something that happened recently that provides a good illustration of how I often feel about my self-worth was when _____

_____

As I inventory and lay aside these patterns of old pain, I am beginning to sense hope that I can shift my love life and my food life in new directions by _____

_____

DAY 2

Step 7. We humbly ask Him to remove our shortcomings.

HUMILITY: WHAT YOU NEED TO KNOW

The life-changing experience of humility requires two awarenesses. First, the use of material things—and the quenching of material needs—will never by themselves bring contentment. Complete the following sentences, naming several things in each category.

I have accomplished _____

_____

_____

I have amassed _____

_____

_____

These things (have, have not) resulted in full contentment and spiritual satisfaction. (Circle one.)

Can you remember times when you've been guilty of "rainbow's end" thinking? Some examples might be:

When I just turn sixteen, then my problems will be over.
If I can just lose twenty pounds, then I'll be happy.
As soon as I get into that new house, then I'll be satisfied.
If I can just land that raise, then I'll have enough.

Now add your own personalized statements. What specific promises of contentment have you made to yourself down through the years?

_____, then _____

_____, then _____

_____, then _____

These things (have, have not) resulted in full contentment and spiritual satisfaction. (Circle one.)

A second awareness you must come to before true humility is possible is simply this: The mere use of material things and the satisfaction of material needs will never satiate your codependent hunger.

The fact that you are halfway through this workbook and the Twelve Steps is a good sign that you have already experienced this awareness to some degree. If material things—including food—could satiate your love hunger, you would not have bought this book. The fact is, consuming every crumb in the cookie aisle in your local supermarket will no more satisfy your love hunger than it will satisfy the physical hunger of the clerk who sold you the cookies.

Think of two situations in the past weeks that have succeeded in driving you to eat. Stress over the job? Anger at your spouse? Loneliness? A fear of letting someone get "too close?"

Frustration at a pattern of overcommitment and inability to protect your own boundaries? Summarize the two incidents.

_____

_____

Now place an X next to any incident that was brought to full resolution as a result of your eating binge. Not one. Right?

The fact is, if you eat to escape the pain of loneliness, the food you consumed may distract you from the pain temporarily but can never satisfy your hunger for meaningful relationships. The coping method you've embraced is, in fact, incapable of achieving the purpose for which it was intended.

DAY 3

FATS ARE FATTENING

Dietary fat is quite possibly the most controversial aspect of the American diet. Everyone has an opinion on types, amounts, fat substitutes, cholesterol, and any number of other similarly related topics. The most important thing to remember with regard to weight loss is—*If you eat fat, it turns into fat.* Granted this is a gross oversimplification, but most Americans have historically consumed an obesity-promoting diet that contains up to half of the total daily caloric intake as fat.

TYPES OF FAT

Dietary fat may be classified in two ways—saturated or unsaturated. *Saturated fats* are primarily found in foods of animal origin including meats, cheese, whole milk, dairy products, and butter. Some fats that are polyunsaturated by nature are made into saturated fats through the process of hydrogenation. For example, an all-vegetable shortening is simply a vegetable oil that has been chemically solidified. It affects your body, and even looks, like lard. In other words, don't use shortening, even if it says "cholesterol free."

Unsaturated fats are usually of plant origin and can be mono-unsaturated like olive oil or can by polyunsaturated like corn and safflower oil. It has been known for years that a higher dietary intake of polyunsaturated fat and a lower intake of saturated fat could lower serum levels of cholesterol. The recent revelation is that olive oil seems to work the best of all the unsaturates since it lowers total cholesterol but does not lower the good cholesterol (HDL-cholesterol) that can help protect you from heart disease.

Dietary cholesterol, also considered a fat, is in a group all its own. Cholesterol is generally found in foods of animal origin. Foods restricted on a low-cholesterol diet include egg yolk, organ meats (especially liver—one of the highest sources of cholesterol), and meat fat. However, meat fat is usually contained throughout the food and cannot simply be cut off when the meat is trimmed.

The most interesting thing about all of this is that no matter what kind of fat you choose, they all have just about the same amount of calories. One tablespoon of the following contains close to 100 calories even though the types of fat may vary: butter, margarine, canola oil, olive oil, corn oil, lard, shortening, mayonnaise, peanut butter, and beef tallow. Thus, from the weight loss standpoint, the most important way you can achieve success is to eat a very low-fat diet.

Answer the following questions and see how much more you will be able to get for your calories once these simple principles are enacted.

Instructions: The following sentences contain two calorie equivalents within the same sentence. You must decide if you would rather have the richer or the lighter but more voluminous of the two selections. Underline the item in the sentence that you would rather have.

Would you rather have one tablespoon of peanut butter or three cups of popcorn (minimal oil, butter sprinkle substitute)?

Week 7

Would you rather have the one and one-half tablespoons of oil used to fry a piece of chicken or have the same piece of chicken oven-fried (baked to resemble fried chicken) plus a small baked potato with butter sprinkles and one tablespoon of sour cream? (Sour cream contains only 30 calories per tablespoon as opposed to the 100 contained by butter.)

Would you rather have a serving of regular house dressing or salad dressing on top of a salad at a local fast food or other restaurant or have light dressing on the salad plus a hamburger (small-sized, no mayo or cheese)?

Would you rather have Chinese vegetables sautéed in peanut oil or the same vegetables sautéed with a nonstick spray and one-half cup of rice?

Would you rather have one-quarter cup of a rich ice cream or one-half cup of a light ice cream or two-thirds cup of nonfat frozen yogurt?

Would you rather have two tablespoons of a processed cheese topping on top of broccoli or a very large salad with light dressing and crackers, plus the broccoli and cheese-flavored sprinkles (a Molly McButter® product)?

Now go back and look at what you have underlined. If you are like most people, you are not usually willing to give up larger and possibly more regular-sized portions for a few added flavorings that can be duplicated with low-fat alternatives.

How Much Fat Is Enough?

Some of our patients wonder if they are ever in jeopardy of having too little fat in their diets. As long as 10 percent of your total caloric intake comes from fat, you will not be at nutritional risk. Most Americans consume a diet that is 40 to 45 percent fat. The Love Hunger Diet Plan is designed to give you about a 25 percent intake. We feel that this will give you your greatest opportunity for weight loss success and at the same time be quite palatable and health conscious.

DETERMINING FAT CONTENT

To help you determine the percentage of the total calories coming from fat in the foods you are eating, we have included this information with the menus in this book. Secondly, the following chart below divides foods into categories to give you an overall view of the percentage of fat that is present in most food. Study this list carefully, and try to avoid foods containing large amounts of fat.

FOODS AND FAT CONTENT

% Fat Compared with the Total Calories	Foods
100%	Meat fat, oils (all types), shortening, no-stick sprays, butter, margarine, oleo
90–95%	Most regular salad dressings (including Italian, French, Ranch, Thousand Island, Green Goddess, etc.), olives (all types), cream cheese, macadamia nuts, sour cream, cream
80–89%	Avocados, fresh coconut, sesame seeds, light cream cheese, most nuts (including walnuts, almonds, pecans, etc.)
70–79%	Most brick cheeses (including cheddar, Swiss, etc.), peanuts, peanut butter, American cheese, ribs or rib roast, egg yolk
60–69%	Whole egg, ricotta, whole-milk cheese, mozzarella whole-milk cheese, Romano cheese, cheese sauce, regular ground beef
50–59%	Mozzarella part-skim milk cheese, parmesan cheese, chocolate bars with nuts, lean ham, whole milk

40–49%	Ground round, beef liver, roasted and lean pork loin, sardines (no oil), cakes with frosting, biscuits, waffles, cream pies, pastries, ice cream
30–39%	Round steak (no fat); dark meat chicken (no skin); dark meat turkey (no skin); fatty fish (flounder, salmon, pompano); creamed cottage cheese; milk chocolate; most granolas; brownies; and many cookies; cheesecake; muffins; fruit pies
20–29%	Light meat chicken (no skin), 2% low-fat milk, low-fat cottage cheese, rice mixes
9–19%	Light meat turkey (no skin), shellfish (crab, oysters, lobster), flour tortillas, ice milk
Less Than 9%	Lean fish (cod, halibut, hake), skim milk, non-fat yogurt, most flakes or nugget breakfast cereals, most breads, corn tortillas, frozen yogurt
0%	Egg white, rice, most vegetables and fruits, sugar candy (jelly beans, hard candy)

Now that you have carefully looked at the list of foods and their fat content, which foods do you need to eliminate from your diet now and possibly your maintenance diet in the future? Keep in mind that when you are consuming an entire dinner, the lean meat may still be 35 percent fat, but when served with low-fat breads or vegetables the average will be only about 20 percent fat.

Week
7

AN EQUATION FOR ALL OCCASIONS

To determine the fat content of any food from the food label information, use the following equation:

$$\% \text{ fat} = \frac{\text{grams of fat per serving} \times 900}{\text{calories per serving}}$$

Just plug the number of grams and calories per serving into the correct spot and you can determine the "true" fat percentage.

Many manufacturers are reporting fat percentages by volume (and it appears to be much lower) rather than by total caloric content. An example might be whole milk, which is reported to be 4 percent fat. Actually, whole milk is 50 percent fat; that is, one-half of the calories in whole milk are fat.

Your goal will be to consume meals that are lower than 30 percent fat. Try taking your calculator with you next time you go to the grocery store. You'll be amazed at what you will learn.

DAY 3

THE ADDICTIVE AGENT

Many people are driven to food in a quest to numb some pain or incompleteness in their lives. And to some degree this effort can be successful: Psychologically and physiologically food can tranquilize pain for a short time. In this way, food is used as a gratifier—something that will make you feel good . . . at least for the moment. Some people use shopping in a similar manner, gaining a temporary rush of satisfaction or relief from the act of making a purchase.

The bad news is that these and other addictions are false gratifiers: they are short lived, typically self-destructive, and do not address the real issue—the cause of the pain.

Take a moment to review the addictive agents in your life. As we have already discovered, persons who are food addicted often show collateral addictions such as shopping, sleeping, chemical abuse, sex, work, performance, or perfectionism. In an attempt to break away from one addictive agent, the addiction may be simply transferred to another agent. This is why those who quit smoking often gain weight or recovering alcoholics take up smoking.

As you strive to break your love hunger cycle, watch for tendencies to switch your addictive behavior to another agent. Frequently, when people cut back on eating, a new addiction will crop up, for example, the urge to run up balances on credit cards.

There are two approaches to dealing with addictive agents: The first approach is to completely abstain from the abused substance or behavior. This has been proven as the best way to deal with addictive agents such as drugs or alcohol.

Then there are addictive agents that simply can't be avoided: An addiction to spending is a hard obsession to break because purchases must be made; the question is how to make them for the right reasons. For these and other addictions (food), work, destructive relationships, spending), as well as which approach is appropriate in overcoming the problem, the road to recovery is paved with balance rather than abstinence.

If your recovery goal is balance, take a moment to be more specific about the boundaries. With food addiction, abstinence is impossible, but there may be some foods that may be reasonable candidates for abstinence: go ahead and list the specific foods that are, for you, toxic and identify exactly what your new boundaries will be regarding those foods. It's not enough to say about your workaholism: "I need to bring my career into balance." A more specific set

Week
7

of boundaries might include working no more than 45 hours per week and engaging in a maximum of 5 hours per week of phone calls outside of work.

I am addicted to _____. My recovery goal for this addiction is (to balance or abstain): _____. If I selected balance, my new, specific boundaries regarding this addictive agent are as follows: _____

_____

Are there any safety measures I can establish that will help me respect my new boundaries?

_____

_____

What are some of the trigger events that have in the past "set off" my addictive behavior, and how can I avoid these events or lessen their impact on me in the future? _____

_____

I am addicted to _____. My recovery goal for this addiction is (to balance or abstain): _____. If I selected balance, my new, specific boundaries regarding this addictive agent are as follows: _____

_____

Are there any safety measures I can establish that will help me respect my new boundaries?

_____

_____

What are some of the trigger events that have in the past "set off" my addictive behavior, and how can I avoid these events or lessen their impact on me in the future? _____

_____

I am addicted to _____. My recovery goal for this addiction is (to balance or abstain): _____. If I selected balance, my new, specific boundaries regarding this addictive agent are as follows: _____

_____

Are there any safety measures I can establish that will help me respect my new boundaries?

_____

_____

Week
7

What are some of the trigger events that have in the past "set off" my addictive behavior, and how can I avoid these events or lessen their impact on me in the future? _____

_____

DAY 3

Step 7. We humbly asked Him to remove our shortcomings.

THE POWER TO TRANSFORM

There is an interesting feature of Step 7 in terms of the wording. Step 7 is the very shortest of the Twelve Steps. As a result, in terms of how it is discussed in recovery groups, it oftentimes is the least talked about of the twelve.

Ironically, this is very likely the most potent step of the bunch. This is the step that embodies the miracle of transformation—the moment when you can take your brokenness and ask God to change it. The following prayer is one which many have prayed through the years in the course of their recovery. Notice the emphasis on the transformation from "defect of character" to "usefulness" and "strength."

My Creator,

I am not willing that You should have all of me, good and bad. I pray that You now remove every single defect of character which stands in the way of my usefulness to You and my fellows. Grant me strength as I go out from here to do Your bidding.

Amen.[1]
—Twelve Steps and Twelve Traditions

The apostle Paul, a man whose life was changed by God, told the Corinthian Christians about the transforming power possessed by God:

Therefore, if anyone is in Christ, he is a new creation; old things have passed away; behold, all things have become new. (2 Cor. 5:17)

DAY 4

THE "MIRACLE" CURES

Todd and Valerie were feeling good about nutrition questions which had once been a puzzle to them and were now becoming clear. They still wanted to know more about vitamins, minerals, and "other factors" which were unabashedly displayed across the tabloids at the supermarket. What about all those miracle cures? Were there really any undiscovered enzymes and vitamins that would help with the weight loss process? Dr. Sneed opened up their workbook to this section and tried to answer those questions for them.

VITAMIN AND MINERAL SUPPLEMENTATION

Many patients will ask us if they need added vitamins and minerals during the weight loss process. If you are consuming the minimum servings of foods from all of the food groups (see the Food Exchanges, pages 353–355), then extra vitamins are probably not necessary. However, you must be careful not to shortchange yourself on either milk or vegetables. If you are going to be deficient in certain nutrients, it would probably pertain to calcium and the vitamins and minerals present in a diverse group of vegetables.

You will no doubt have noticed that it is only vegetables and not fruits which have been emphasized in this manual. Fruits are also wonderful sources of nutrients, but they do contain more calories and fewer nutrients than do the lower calorie vegetables.

If you do not eat many vegetables and dairy products, you should consider a general vitamin and mineral supplement which contains no more than 100 percent of the Recommended Dietary Allowances (RDA) for any particular nutrient. *Megadoses of vitamins and minerals will not help you* and can in fact make you sick by irritating the lining of your stomach.

Calcium supplementation for women is another important issue. All women need at least 800 to 1,200 mg of calcium per day. This is particularly difficult to obtain at the 800-calorie level. A woman using this diet plan might do well to supplement herself with 600 mg of calcium per day and depend on getting the rest from her dietary choices.

One thing we can't emphasize enough is that you will never make up for a poor diet with a pill. For example, calcium is absorbed better from a real dairy product than from a pill. Or another example might be that all of the micro-nutrients which occur in a slice of whole wheat bread will not be present in most vitamin-mineral preparations. Take care to choose your food wisely, when on a diet. There is really no room for much "junk" since your calorie intake is so low.

OTHER FACTORS

Every Sunday newspaper across America, as well as the supermarket tabloids, includes some miraculous new weight loss remedy. Let's face it, diets sell. It's a multibillion-dollar business, and some folks are in it for the greenbacks only. The government tries to protect us against most of these scams, but the companies just reorganize, relabel their products, and appear as one of those $19.95 specials on late night television the next week.

There are no new miracles out there. There are no pills that can increase your metabolism (unless you are taking amphetamines). There are no enzymes that can render the calories you have eaten unusable. There are no undiscovered vitamins and minerals which will help you lose two pounds per day. In short, there are no quick fixes. If there were, we happily would tell you about them. Finally, be advised that certain people will tell you what you want to hear in order to sell you a product you don't need.

DAY 4

GUILT AND SHAME

Consequences associated with "shortcomings" can generate large doses of guilt as you sense the greater impact of your food addiction. It is possible that the guilt you feel as a result of consequences is authentic. For example, you may feel guilty that your food addiction has posed a dangerous model for your children. The fact is, you are probably right. Your addiction may have helped set the stage for your son's or daughter's own journey into addictive behavior somewhere in their future.

Guilt in limited doses can be a helpful emotion, serving a positive purpose. Guilt—regarding a valid infraction or wrong—may be the emotion that alerts you to harmful behavior and motivates you to correct or change that for which you are responsible. At that point, guilt has served its purpose and must be discarded. If it isn't, you may become mired in unnecessary guilty feelings which can *demotivate* you and actually strengthen your bond to the destructive.

Another more virulent and prevalent form of guilt, however, is false guilt. False guilt can occur when you, at some level, assume responsibility for something that is out of your control. Many adults carry false guilt from their childhood days in their families of origin. It is a normal developmental dynamic that young children have a sense that the world does, indeed, revolve around them. This dynamic, however, will lead a child to believe that if tragedy or dysfunction occurs in his family, he is fully responsible. If parents divorce, it's the child who suffers a nagging sense that if she had only been better behaved, the family would still live together. If a parent dies, it's the child who feels responsible, even though she may not be able to identify exactly how she brought about daddy's death. If a parent is rageaholic or alcoholic or addicted to drugs or food or whatever, it is the child who points an internal finger in accusation back at self. In Week 8, you will discover how to say "good-bye" to false guilt—now it is important to simply realize that you may need to let yourself off the hook for a lot of the false guilt you may be experiencing.

DAY 4

Step 7. We humbly asked Him to remove our shortcomings.

GUILT

Guilt—authentic or false—can readily result in shame. Shame is more than an acknowledgment of your part, real or imagined, in a mistake, crisis, or tragedy. Shame is a reflection of the resulting impact on the way you view your self-worth.

Guilt says: I shouldn't have eaten that bag of candy.
Shame says: I'm such a bad person. I don't deserve to lose weight or to look better or to feel good about myself.

Guilt says: I made a mistake.
Shame says: I am a mistake.

Authentic guilt imparts humility and inspires right action. False shame paralyzes and erodes healthy identity. As you examine your life for sources of guilt and shame, it may help to respond to the following statements and questions.

I feel guilty or ashamed whenever I think about _____

Was I the person who physically produced the behavior? ____ yes ____ no

If not, who was? _____

Exactly how did I influence this event, crisis, or behavior? _____

_____

If I am, indeed, responsible for this event, crisis, or behavior, are there any persons, including myself, who have been hurt as a result? ____ yes ____ no

If so, who are they, and how have they been injured? _____

_____

If I am, indeed, responsible for this event, crisis, or behavior, is it morally or legally wrong?
_____ yes _____ no

Is there anything I can do now to remedy the situation and thus move past the authentic guilt?

_____

When there is true guilt—where you have practiced your addiction and hurt yourself or others—it is important to dig deep into your feelings about the loss and damage. For example, if you are an overeater and workaholic and as a result never played sports with your son, you may realize that you lost a huge piece of quality time with your son. It's important, then, to get in touch with the authentic guilt and remorse that you may feel as a result. The goal is not to get stuck in guilt and shame—even authentic guilt. The fact is, saying "hello" to the painful feelings lays the groundwork for being able to say "good-bye," releasing yourself from their grip, and moving on with your life. This process of saying "good-bye" will be thoroughly examined in Week 8. Right now, however, take the time to get in touch with any feelings of authentic guilt. If you have hurt yourself or someone you love in any way, write a letter pouring out your feelings about the damage you inflicted—address the letter to yourself if you are the victim. For the time being, assume you will never deliver the letter if it is to a second party. Let your focus rest on what the letters means to *you* as you get in touch with the painful feelings.

Dear _____,
I've been thinking about _____ and the way you have
been hurt by this. I realize that I'm the one responsible—that I should have

_____

_____

_____

_____

_____

_____

_____

_____

_____

DAY 5

PUTTING IT ALL TOGETHER

Valerie and Todd were letting everything soak in and had come to a greater appreciation for the very complex nature of a thorough weight-loss program. With so much new information to understand and assimilate, Valerie was still a little bewildered as she asked Dr. Sneed, "How can you help us put all of this together into the perfect diet program?"

"Well, Valerie," said Dr. Sneed, "you have done most of that already all by yourself. First, you should review everything you wrote down this week and then we will summarize some of that information together as we go through the lesson today. One summary concept I would like to talk about, that we have not addressed directly, is the issue of calories."

CALORIES DO COUNT

Though calories have not been discussed as of yet, they represent the summary of whether weight loss will occur or not. It is ultimately impossible to lose weight unless more calories are going out than are coming in. This simplified verbal picture of calorie balance can help us see that weight control is like a child's seesaw, tipping in one direction to cause weight gain or the other direction to cause weight loss. Examine those factors which can cause weight loss and then answer the related questions.

EXERCISE

Exercise helps you burn more calories during the actual exercise period and afterwards for the following four to six hours when your metabolism is still elevated. You have been in the program for about two months, now, and should be exercising (walking, jogging, exercise class) about 30 to 60 minutes per day, unless you have a medical restriction. You will burn at least 100 calories for every mile you walk. Keep that in mind next time you put on those walking shoes.

Are you currently exercising at least 30 minutes per day? _____ yes _____ no

If your answer is no, examine the reasons. _____

_____

_____

Are you providing yourself ample opportunity and time to exercise daily?
____ yes ____ no

If not, how can you make further changes? _____

_____

_____

Exercise is one of the greatest factors in helping you get weight off and keep it off. It tips that seesaw in your favor and keeps it there.

ADVANCING AGE

Advancing age is something you can't do anything about. But it is important to know that past age twenty-five, your basal metabolic rate decreases by two percent per decade. This may not seem like much, but if you don't adjust your food intake accordingly or increase your energy output (amount of exercise and activity), then you can count on gaining about three to five pounds per year.

At what age were you when you began having trouble with your weight? ____ If you were an adult, then you can count on the fact that the advancing age factor had something to do with it. Now that you understand this issue, does it help to know that anytime you can save twenty or fifty calories worth of food intake (equivalent to one pat of margarine), this might be the little effort that keeps the extra three pounds a year from accumulating? What small food intakes can you avoid each day which don't contribute to your taste buds or eating satisfaction, but do contribute to an increase in weight? _____

_____

_____

Fat is more fattening. This factor has been discussed earlier this week to show you that no more than 25 percent of your total daily caloric intake should come from fat.

Remember this, the more fat you have in your diet, the fewer calories you will be able to eat and still maintain or lose weight. Fat contains nine or more calories for every gram while protein and carbohydrate both contain only four calories per gram. Thus, they are much less concentrated sources of calories. And, because of the close chemical similarities between dietary fat and human body fat, if you eat fat, some of it will turn into fat, even on a calorie restricted program.

Do you feel you have made the jump to a lower fat diet? ____ yes ____ no

What changes do you still need to make? _____

_____

Are you still consuming any high fat comfort foods? _____ yes _____ no

Can you see that eventually these will no longer taste good to you as you form new habits?
_____ yes _____ no

CALORIE DISTRIBUTION

Distribution of calories is a key. Twenty-five percent of your calories should come from fat (even less would be good if you can manage it). Another twenty-five percent should come from protein and the remaining 50 percent from carbohydrate. These represent average amounts while you are on the Love Hunger Diet Plan program. The ranges will vary depending on the number of calories you are having per day and the individual choices you make.

Protein	25 to 35 percent of your total daily caloric intake
Carbohydrate	40 to 60 percent of your total daily caloric intake
Fat	15 to 25 percent of your total daily caloric intake

How does your diet measure up to these standards? _____

_____

Are you following the menu exchange program carefully or are you including extra foods that may be higher fat items than we would normally recommend?

_____

Can you see that after you have lost your weight the same type of diet will work well as a maintenance diet except that it needs to be of a higher caloric content?
_____ yes _____ no

(*Note:* The maintenance diet will actually contain many of its added calories from carbohydrate, decreasing total protein intake about 20 percent.)

FIBER

Increased fiber content in your diet will help move digesting food in the intestine along at a faster rate. The inclusion of one-half cup per day of a very high fiber cereal will provide all the extra fiber that you need. This should save you as much as fifty calories per day in foods that are not absorbed as completely because of the decreased transit time in the colon.

Even though we first talked about fiber yesterday, have you thought about making any changes in your daily eating program? _____ yes _____ no

What do you anticipate changing? _____

_____

A SUMMARY OF WEIGHT LOSS FACTORS

1. Exercise regularly.
2. Plan on decreasing your caloric intake slightly with advancing age.
3. Decrease your fat intake.
4. Eat very lean sources of protein and include complex carbohydrates in your diet.
5. Consume at least 25 grams per day of dietary fiber.

These suggestions will help you lose the same amount of weight as you would have on a diet that contained as much as 400 calories per day less than the one you have designed for yourself using the menu exchanges in this notebook.

DAY 5

SELF-HATRED

Whereas guilt says, "I shouldn't have done that," and shame says, "I'm a bad person and don't deserve to be happy," self-hatred takes the cycle a step further and says, "I don't even deserve to live."

Your addiction to food is, as we have examined, a form of slow suicide. Whereas it may ultimately result in your early death, it certainly is the death of quality living even now. How many athletic activities or social events have you declined because of your weight? How many relationships have died because you used your weight to barricade yourself against emotional or physical intimacy?

What are some of the specific, self-destructive features of my food addiction? _____

_____

If I didn't already include them in my previous response, what are several health risks that are associated with obesity or with diet high in fat or sugar?_____

_____

_____

_____

_____

Regarding the thought of death, I . . . (Check all that apply.)

____ feel scared.

____ think death would be a relief.

____ wonder what it would be like to escape all the pain.

____ think about who would miss me.

____ feel anxious.

____ wonder how I'll die.

____ keep waiting for life to really begin for me.

____ think about how I've mistreated my body.

____ feel sad, but sometimes I think I deserve it.

____ try not to think about it.

____ think about disease a lot.

____ am afraid of any pain involved.

____ look forward to a happier afterlife.

____ don't feel like I'm really living very fully now.

The final point on the addictive cycle is the self-destruct mode. Yet it doesn't end here. This kind of self-hatred and self-inflicted damage carves out a hungry place in the addict's emotional heart, enlarging the love hunger cavity. Suddenly you find yourself at the top of the cycle, gaining momentum for a second spin, this time driven more intensely than before.

You can get off the cycle. Diet and exercise alone won't do it; it takes a thorough examination of each of the five points on the spiral. As you progress into Week 8 and learn how to say healthy good-byes, you will be receiving tools that can help you begin to release yourself from the vicious cycle of addiction.

DAY 5

Step 7. We humbly asked Him to remove our shortcomings.

MAKING THE REQUEST

In the previous segments, you've read one example of a seventh step prayer used in Twelve Step groups for decades. You've also received direction on how to make your request—embracing your God-given needs while rejecting defective means of meeting or expressing those needs.

Now is the moment to approach God with your request. Because this is such a significant step toward transformation, take the time to write your prayer as a letter to God in the following space. As you write your letter, do so with one eye on the photocopied inventories you saved from Step 6. These are the specific shortcomings you are offering into the powerful hands of a God who is experienced in the transformation of lives.

Most important, consider the attitude of your heart as you approach God; willingness and humility are all that are required from you at this moment. The actual work of transformation is an undertaking that belongs to God. If you do your part, He'll come through with His.

Now that your letter/prayer is complete, take the photocopied inventories you have just submitted humbly to God and relinquish them in a fashion symbolic of the spiritual relinquishing you have just achieved. You may want to take the inventories to a safe place and burn them. Perhaps you feel like sending them through a paper shredder or simply tearing them into shreds by hand.

Whatever you choose, know that you have taken a great step in the process of finding full recovery from your codependencies.

> Dear God of the Universe,
> I humbly and expectantly invite You into my recovery process, and specifically, I ask that Your bold transforming power touch the following areas of my life . . .
>
> _____
>
> _____
>
> _____

WEEKLY FOOD AND EXERCISE JOURNAL

Date _____
Weight (First day of week only) _____

	Breakfast/ A.M. Snack	Lunch P.M. Snack	Dinner Nite Snack	Exercise	Feelings and Major Events of the Day
Day One					
Day Two					
Day Three					
Day Four					
Day Five					
Day Six					
Day Seven					

Week
7

DAY 1

CREATIVE COOKING

BECOME A GOOD COOK

Valerie had always wanted to be involved with a weight loss program that was practical and helped in everyday matters like cooking. She was pleased when Dr. Sneed explained that Valerie's favorite recipes could be a part of her Love Hunger Diet Plan.

"Almost any recipe you can think of can be modified to fit into your diet plan, Valerie," said Dr. Sneed. "You can learn to make great tasting but lower calorie pizza, Mexican food, and even cheesecake. We have some of our best recipes in the *Love Hunger* book—that might be a good place to start. I'm sure you have other cookbook resources at home. This week we will talk about general principles of cooking that will help you "de-fat" or reduce the calorie content of some of your favorite meals."

During Valerie's next few appointments, Dr. Sneed explained this.

1. Learn to cook well. Many people don't eat certain healthy foods—specifically fish and vegetables—because they did not grow up with them. If their mother did not fix them, they never learned to cook these foods properly. If you have not learned to cook well, enroll in a community education class or some type of cooking class. The recipes in *Love Hunger* use healthy ingredients and cooking methods. Investigate other cookbooks that feature low-calorie and/or low-fat recipes.

2. Be an organized cook. Plan your meals and make your grocery list accordingly. This takes less time than having to make do with other ingredients or running to the store every day at the last minute.

Is it your current habit to make a shopping list when you go to the grocery store?

____ yes ____ no

When you don't make a list, do you find yourself doing more impulse buying and perhaps purchasing specials that are not good food choices but are on sale?

_____ yes _____ no

Do you really think these are bargains? _____ yes _____ no

Do you ever overbuy because something is a good deal and then feel compelled to eat it before it spoils? _____ yes _____ no

3. Develop your own recipe file. Of course, your family has certain foods that they favor. Go through your cookbooks and try the recipes that appeal to you. Take the ones you like best, write them down on cards, and you will have a collection of healthy dishes that are all winners.

Are you willing to put away your personal recipes that include ingredients which are not good for either your weight loss or your weight maintenance program?

_____ yes _____ no

Which recipes do you think will have to be eliminated or used very infrequently?

_____

_____

_____

4. Use the right equipment. Nonstick cookware means that you don't have to cook with fat. In the past, fat in a cast-iron skillet reduced scrubbing. Today, a very important part of low-fat cooking is good nonstick cookware and nonstick cooking sprays which come in regular flavor, butter, or olive oil flavors. Another important feature of good cookware is its weight. Heavier pans distribute heat through food more evenly.

Do you have some nonstick or very heavy cookware that allows you to cook without added fat? _____ yes _____ no

5. Make use of the microwave and other helpful kitchen appliances. Microwaves are excellent for cooking vegetables. To microwave a vegetable, put it in a small bowl, add two tablespoons of water, cover the bowl with plastic wrap, and zap it for about ten minutes, depending on the type of vegetable. Flavor it with herbs, spices, or sprinkle with a butter substitute. This is also the easiest way to make non-fat popcorn. Take plain, microwave popcorn, spray it with the butter-flavored, non-stick spray, and sprinkle with a butter substitute. A food processor or a blender is also a useful item to save you time and effort on many vegetable dishes. Ask for one of these items next time a gift occasion rolls around if they are not already in your kitchen.

Week
8

DAY 1

SAYING GOOD-BYE

Psychologists and others often view life as a series of hellos and good-byes. Experiences, phases, stages, even relationships come and go, and if you are living life well you will find yourself facing frequent transitions and the need to say good-bye in every realm of your life.

As a recovering food addict, there are some special good-byes that you may need to get tough with. If you have trouble letting go of these hurts, experiences, or relationships, it will cripple your capacity to say hello to many good things in your present and future.

People can become literally fixed—obsessed—with some feature of their past.

The irony is that while it's always hard to say good-bye to any family we've grown up in, it seems to be more difficult to say good-bye to a dysfunctional family and the pain experienced there than a healthy family. Logic tells us it should be the other way around. If we grew up in a warm and loving family, it might be hard to leave that nest and move on. Yet reality proves otherwise. If a child has been reared in a warm, loving family, his or her needs have been adequately met, and he or she is actually ready to move on to the next phase of life. Think for a moment of the relationship between a battery and its recharger. If the battery has been there long enough and received enough input, it is ready to go on and fulfill its purpose.

On the other hand, if a child has been exposed to dysfunction, he or she has needs that have never been met. There exists a part of that person, even upon reaching adulthood, which still cries for those needs to be met by Mom and Dad. This person remains emotionally and spiritually rooted to home, carrying pains from that family around inside almost like a ghost.

There are three specific areas related to your family of origin to which you need to say good-bye.

1. Say good-bye to whatever residue of pain you've carried with you out of the experience of growing up in the family you did. In Week 9 of the Mind track, you will examine further ways to release yourself from this pain, but for this week it's important to recognize the pain and make a conscious effort to say "good-bye." Complete the following statements, using the example as a guide.

(It's time to say good-bye to the pain of my parents' divorce. As a part of that good-bye, I realize that while I suffered, there was no intent to hurt me. My parents, like the rest of the world, are imperfect human beings and make mistakes; it's unfortunate, but sometimes innocent bystanders get hurt, too.)

It's time to say good-bye to the *pain* of _____

_____

As a part of that good-bye, I want to say hello to new life by _____

_____

(It's time to say good-bye to my anger over my physical abuse at the hands of my parents. As a part of that good-bye, I want to move past my personal pain and toward helping other victims through the support network of a local community service.)

It's time to say good-bye to my *anger* over _____

_____

As a part of that good-bye, I want to say "hello" to new life by _____

_____

(It's time to say good-bye to my resentment toward my inattentive father. As a part of that good-bye, I realize that he hurt me, but I'm multiplying that hurt by living my life bitterly and full of anger. I want to become more caring in the key friendships of my adult life.)

It's time to let go of my *resentment* toward _____

As a part of that good-bye, I want to say "hello" to new life by _____

_____

DAY 1

STEP 8: WE MADE A LIST OF ALL PERSONS WE HAD HARMED AND BECAME WILLING TO MAKE AMENDS TO THEM ALL.

Implicit in Step 8, as well as in Step 9, is the assumption that you carry a shame or guilt residue from virtually every incident where you have hurt, rejected, or ignored others. The assumption here is that every time you hurt someone, it leaves a toxic residue. Even though you feel some guilt and shame, you may be able to go along for months, years, even decades tolerating that toxic residue. But at some point it reaches a breaking point—which is why Steps 8 and 9 are so important as ways of reducing that shame and guilt and burying the "ledger."

This step also recognizes the pivotal role of relationships in the recovery process. Remember, your relationships with people play a greater role in your addiction than even your relationship to the addictive agent. Another way to phrase this key point—as we've stated before—is that your relationship with food has much more to do with your relationship with people than it has to do with calories, nutrition, and diet.

Realize that this process of repairing relationships is one-sided and one-directional. That means it's not contingent on the other person's returning the apology; it's not necessarily reciprocal. This process also does not ignore, excuse, or condone harm that may have come to you from others. You need to recognize those hurts—don't deny or bury them—but go ahead and make the amends for your own peace of mind so you feel cleared of your responsibility for what went wrong in that relationship.

In the following days you will be compiling lists of people you have hurt in any ways. Today, however, it's important to set the foundation for the work that will follow by examining any fears you may have about admitting fault or guilt.

In your family of origin, how did your parents resolve relationships when they had done something to damage the bond? _____

_____

Did members of your family readily admit fault or guilt to one another?

____ yes ____ no

When such an admission was made, how did your parents react? _____

_____

Were your parents able to admit their own imperfections to their children?

____ yes ____ no

If not, what image did they present instead? _____

_____

In your adult life, are you able to easily apologize to people you have hurt?

____ yes ____ no

If not, what is your alternative approach when you realize that words or actions of yours have damaged a relationship? _____

Looking at your present-day relationships, do they "go back" any length of time or are they all fairly new relationships? _____

When you hit a "glitch" in a relationship, is it easier to let the relationship fade and begin a bond with someone new, or have you learned to work the relationship past the troubled spot?

Looking at your present relationships, identify the ones which have survived hurtful or troubled times and which represent a closer bond because of working through the mistakes and problems.

Relationship with	*Offending party, you or them*	*How resolved*
_____	_____	_____
_____	_____	_____
_____	_____	_____

Identify relationships which have faded and died because one person offended the other and things were never patched.

Relationship with	*Offending party, you or them*	*How resolved*
_____	_____	_____
_____	_____	_____
_____	_____	_____

DAY 2

MODIFY, LIMIT, DILUTE

1. Read labels and recipes carefully. Modify recipes when you can. Learn which ingredients are good for you and which are not. Learn how to determine fat percentage from the label (see page 185). Remember that many of your old recipes call for too much fat and too much sugar. You might be able to take, for example, your all-time favorite oatmeal cookie recipe, reduce the fat content by one-third, reduce the sugar content by one-half, substitute two egg whites for one whole egg, and have a great-tasting lower-calorie, lower fat, healthful cookie.

2. Dilute recipes. Extend the volume of your recipes with high fiber, low-calorie foods. For example, if you're going to make a tuna salad, you can double the volume size and dilute the calories by adding things like chopped celery, chopped dill pickles, and chopped apples—turning a lovely recipe into one that is also low-calorie and healthy. You might use this same calorie dilution principle in making a hearty vegetable beef soup, by using more low-calorie vegetables than anything else. Or what about a spicy Southwestern chili full of peppers, onions, fresh tomatoes, and even sliced carrots?

3. Limit oils. When sautéing, use only a very small amount of oil or a combination of a very small amount of oil and perhaps bouillon or water. Fat-absorbing vegetables such as potatoes should be cooked with as little oil as possible.

4. Watch the cholesterol. Cholesterol intake still makes a difference in your overall serum concentration, and lower serum levels of cholesterol help prevent heart disease. The added benefit is that a low-cholesterol diet is usually a low-fat as well as a low-calorie diet. The chart below shows some low-fat alternatives you can try when you do cook.

Low-Cholesterol and Low-Fat Alternatives

Skim, 1/2%	Lean fish, turkey, chicken (no skin),
Skim milk or part skim milk cheese	beef (no visible fat), pork, lobster, crab
Soft margarine	Olive oil, vegetable oils
Ice milk, fruit sorbet, frozen yogurt,	English muffins, bagels, bread, French
sherbet	bread, muffins, pita bread
* Egg whites, egg substitutes	Baked chip alternatives, pretzels,
	homemade dip

*Two egg whites may be substituted for one whole egg in most combination recipes.

5. Use a separating cup. Separating cups may be obtained at culinary shops. Take the stock from any roast or baked chicken dish, pour it into the separating cup, and the fat will float to the top. Pour the fat-free bouillon off and throw the fat away to make all types of fat-free gravy. For example, if you have a pot roast—a very lean pot roast, like the eye of the round roast— go ahead and Dutch oven cook it, pour the stock into the separating cup, pour the bouillon back into the pan, thicken it with cornstarch and water, and you have a very nice fat-free brown gravy. You can use the same principle with the stock from your Thanksgiving turkey.

Week
8

DAY 2

SAYING GOOD-BYE TO YOUR PAST

You need to say good-bye to the hope, wish, or fantasy that you could ever change your family of origin. You could be in midlife or beyond and still clinging to the unconscious fantasy that if you just become good enough or thin enough or successful enough, then "Dad will accept me" or "Mom will see that I turned out okay and love me" or "Dad will admit how wrong he was to molest me" or "Mom and Dad will learn to value me more than their careers, or money, or whatever." Parallel to this is the thought that you have the power, somehow, to make your parents give you whatever it is they *didn't* give you when you were growing up. For better or worse, members of your family of origin are who they are, and you need to accept that. You can't change them, you can't make them meet the needs they've ignored for years, you can't solve their problems. You aren't responsible for their dysfunctions, and saying good-bye to that notion is important because if you, at any level, believe that you *are* responsible then the sense of failure you may experience can propel you deeper in the food addiction cycle.

(It's time to say good-bye to the fantasy that I could change Mom and Dad's marriage by being the "perfect daughter.")

It's time to say good-bye to the fantasy that _____

_____

(It's time to say good-bye to the fantasy that we could be one big happy family if I play the peacemaker and bring everyone together.)

It's time to say good-bye to the fantasy that _____

_____

(It's time to say good-bye to the fantasy that my sister would approve of me if only I was more like her.)

It's time to say good-bye to the fantasy that _____

_____

These emotional good-byes release an enormous weight, reduce the shame base, and equip us to become energetic and unencumbered expressions of God's love in action.

DAY 2

Step 8. We made a list of all persons we had harmed and became willing to make amends to them all.

ACKNOWLEDGING THE VICTIMS OF MY ADDICTIONS

This is the day where you begin drawing up the list of persons to whom you are willing to make amends. Begin now by identifying those persons who have been unwilling victims of your addictions.

You might include a spouse for whom your weight became a barrier to intimacy; or your children who have experienced the impatience of a parent distracted by food and the other addictions you identified in Week 2. These are the same children who have watched, possibly during very formative years, as you've modeled food codependency.

Maybe another victim has been a boss for whom you've worked less efficiently because of your compulsive behavior; or dating partners who never fully understood some of the dynamics—related to your codependency—which impacted the relationship. Friends, family members, members of your church or neighborhood—think deeply about the many relationships that might have been different or better somehow if not for your food addiction.

I realize now that my addiction to food has influenced my relationship with _____ _____ . Until now, I haven't tried to resolve this matter with this person because I felt _____

_____

Realizing that relationships are two-way streets, this individual may have contributed to the problem by _____

Nevertheless, I am not responsible for his or her wrongs, only my own. Regarding the manner in which I have negatively impacted our relationship, I would like to say to this person:

_____

_____

_____

I realize now that my addiction to food has influenced my relationship with _____

_____ . Until now, I haven't tried to resolve this matter with this person

because I felt _____

_____

Realizing that relationships are two-way streets, this individual may have contributed to the problem by _____

Nevertheless, I am not responsible for his or her wrongs, only my own. Regarding the manner in which I have negatively impacted our relationship, I would like to say to this person:

_____

_____

_____

DAY 3

HERBS AND SPICE AND EVERYTHING NICE

1. Fish is your best meat choice. If you've never learned to like fish, make the effort. It is worth it because fish is decidedly different from chicken or other types of poultry. Fish will help you decrease your serum levels of triglycerides and cholesterol, and it is lower in fat and calories than either chicken or beef. On the generic menu, you may always have a four- to five-ounce serving of fish whereas if you choose beef, it should be a three-ounce serving.

If fish is not a regular part of your diet, are you willing to make more effort to try recipes you might like? _____ yes _____ no

2. Remove visible fat and skin from meat. Always choose the leanest cuts of beef. Cutting away visible fat and skin from any meat you are preparing is a given. You know that already. But did you know that there is a lot of fat that cannot be cut away because it is located between the meat fibers and permeates the entire portion? The cuts of beef that have the least amount of this marbleized fat include lean round steak, eye-of-the-round roast, ground round, tenderloin, and sirloin. Do not buy the fattier ground beef or cuts such as T-bones and ribeyes. Also, veal is usually 20 percent lower in fat than beef because veal comes from a younger animal and has less time to develop fat.

One additional tip: Beef is an especially good source of certain trace minerals, including iron and zinc. Americans consume only marginal amounts of these nutrients.

Let's name some recipes in which round steak might be used. Check off the ones that you have tried in your kitchen before or would like to try. Remember that you can have a three-ounce serving of any of these during your lunch and/or dinner meal.

____ Smothered steak

____ Pepper steak

____ Chinese beef and broccoli

____ Beef shish kebab

____ Swedish meatballs

____ Hamburgers

____ Meatloaf

____ Spaghetti with tomato and meat sauce

____ Chili

3. Substitute herbs and spices for fat and salt. Use herbs and spices in everything to reduce the need for fat and salt. If you are using fresh herbs such as fresh chopped parsley, use about two to four times more fresh than dried. Use the chart below to help you determine which spice or herb will work for which food.

Food Flavorings as a Replacement for Salt

Beef	Bay leaf, dry mustard, green pepper, red wine, sage, marjoram, mushrooms, nutmeg, onion, pepper, thyme.
Chicken and poultry	Cranberries, mushrooms, paprika, parsley, poultry seasoning (unsalted), thyme, sage, lemon juice, orange juice, lime juice, white wine.
Lamb	Curry, garlic, mint, pineapple, rosemary.
Pork	Apple, applesauce, garlic, onion, sage, cranberries.
Veal	Apricots, bay leaf, curry, currant jelly, ginger, marjoram, oregano.
Fish	Bay leaf, curry, dry mustard, green pepper, lemon juice, lime juice, marjoram, mushroom, paprika, onion, dill weed parsley.
Eggs	Curry, dry mustard, green pepper, jelly, mushrooms, onion, paprika, parsley, tomato.
Asparagus	Lemon juice.
Corn	Green pepper, tomato, sugar.
Green beans	Marjoram, lemon juice, nutmeg, dill seed, sugar, unsalted French dressing.
Peas	Onion, mint, mushrooms, parsley, green pepper.
Potatoes	Onion, mace, green pepper, parsley.
Squash	Ginger, mace, onion, basil, nutmeg.
Tomatoes	Basil, marjoram, onion, sugar.

DAY 3

SAYING GOOD-BYE TO YOUR NEED TO MIMIC OR REBEL

You also need to say good-bye to your need to mimic or rebel against members of your family of origin. In Week 6, when we talked about how family members become locked into roles, we discussed the possibility of becoming mechanically locked in a state of rebellion or a state of mimicking the role of one of your parents. The goal here is to say good-bye to either of those extremes. This "good-bye" *must* take place before you can choose the parts of your emotional heritage you want for yourself, and freely leave the parts you don't want.

> Imagine all the traits, characteristics, strengths, and weaknesses belonging to your parents being set out before you, like a cafeteria buffet. Instead of accepting everything dumped blindly on your plate, now as an adult you have the opportunity to go back and pick and choose: "Here's a positive quality of Dad's. I choose to make that a part of me. Here's a negative: I'm not judging him, but I'm putting that back on the shelf."

(An aspect of Mom's role that I choose to reject for myself is her perfectionism.)

An aspect of _____'s role that I choose to reject for myself is _____

_____

An aspect of _____'s role that I choose to reject for myself is _____

_____

An aspect of _____'s role that I choose to reject for myself is _____

_____

(An aspect of Mom's role that I choose to incorporate in my life is her commitment to her marriage.)

An aspect of _____'s role that I choose to reject for myself is _____

_____

An aspect of _____'s role that I choose to reject for myself is _____

_____

An aspect of _____'s role that I choose to reject for myself is _____

_____

(I no longer need to mimic Mom's compulsive eating. Instead, I can accept food in my life for its nutritional value and nothing more.)

I no longer need to mimic _____

Instead, I _____

_____

Week
8

(I no longer need to mimic Dad's need to be in control. Instead, I can feel good about myself even when things aren't going my way.)

I no longer need to mimic _____

Instead, I _____

_____

(I no longer need to rebel against Dad's workaholism by being irresponsible just to irk him. Instead, I can accept or reject responsibility in my own life based on how it impacts me, not him.)

I no longer need to *rebel* against _____ by _____

_____

Instead, I _____

_____

(I no longer need to rebel against my parents' messages that I am unworthy by seeking sexual affirmation from many partners. Instead I will seek to build my own self-esteem through positive self-talk and reinforcement from nonsexual relationships.)

I no longer need to *rebel* against _____ by _____

_____

Instead, I _____

_____

Week
8

(I no longer need to rebel against my father's compulsive spending by hoarding my money. Instead, I will allow myself [and my family] more opportunities to enjoy what money we have.)

I no longer need to *rebel* against _____ by _____

_____

Instead, I _____

_____

Finally, have you established appropriate physical and financial boundaries between you and your family of origin? If you, as an adult, are still living at home or are dependent financially upon a member of your family, particularly one or both parents, it will be very difficult to say the necessary generational good-byes that will help you resolve the food addiction cycle.

DAY 3

Step 8. We made a list of all persons we had harmed and became willing to make amends to them all.

REVIEWING YOUR RELATIONSHIPS

Now take a moment to review the relationships that we've talked about, spanning several steps—particularly relationships within your family of origin and current relationships with friends, family, and coworkers. As a rule, you may owe amends to most of the people who have entered your life in a significant manner. You have probably, at some level, even managed to hurt the people who have first hurt you—so don't rule out any relationship just because their violation of you might seem more significant than your violation of them.

Please note that your willingness to make amends does not absolve other parties of the wrongs they may have committed against you. This step does not ignore or whitewash sufferings inflicted on you by others. Rather, it is a way to release you from the shame and guilt that play a part in driving your obsession. This step is primarily for your sake. A secondary function is what your amends might do for the person you have wronged, but the key emphasis is on the release the amends generate for you.

In this section, don't limit the wrongs to those related to your food addiction. Thinking back over all your significant relationships—even those that were remote or based on acquaintance only—write down any instance that comes to mind regarding something you did that hurt someone else. It is important that you identify intentional as well as nonintentional grievances. The shame and guilt you may experience as a result of "accidentally" harming a friend is no less than that which you may experience over a malicious act.

I realize now that I harmed my relationship with _____ when I

As a result, my carelessness has impacted the relationship in the following manner:

_____

The reason I have not sought to repair any hurt resulting from this event is that _____

_____

Clearing the air at this point:

____ is important to me because _____

_____

____ is not important to me because _____

_____

Regarding this violation of the relationship, I would like to say to this person: _____

_____

I realize now that I harmed my relationship with _____ when I

_____

As a result, my carelessness has impacted the relationship in the following manner: _____

_____

The reason I have not sought to repair any hurt resulting from this event is that _____

_____

Clearing the air at this point:

____ is important to me because _____

_____

____ is not important to me because _____

_____

Regarding this violation of the relationship, I would like to say to this person: _____

_____

DAY 4

FIGHTING FAT IN THE KITCHEN

1. Avoid high-fat breads, chips, and dips. When considering breads, steer away from high-fat breads such as biscuits, doughnuts, croissants, and any other type of pastries. Choose lower-fat breads including English muffins, bagels, French bread, regular bread, muffins, and pita bread. For chips and dips use the baked chips or the lighter chips and homemade dips made out of low-fat cottage cheese, ricotta, or yogurt instead of sour cream. Making sandwiches, toast, or anything else requiring bread is not a problem as long as a low-fat variety has been used.

2. Don't fry. Mock frying by coating a food and baking it in the oven in a crispy coating can satisfy most of your desires for fried foods. This form of cooking can be applied to "oven-fried" chicken, fish, French fries, fritters, and several other recipes.

Are you aware that frying can double or even triple the caloric content of a food?

____ yes ____ no

Did you know that when you turn a 30-calorie onion into onion rings, it will contain more than 350 calories and be about 85 percent fat? ____ yes ____ no

Are you prepared to stop any frying that you are doing now and prepare the foods by a different method? ____ yes ____ no

3. Avoid high-fat crackers. When making a cracker selection, don't be fooled by high-fat crackers. Many varieties of crackers, even some which are whole wheat, are extremely high in fat. Take a facial tissue and place the cracker on it. A high-fat cracker will leave a little grease mark on the tissue. Also check the food label. Unfortunately, many labels list only the ingredients, not the calorie and fat contents specifically. If one of those ingredients is hydrogenated fat, be suspicious as this usually indicates a high-fat cracker. Even a "baked" cracker may not be low-fat. We recommend melba toast and rice cakes.

Are you currently incorporating any high-fat crackers like Wheat Thins®, Triscuits®, or variety crackers into your diet thinking that they are a good nutritional choice?

____ yes ____ no

Name a lower fat cracker you would be willing to substitute for these. _____

4. Substitute egg whites for whole eggs. To decrease cholesterol, substitute two egg whites for each whole egg in most recipes. This will also save you fifty calories and five grams of fat per egg. (One-half cup of Egg Beaters® may be used instead of two egg whites.) You can use egg whites as a substitute in the following recipes. Check the ones that you use and add some of your own in the second column.

____ Muffins   ____ _____

____ Cornbread   ____ _____

____ Casseroles   ____ _____

____ Meatloaf   ____ _____

____ Batter mix for oven-fried foods   ____ _____

____ Egg entrees for breakfast   ____ _____

5. Use butter substitutes. These are primarily spray or dried butter products which have been defatted. They have the essence of the butter flavor without all of the fat. They may be used during the cooking process or after the fact.

6. Avoid regular salad dressings. Never even consider a regular salad dressing. If you put one scoop of regular salad dressing on top of a salad, just imagine that, in terms of calories, you've put a cheeseburger on top of your salad. Regular salad dressings are about 80 to 90 calories per tablespoon, and we recommend 25 calories or less per tablespoon. Read the label and make sure that the calorie content, which is going to reflect the fat content, is 25 calories per tablespoon or less.

DAY 4

SAYING GOOD-BYE TO A LIMITING BODY IMAGE

Your path to recovery must include the process of saying good-bye to the distorted body image standing between you and freedom from your food compulsion. This can mean several different things.

If you have been chronically obese, you may have come to a point of resignation, throwing your hands in the air and accepting the unnecessary statement that you will always look this way and can never really improve your appearance. If this is the case, then you have locked yourself into an image that is a distortion of the truth. The truth is you may look this way today; the truth is also that you can look a great deal different this same time next week, next month, or next year. A distorted body image that limits you to your present size can become a self-fulfilling prophecy. To continue in recovery, you need to say good-bye to that distorted image and begin to nurture a new image of the way you want to look.

On the other end of the spectrum, if you are bulimic or anorexic you may—no matter how trim or fit you get—see fat or obesity that is not there. To progress into full recovery you, too, must say good-bye to that distorted body image and work on a new view of yourself that reflects reality.

The third possibility is that you are a compulsive overeater who may be in denial about his or her obesity. An example is the client who was approaching 400 pounds; he looked one of our counselors straight in the eye and admitted that he knew he needed to lose 40 or 50 pounds. He actually needed to lose several hundred pounds but honestly couldn't see that. Before he could get serious about any recovery program, he needed to say good-bye to his false body image and acknowledge the reality of his life-threatening obesity.

Take a moment and record your perception of your body image: What do you look like? What words would you use to describe your body shape? Are you plump? Obese? Chubby? Fat? How much weight do you need to lose?

_____

_____

_____

Now approach two people whom you know and trust. Ask them to describe, orally or by writing it down, how they see you. Ask them to answer the same questions you just asked yourself.

1. (1st respondent): _____

_____

_____

2. (2nd respondent): _____

_____

_____

Are the people you approached fairly consistent in their perceptions of the amount of weight you need to lose? Approximately how much is that? _____

How does this amount of weight differ from the amount of weight you said you thought you needed to lose? _____

Are there any other differences between your perception of your body and the response of the friends you approached? _____

_____

What about the potential for the future? How did your friends' responses differ from yours regarding the likelihood of your moving toward or reaching your ideal weight?

_____

_____

Describe the beauty, balance, and proportion that you want for your body size and shape as a long-term blessing from your food recovery. _____

_____

DAY 4

Step 8. We made a list of all persons we had harmed and became willing to make amends to them all.

MEMBERS OF THE NEXT GENERATION

Chances are, even if you aren't a parent you come in contact on a regular basis with members of the next generation. Through the families of friends and relatives, through your involvement at church, or perhaps even through your job, you meet and mark young people, leaving impressions that may last a lifetime. As a parent, you have an even greater privilege and responsibility in the arena of molding young lives.

As you consider the members of the next generation in whose lives you have played a role, think about how these children and youth have been impacted by the more destructive aspects of your life. This section is not unlike a portion of the exercise from Day 2—but today you have an opportunity to explore this issue on a deeper level. Whereas on Day 2 it was enough to acknowledge that your children had been impacted by your food addiction, today presents the chance to take a closer look at exactly how they have been marked, exactly what they have learned from you.

A child in whose life I play a significant role (or played a significant role if that child is now an adult) is _____

Do/did I ever binge in the presence of this child? ____ yes ____ no

Do/did I allow this child to participate in unhealthy eating habits? ____ yes ____ no

If so, what habits? _____

Have I ever lashed out at this child when I was, in fact, frustrated with the issues and dysfunctions in my own life? If so, mention a specific or representative incident: _____

_____

_____

Have I ever been distracted or depressed with my food addictions in such a way that it caused me to be negligent in meeting any of my child's needs? If so, what needs and how did they go unmet? _____

_____

_____

In what ways has this child modeled any part of my life (such as in areas of personality, career choices, values, communication, people skills, habits)? _____

_____

When I think of the possibility of this child's mimicking my addictions to food or other agents at any point in the future, I feel _____

_____

In response to any wrongs I may have inflicted on this relationship, I would like to say to this child: _____

_____

_____

A child in whose life I play a significant role (or played a significant role if that child is now an adult) is _____

Do/did I ever binge in the presence of this child? ____ yes ____ no

Do/did I allow this child to participate in unhealthy eating habits? ____ yes ____ no

If so, what habits? _____

Have I ever lashed out at this child when I was, in fact, frustrated with the issues and dysfunctions in my own life? If so, mention a specific or representative incident: _____

_____

Have I ever been distracted or depressed with my food addictions in such a way that it caused me to be negligent in meeting any of my child's needs? If so, what needs and how did they go unmet? _____

_____

_____

In what ways has this child modeled any part of my life (such as in areas of personality, career choices, values, communication, people skills, habits)? _____

_____

When I think of the possibility of this child's mimicking my addictions to food or other agents at any point in the future, I feel _____

_____

In response to any wrongs I may have inflicted on this relationship, I would like to say to this child: _____

_____

_____

The purpose of this exercise is not to drive you into guilt and shame regarding the impact your addictions may have had on young lives. On the contrary, this and the other exercises in this section are designed to help you purge guilt and shame from the realm of the unspoken where they may well have hidden and festered. Acknowledging any wrongs for which you are responsible is the only way you can go on and make amends for these wrongs, thus fully releasing yourself from the guilt and shame which may, festering, have further driven your food addiction.

One more thought: Particularly in our relationships with children, it is not our responsibility to model perfection. If we hold ourselves to the unrealistic expectation that the next generation will never see us fail, we will reap havoc in our lives as well as in the lives of the children we are hoping to influence.

Rather, one of the greatest gifts we can give our children is to let them observe us in our wholeness. Living with a two-dimensional parent who struggles to appear perfect offers much less than life with an adult who models what it's like to fail and rebuild. The process of apologizing to children you may have impacted through your addictions offers much more than a chance to repair past mistakes: it offers the chance for you to model key principles—that no one is perfect, that relationships are treasures worth protecting, that there is an appropriate way to respond if and when you hurt someone you love. These are the kinds of lessons that can prepare the next generation for successful living—now and in the years to come.

DAY 5

TRIM YOUR DAIRY FAT

1. Use skim milk or ½ percent milk. Don't even consider using whole milk or 2 percent milk. Whole milk is half fat. That is, every other calorie in whole milk comes from saturated fat. No one past the age of two needs to drink whole milk. Nutritionally speaking, skim milk contains just as much calcium, phosphorus, and all the other good things that whole milk does, and it does not have the calories and the fat. And don't stop at 2 percent milk either. One-quarter of the calories of this "so-called low-fat milk" is still from saturated fat. Skim milk is the only way to go (½ percent is essentially the same as skim).

Have you made the jump to skim or ½ percent milk? _____

_____

What about the rest of your family members? _____

_____

Do you realize that even your children need lower fat milk if they are not underweight and are over the age of two? _____

_____

Is your roommate or spouse open to drinking skim milk? _____

_____

2. Use a part-skimmed cheese or one that is lower in fat. The whole milk cheeses are out of the question since they contain about 85 percent fat. The next time you eat a piece of whole milk cheese think of it this way—over three-quarters of the piece is nutritionally akin to a piece of beef fat. The only exceptions might be when you use very small amounts of cheese by using an angel hair grater (grates very fine) or when you use a slight bit of a very sharp cheese just for flavor. You can use about a quarter of what you would have needed if you cook with the sharpest cheddar you can find. See the Shopping Guide on page 63 for details on low-fat cheeses.

Check off the following lower fat dairy products that you might incorporate into your recipes:
_____ Low-fat yogurt and yogurt cheese (see *Love Hunger* for recipe)
_____ Low-fat cottage cheese
_____ Mozzarella cheese and others made with part-skimmed milk (Be cautious—they still can contain up to 65 percent fat.)

3. Use skimmed evaporated milk. Skimmed evaporated milk that comes in little cans is a versatile product. It can be used in pies at holiday times; it can be whipped and used in place of whipping cream; it can be substituted for cream or half-and-half; and it goes very well in quiche, pumpkin pie, and in anything that you might need a thicker milk or cream base.

Week
8

4. Use lean sandwich meats. Sandwiches can be an excellent food choice. Just make sure that you're not choosing one of the fatty processed meats such as bologna, salami, canned meats, sausages, or any other type of pressed meats. The only meats to consider for your sandwiches are the very lean deli cuts such as turkey breast, lean ham, chicken breast, lean roast beef, or tuna packed in water.

How can you make your favorite sandwich using ingredients that are good for you? Remember, you can even make a grilled sandwich if you are utilizing a nonstick spray or a diet margarine.

_____

_____

_____

_____

5. *Substitute yogurt for sour cream and cream cheese.* Instead of sour cream, use nonfat or low-fat yogurt (custard style yogurt won't work), and instead of cream cheese, use yogurt cheese. Yogurt cheese is easily made in your own home using a specialty funnel, available in many cooking stores, or by using a coffee filter. You simply place yogurt in the funnel draining over a glass and leave it in your refrigerator for two days. The whey drains out leaving essentially a dehydrated yogurt. The product may be substituted for cream cheese in recipes.

6. *Low-calorie ice milk can be okay as a frozen dessert.* Whether a product is a good dieting food choice depends on the fat content. You need to use your percent fat formula (see page 185) to determine that it is 25 percent fat or less. This will usually make it 100 calories per one-half cup serving. You might use this in recipes such as milkshakes, strawberry shortcake, baked Alaska, ice cream cones, frosted Cokes (list a diet Coke with ½ cup light ice cream for one of your 100-calorie snack options).

7. *Use angel food cake.* Angel food cake, which is made from egg whites, contains no fat or cholesterol at all. Homemade or commercially made, it is delicious with strawberries over the top.

8. *Avoid soggy, packed lunches.* If you're packing sandwiches, take your vegetables in a separate plastic wrap, so that they won't become soggy. This is especially important if you pack your lunch the night before.

DAY 5

SAY HELLO TO YOUR IDEAL WEIGHT

Particularly if you have been overweight for some time, the concept of your "ideal" weight may seem vague and nebulous. To help you realign your body image and establish realistic goals, try the following exercise.

On a large piece of paper, draw a line separating the right and left halves of the sheet. Thumbing through a number of magazines, cut out images or draw pictures that represent to you your current body image. These may be clippings or drawings of people, or even of non-human subjects as symbols. One woman chose photos of animals—hippos and elephants—to represent the way she viewed her body. Paste these images in collage-style on the left half of the sheet, beneath a title that says simply, "Good-bye." These are, indeed, the body images to which you want to bid adieu.

On the opposite side, write the heading "Hello," then select pictures or images that represent the way you want to look. The woman who used animal images to represent her present self, when it came to the second stage of the exercise, selected photos of women who were her approximate age and of similar bone structure but who were at healthy weight levels. Notice that she didn't select pictures of women half her age. She set a realistic goal in the images she chose to represent her future body.

This kind of visual process can become a beacon light guiding you toward your ideal weight. With specific images in mind and in hand, it becomes easier to say to yourself, "Yeah, that's what I'm working toward" rather than thinking vaguely about some fuzzy image that seems as unreachable as it is undefinable.

DAY 5

Step 8. We made a list of all persons we had harmed and became willing to make amends to them all.

MEMBERS OF NONBIOLOGICAL FAMILIES TO WHICH YOU BELONG

So far we have focused on relationships in your family of origin, family of procreation, and other key relationships that play a significant role in your life. In this final stage of making your "amends inventory," consider the relationships in some of the "larger" families to which you belong: your work family, remembering persons that you have hurt or run over or harmed in your work relationships; your community family, including neighbors and whoever else constitutes your community; and your church family. In the family of God, are there members you have hurt or harmed?

Finally, you'll want to include any members of the larger family of man. One alcoholic who sought counseling was an angry and intolerant person, and on his amends list he identified certain racial minority groups. He realized that for most of his life he had carried strong racial prejudice, and that he had to acknowledge that as a major area in which he had hurt an entire portion of the family of man.

Regarding my work family, people that I have wronged include:

Name: _____

How I injured this person or our relationship: _____

_____

How has our relationship changed as a result? _____

_____

What long-term effects have come about because of the wrong for which I was responsible?

_____

Name: _____

How I injured this person or our relationship: _____

_____

How has our relationship changed as a result? _____

_____

What long-term effects have come about because of the wrong for which I was responsible?

_____

Regarding my relationship with my community and my church family, people that I have wronged include:

Name: _____

How I injured this person or our relationship: _____

_____

How has our relationship changed as a result? _____

_____

What long-term effects have come about because of the wrong for which I was responsible?

_____

Name: _____

How I injured this person or our relationship: _____

_____

How has our relationship changed as a result? _____

_____

What long-term effects have come about because of the wrong for which I was responsible?

_____

Regarding corporate, nonbiological families in which you play a role, it may be difficult to establish the circumstances under which you can make appropriate apologies or amends for any pain or hurt you inflicted. In Week 9, you will have a chance to work through specifics regarding to whom and when and how you might want to carry through with the actual process of apology and restoration.

WEEKLY FOOD AND EXERCISE JOURNAL

Date _____
Weight (First day of week only) _____

	Breakfast/ A.M. Snack	Lunch P.M. Snack	Dinner Nite Snack	Exercise	Feelings and Major Events of the Day
Day One					
Day Two					
Day Three					
Day Four					
Day Five					
Day Six					
Day Seven					

DAY 1

MARVELOUS MENUS*

ORIENTAL CUISINE

Last week you learned about general principles of cooking that may be applied to almost any recipe you have in either low-fat or traditional cookbooks. This week you will apply that information in weekly menus suitable for both individuals and large families. At the end of each weekly menu, there will some questions that will help you identify which new cooking procedures may help you the most.

In case you are tempted to skip this section because you have "never been a cook," keep this in mind—mastering low-fat cooking is one of the top three maintenance techniques that will help you keep weight off once your ideal weight has been achieved. Think of it this way: would you rather have the small hamburger at most fast food places or the complete meal described below for the same 300 calories (does not include dessert)?

MENU FOR TODAY

Stir-Fried Chicken-Vegetable Medley
Oriental Rice
Mandarin Orange and Spinach Salad
Japanese Green Tea
Fortune Cookies

Serves 4
Total calories per meal: 305

---

*NOTE: For more recipes, see the last half of the book, *Love Hunger*.

STIR-FRIED CHICKEN-VEGETABLE MEDLEY

4 boneless, skinless chicken breast halves
   Buttery-flavored, nonstick, vegetable cooking spray
½ medium purple onion, slivered
3 cups Chinese cabbage, cut into 1-inch strips
3 green onions, cut in 1-inch strips
½ cup fresh mushrooms, sliced
1 large green or red bell pepper, cut into strips
8- ounce can sliced water chestnuts, drained
1 teaspoon cornstarch
3 tablespoons soy sauce
3 tablespoons water
Dash of pepper

Slice the chicken into one-inch cubes. Lay the chicken out on a tray and spray with the buttery-flavored nonstick spray. Now spray a nonstick wok or skillet with the coating spray. Sauté the chicken on medium heat until cooked throughout and then remove from the pan. Now add the sliced peppers and slivered onion to the skillet to soften. After two minutes add the fresh mushrooms and green onions. Finally add the water chestnuts to the vegetable mixture and sauté an additional one minute. Remove all vegetables and add to the already cooked chicken. Now combine all remaining ingredients in a small bowl and stir until lumps have been dissolved. Add this cornstarch mixture to the wok and stir until thickened. Add the cooked chicken-vegetable medley to the wok to reheat in the sauce. Serve hot with Oriental Rice.

Yield: 4 servings, 180 calories per recipe, 21 percent fat

Variation: Substitute twelve ounces of very lean round steak for the chicken and add one-half pound of fresh snow peas to the sautéed vegetables for a variation on this same recipe. The servings and nutritional values will be almost identical.

Week 9

ORIENTAL RICE

⅓ cup uncooked rice, preferably brown rice
⅔ cup water
1 chicken bouillon cube
1 teaspoon soy sauce
1 teaspoon margarine
⅔ cup of celery, cut on the diagonal
⅓ cup green peas, frozen
Dash of pepper

Combine the first four ingredients and cook until rice is tender. Add the celery and continue to heat gently for two minutes. Now add the pepper and the frozen peas. Heat until peas are warm. Serve immediately. (Store extra rice in the freezer to use later in a soup.)

Yield: 6 one-half-cup servings, 65 calories per serving

MANDARIN ORANGE AND SPINACH SALAD

12 **to 16 ounces of fresh, washed spinach**
1 **small can Mandarin orange slices, drained**
½ **cup frozen artichoke hearts, nonmarinated**
½ **cup Kraft® Zesty Italian reduced-calorie salad dressing**
1 **tablespoon Balsamic vinegar**

Marinate the artichoke hearts overnight (if possible) in the salad dressing and vinegar. Prepare the spinach in a glass salad bowl and add the drained orange slices. Add the artichoke marinade, toss lightly and serve cool.

Yield: 4 servings, 40 calories per serving, 10 percent fat

Additionally, serve Japanese green tea and one fortune cookie to enjoy a delicious meal containing only 305 calories.

TODAY'S COOKING REVIEW

Check off the cooking techniques you enjoyed from today's lesson as an indication that you will use them in other similar recipes in the future.

_____ Oriental stir-fry recipes are usually low in calories and high in bulk and nutrition. The chicken recipe does not involve extra peanut oil as in traditional recipes. Instead it uses a nonstick vegetable cooking spray. For every tablespoon of oil you do without, you have just eliminated 100 calories from your total recipe count. Also, the generous use of Oriental vegetables "dilutes" the calorie content giving you larger volumes of food for fewer calories.

_____ Bouillon cubes (either beef or chicken) are a wonderful way to flavor rice. They may be found in low-sodium form if that is a concern for you. Almost any kind of vegetable lends itself to being added to a rice pilaf. This can be a handy way to use small amounts of vegetable leftovers.

_____ Spinach is much more nutritious than lettuce. Use it frequently as a fresh salad or on sandwiches to add flavor and nutrition to your diet for very few calories.

DAY 1

SUCCESSFUL GRIEVING

Everything you have been doing so far has been preparing you for the grief process. In fact, if you've been doing the exercises in this book faithfully to this point, you already have been, no doubt, catapulted into the process. If so, then this week will describe and define things you have already been experiencing.

Even the positive steps you've taken as a recovering food addict have their connection to grief. Something as simple as setting new and healthy food boundaries represents a major loss in your life: you've given up your old coping mechanism. Even an alcoholic or drug addict will tell you that as much as he needs to give up his addiction, it's like losing an old friend. Now, and in the coming months of recovery, you may feel great pain at the loss of the "friend" called food. You may actually feel sad that your new boundaries prevent you from experiencing the familiar rush of a binge no matter how short-lived that intoxication was before the shame and guilt and pain set in. The feelings may surprise you and you may be tempted to try to ignore or deny their existence. Don't. Saying hello and good-bye to these and other losses are pivotal steps in the grieving process. Remember, the way beyond grief is *through* it, not *around* it.

This week you will deal more with the concept of saying "hello" and "good-bye" to pain. You will also examine five other milestones or markers on the footpath of grief.

Becoming familiar with all the dynamics of grieving—and even learning to grieve well—is important for this reason: if you don't complete the grief cycle with regard to any loss, you will remain under the influence of that loss. Future decisions, behaviors, and relationships may all be impacted by the ongoing pain of that ungrieved loss. And going back to the concept that life is a series of good-byes—thus a series of losses—learning how to grieve becomes a key ingredient in learning how to really live.

The goal in Week 9 is to help you develop a grieving mechanism or pattern that you can use to deal with past, present, or future pain. Learning to grieve well enables you to let go of the pain as it comes into your life day by day. This prevents pains from being stored up and harbored, ultimately festering until they poison every area of your life.

The grief process is the only method of coping with pain that actually works. Sometimes patients say, "Wait a minute . . . I've cried buckets of tears. That means I've grieved about it, right?" Not necessarily. Grief, in its fullest form, must be done in three realms.

1. It's important to grieve alone. These are the private tears that come when no one else is near. Many compulsive overeaters admit they cry often alone, yet don't let anyone else see how much they hate themselves for their obesity. This first stage of solo grieving is important, but it cannot, by itself, complete the process.

Regarding what loss or pain have you allowed yourself to grieve alone only?

_____

2. The process also involves grieving with other human beings. This is the reason a therapist can be so valuable, even if he or she simply sits and listens without excessive comment. People are often surprised at the tears and anger that surface in therapy. Even in a support group meeting like OA, you may start talking about yourself and suddenly find yourself in tears, surprised at the outburst of emotion.

3. Vicarious grieving is a third key. When listening to others talk about their pain, your grieving with them about their loss prompts personal grieving about your own losses as well.

Through what avenues are you exposed to the grief process of others? (Someone in your family who is hurting; your membership in a support group; membership in a close-knit group of friends from church.) _____

_____

Describe a difference between empathizing with someone's pain and emotionally carrying that pain for him or her. _____

_____

DAY 1

STEP 9: WE MADE DIRECT AMENDS TO SUCH PEOPLE WHEREVER POSSIBLE, EXCEPT WHEN TO DO SO WOULD INJURE THEM OR OTHERS.

This is the week to take the lists you compiled in Step 8 and begin the process of making direct amends to as many people as possible. This is not an easy process, nor is it one that will necessarily be completed in short order. But this is not a step that can be skipped on your road to recovery. If these amends are approached cautiously, they can be:

1. Sincere efforts to offer apology for past harm and hurt;

2. Wonder bridge-builders for more positive future relationships;

3. Effective tools in removing that tremendous weight of guilt, shame, and remorse.

There are two things that these apologies and retributions should not become. They should not become "installment payments" on guilt and shame. Watch the tendency to drift into a kind of legalism and perfectionism where you begin to accept the false premise that if you just apologize enough or do enough in the way of penance, you might somehow earn or win your own redemption. Particularly for the codependent person who tends toward false guilt and shame, this kind of dangerous thinking could creep into Step 9 at an unconscious level.

Secondly, these amends should not become a source of injury or pain for anyone else. Before you apologize to your best friend for having repeatedly flirted with his wife as a means of compensating for your own poor body image, you need to consider if your emotional honesty outweighs the pain you will bring into that man's life and his marriage. There is also an important disclaimer in the second half of this step that says "except when to do so would injure." Notice in Step 8, when you became *willing* to make the amends, you needed to list everyone you may have wronged intentionally or nonintentionally. No one was left off that list. You must be willing to make amends to all. But now in Step 9, as you consider the actual execution of the step, it's a different picture. You have to use a high degree of discretion about to whom and when to make the person-to-person exchange.

There are several categories that can help you decide whether or not you should actually contact each person and carry out a face-to-face apology. The first category is people to whom you can and should apologize. This includes people close to you, often family members, to whom you owe an obvious apology, as well as people who may not come as readily to mind because you're still in denial over the hurt you inflicted.

In the following spaces, you'll have a chance to identify people to whom you owe obvious apologies, as well as how, when, and where you intend to meet with each person. As you think through what you would like to say to this person in terms of a verbal apology, stay away from the following two words: *sorry* and *blame.* The first reaction many people have is to say "I'm sorry"—sometimes over and over again. Rather than using a phrase that implies you are a sorry or a bad person, use phrases like "I apologize for the hurt I caused," "I regret . . . ," "I feel remorse for . . . ."

When possible, consider a more substantive form of apology. For example, where there has been financial damage, consider financial reparation if it is at all possible. If you realize that your depression, preoccupation with weight and low self-esteem have caused you to present your employer 50 percent effort, you may want to approach your employer with a verbal pledge that from here on out you will perform at high capacity and that your employer can expect this kind of quality effort from you.

Who are three people on whom you have inflicted the most obvious hurts?

Name: _____

Nature of how relationship was hurt: _____

_____

Verbal amend: _____

More substantive amend: _____

_____

Commit to a time and place when you will meet with this person to take steps toward restoration and healing in the relationship. _____

Name: _____

Nature of how relationship was hurt: _____

_____

Verbal amend: _____

More substantive amend: _____

_____

Commit to a time and place when you will meet with this person to take steps toward restoration and healing in the relationship. _____

Name: _____

Nature of how relationship was hurt: _____

_____

Verbal amend: _____

More substantive amend: _____

_____

Commit to a time and place when you will meet with this person to take steps toward restoration and healing in the relationship. _____

DAY 2

MENU FOR TODAY

Oven-Fried Ginger Chicken
Old-Fashioned Mashed Potatoes
White Cream Gravy
Steamed Vegetable Medley
Strawberry Shortcake (counts as 1 snack)
Coffee or Iced Tea

Serves 4
Total calories per meal: 300 without dessert, 400 with dessert

OVEN-FRIED GINGER CHICKEN

3 tablespoons sesame seeds
2 tablespoons all-purpose flour
⅛ teaspoon white pepper
½ teaspoon ground ginger
3 tablespoons soy sauce
4 chicken breast halves, skinned and deboned
   Butter-flavored, nonstick, vegetable cooking spray

Mix the flour, pepper, sesame seeds, and ginger together in a small bowl. Spray the chicken with vegetable cooking spray and then dip in soy sauce. Coat with the ginger mixture and place in a metal baking dish that has been coated with nonstick spray. Now lightly spray one more time with the vegetable cooking spray and drizzle the remaining soy sauce evenly over all chicken breasts. Bake in a 375 degree oven for about 40 minutes or until tender.

Yield: Four servings, 150 calories per serving, 23 percent fat.

Note: If you like chicken fillet sandwiches, this is the recipe to use. Make several extras and package them individually for storage in your freezer. Use either lite bread or one of the 110 calorie onion buns, add mustard, lettuce, and tomato, and you will have your 300 calorie lunch or supper taken care of. It is a particularly good choice for a brown bag lunch.

OLD-FASHIONED MASHED POTATOES

4 large baking potatoes
½ cup skim milk
1 tablespoon margarine or butter
Salt and pepper to taste
Dry butter substitute (Butter Buds® or Molly McButter®)

Peel, cube, and boil potatoes until soft. Mash with a potato masher and add remaining ingredients. Continue mashing until smooth.

Yield: Eight servings, ⅔ cup per serving, 94 calories per serving, 18 percent fat.

WHITE CREAM GRAVY

1 cup skim milk
2 tablespoons all-purpose flour
1 teaspoon Molly McButter® or some other butter substitute
Salt and pepper to taste

Mix all ingredients together in a cold saucepan with a wire whisk. Heat over medium heat until bubbling slightly

Yield: Eight servings, 1/4 cup per serving, 38 calories per serving, 5 percent fat.

STEAMED VEGETABLE MEDLEY

Use any prepackaged vegetable mixture that does not contain starchy vegetables such as corn, green peas, and dried beans. For example, use one that has a combination of broccoli, cauliflower, and carrots. There are numerous others, and they are very easy to use. The key is to spice them up with one or more of the following spices or seasonings. Be imaginative and find out what your taste buds prefer.

Basil	Butter substitutes
Dried onion flakes	Celery salt
Parsley	Bouillon cubes
Cavendar's® Greek Seasoning Mix	Diced bell pepper or pimiento
Italian Seasoning Mix	Salt and pepper
Mrs. Dash®, any variety	Tarragon

Yield: Most of these vegetables will be about 25 to 40 calories per 2/3 cup serving.

Week 9

STRAWBERRY SHORTCAKE

Angel food cake, slices should each be ½4th of the cake
2   cups light vanilla ice cream (50 calories per ¼-cup serving)
1½ cups fresh strawberries
1   tablespoon sugar
2   tablespoons water

Use either a commercial or homemade angel food cake for this recipe. Remember that angel food cakes do not contain fat or cholesterol and are naturally low in calories. Slice the cake into twenty-four equal slices. This recipe is based on four servings. Place a slice of the cake on a dessert plate. Wash and thinly slice the fresh strawberries and mix with the sugar and water. (They will be better if you do this one day in advance and then let them sit in the refrigerator until time to serve.) Use a ¼-cup scoop, place one scoop of the light vanilla ice cream on top of the cake. Then cover with ¼ cup of the strawberry mixture.

Yield: Four servings, 107 calories per serving, 10 percent fat.

TODAY'S COOKING REVIEW

Check off the cooking techniques you enjoyed out of today's lesson as an indication that you will use them in other similar recipes in the future.

_____   What seem to be fried foods are not necessarily always fried. They may be oven-baked in a crunchy crust to simulate their higher fat and higher calorie fried counterparts. The vegetable cooking sprays (which now come in plain, butter, or olive oil flavors) can be a beginning to almost any coating mix.

_____   Mashed potatoes and other starchy foods, which are commonly thought to be off-limits in a weight reduction diet may be enjoyed if there are simple modifications in the recipe that alter the fat content of the final recipe. It is not the starch you want to avoid but the heavy fat. This same principle might apply to recipes using corn, beans, or rice. Using the butter substitutes, including Molly McButter®, Best o' Butter,® and Butter Buds® will help give your foods the buttery flavor without the fat.

_____   Nonfat gravies may be enjoyed every day—even more than once a day. Old-fashioned nutrition information which blanketly suggests avoidance of sauces and gravies can be detrimental to dieting success. The recipe used today is nothing more than thickened skim milk with added flavor from a butter substitute. Mix your ingredients cold and then heat for almost any low-fat sauce or gravy.

Week
9

_____ Vegetables don't have to be laden with butter or margarine in order to exude savory taste. Herbs and spices can make almost anything taste better and alleviate the need for both salt and fat in the recipe.

_____ Angel food cake is low in calories, fat, and cholesterol. It may be used in a variety of desserts, including the one suggested here. Small amounts of low-fat ice cream may also be incorporated into desserts to give the illusion of richness. Fruits are a good "diluter" of calories in dessert recipes and should be used often with other higher calorie items.

DAY 2

THE FIRST TWO STAGES OF GRIEF: SHOCK AND DENIAL

Elizabeth Kübler-Ross was the first to identify the five stages of grief. In the process of studying persons with terminal illness, she discovered that patients facing death went through predictable stages of grieving.

We now know that these same predictable grief stages apply to any loss or pain. Perhaps someone you love has died or your "baby" has just left for college leaving you with an empty nest or you've just learned that your parents are divorcing after nearly forty years of marriage. These losses have something in common: each will very likely prompt some form of _shock, denial, anger, true grief or sadness, and_—if you allow yourself to work through the entire cycle of grief—_acceptance and/or forgiveness._

You've learned about denial in previous weeks: how you may lie to yourself about the gravity or severity of a problem. Shock, on the other hand, represents a delayed reaction to the severity of that problem. For example, if you were physically abused as a child, denial might cause you to rationalize, "But a lot of parents discipline their kids; my family wasn't different from any others." Shock, on the other hand, might cause you to go through life seemingly unscarred by the experience . . . until your midtwenties when you suddenly abandon your family for the alcohol that numbs the denied pain of your childhood.

An example of physical shock might be the man who is in a serious car accident. He may do fine for several hours, walking around, helping to rescue other victims, filling out forms. Later, after the shock wears off, pain hits him like a sledgehammer and he realizes that all along he was suffering from a broken foot or hand.

We've heard about the unraveling of Vietnam veterans: another example of shock, although this time emotional shock. A man or woman who experienced the trauma of the Vietnam war might return home, functioning in shock or denial for months, years, or decades. Then all of a sudden things begin to explode or fall apart, a delayed reaction to the trauma inflicted years before.

Many people now believe that persons addicted to food, drugs, work, or other things, may actually be walking around in a state of post-traumatic stress or shock. Shock creates an emotional time bomb. People caught up in food addiction may have experienced trauma years ago, staying in shock or denial for years or decades and using food to help perpetuate the denial.

Think back through any traumas in your past; you might identify single events or blocks of time characterized by loss or disappointment. After you have identified these traumas, think about any behavior or actions that you have felt driven toward, perhaps without knowing exactly why. Pay particular attention to any form of destructive behavior aimed either at yourself or other people. For instance, getting pregnant out of wedlock could have been a traumatic experience, while being sexually active and flirting with pregnancy was a behavior you felt driven toward.

Traumas

Examples:

> *Being molested by my stepfather between the ages of 11 and 14*
> *My parents' divorce when I was 6*
> *My two-year marriage to a wife-beater*
> *The loss of a son to cancer*

My List:

_____

_____

_____

_____

Compulsive or Destructive Behavior

Examples:

> *Sexually acting out as a teen*
> *My addiction to food beginning in my late twenties*
> *Rageaholism*
> *A nervous breakdown in 1982*

My List:

_____

_____

_____

_____

DAY 2

Step 9. We made direct amends to such people wherever possible, except when to do so would injure them or others.

PEOPLE TO WHOM AMENDS ARE NOT DUE

As you are evaluating the practical execution of the restoration of your relationships, you need to consider that there may be some people to whom you think you owe amends but do not. False guilt and shame may be driving you to approach people when you, in reality, were responsible for very little, if any, of the pain involved in the relationship.

It's possible that there may be painful relationships that, at first impulse, you feel the need to restore through apology. Yet, if that relationship is with someone who has inflicted the majority of the injury, your contribution to the problem may have been so small so as not to require your effort at making amends.

For example, if you suffered emotional or physical injury at the words or hands of an abusive, dysfunctional person, it's likely that part of the dysfunction included making you feel deserving of the abuse. A child who is physically battered is often made to feel that he somehow egged on the violence. As a result, the victim may leave the series of encounters with a large quantity of false guilt and shame.

Making amends in a relationship where you were, in fact, victim rather than victimizer only serves to set the false guilt and shame with which you are already burdened. In earlier weeks we examined false guilt and shame—how to identify it, say good-bye to it, and grieve through the unnecessary sting of it. Today, you will focus on another means of identifying false guilt and shame.

In the following spaces you'll find sets of questions similar to those in yesterday's exercise. Yesterday you identified several painful relationships for which you recognized the need to apologize—relationships over which you may or may not have been in denial.

Today, identify any painful relationships for which you feel the responsibility to apologize—when these relationships were with family members or friends who had strong abusive tendencies. For example, if you struggle with the pain in your relationship with a stepfather who rarely acknowledged your presence in the house or the pain in your relationship with an uncle who molested you or a former spouse who was repeatedly unfaithful, take a moment to evaluate the precise part you may have played. An accurate accounting of your contribution to the dysfunction may give you a clearer picture of how much of your guilt and shame is valid and how much is false.

Regarding my relationship with _____

How have I been responsible for any portion of the hurt? _____

_____

_____

How has this other person been responsible for any portion of the hurt? _____

_____

_____

Does either one of us carry a vast majority of responsibility for the problems in our relationship? If so, who? _____

If I carry a small portion of the responsibility—for example, 10 percent compared to the
other person's 90 percent—how realistic are my feelings of guilt and shame? _____

_____

In conclusion, I (do, do not) have a responsibility to apologize for this damaged relationship.
(Circle one.)

Regarding my relationship with _____

How have I been responsible for any portion of the hurt? _____

_____

_____

How has this other person been responsible for any portion of the hurt? _____

_____

_____

Does either one of us carry a vast majority of responsibility for the problems in our relationship? If so, who? _____

If I carry a small portion of the responsibility—for example, 10 percent compared to the
other person's 90 percent—how realistic are my feelings of guilt and shame? _____

_____

In conclusion, I (do, do not) have a responsibility to apologize for this damaged relationship.
(Circle one.)

DAY 3

MENU FOR THE DAY

Sometimes you just feel an urge to eat "junk." Though the menu below is not perfectly balanced in that it is a little high in fat and starch and does not contain as many vegetables as we would normally want, it is clear that not all perceived junk food is actually bad for you. These recipes are given here to show you that almost anything can be altered into a more healthy rendition of age-old favorite foods. Use these to add diversity to your diet plan and keep you on the straight and narrow as you continue down the path of weight loss and maintenance success.

Hamburger
Skinny French Fries
Buttery Popcorn (counts as 1 snack)

Serves 4
Total calories per meal: 340 calories for the hamburger and fries; 100 calories for the popcorn. When popcorn is ready, spray with butter-flavored cooking spray and sprinkle with Molly McButter® and Mrs. Dash®.

HAMBURGERS

The key to low-cal/low-fat hamburgers is to use the leanest meat possible. You may either use 3 ounces of ground round or 3 ounces of ground turkey (raw weight) for the hamburger patty. This will yield a 2½ ounce cooked patty. Also, avoid all mayonnaise on these sandwiches, including the light varieties. Use mustard instead—you can develop a taste for it if you haven't already. The bun should be one of the new light varieties, which are about 80 calories per bun. These are "light" versions produced by the same bakers who make the light breads.

Yield: Make as many or as few as you like. Though hamburgers will vary, most will have about 225 to 275 calories when made according to the guidelines listed above.

SKINNY FRENCH FRIES

2 **large Idaho potatoes, unpeeled and cut in strips**
   Nonstick vegetable cooking spray
   Seasoned salt, pepper, or Cajun seasoning mix

Wash and prepare the potatoes. Dry the surface of the potato strips by placing them on paper towels. Spray a nonstick cookie sheet and the potatoes with vegetable cooking spray and then sprinkle with seasoning of choice. (You might try shaking them in a clear plastic bag.) Bake at 350° for 30 to 35 minutes until tender and golden brown. Turn occasionally with a spatula.

Yield: Four servings, 120 calories per serving, 15 percent fat.

TODAY'S COOKING REVIEW

Check off the cooking techniques you enjoyed from today's lesson as an indication that you will use them in other similar recipes in the future.

_____ Buying the less expensive, higher fat ground beef should be a thing of the past for you. Ground round, ground turkey, or ground venison should be your only purchases. Soy product meat substitutes that are no more than 25 percent fat are also good choices. With these things in mind, ground meat is no longer on the taboo list even if you are following a low-cholesterol or low-fat diet due to medical reasons. The same principles will apply when making spaghetti sauce, meatloaf, or casseroles using ground meat.

_____ The Skinny French Fries are another example of having pseudo-fried foods. This recipe is sure to please your whole family and will make them think they are getting their old favorites. You can vary the spices you sprinkle on the fries during cooking. No one will believe they are on a diet with this recipe.

_____ The popcorn recipe is a convenient way of making virtually fat-free popcorn that is not tasteless. Try using one of the new cheese flavored butter substitute sprinkles for a cheese popcorn.

DAY 3

THE THIRD STAGE OF GRIEF: ANGER

Following shock and denial, many people in the grip of grief will experience anger. Anger is multileveled: at the very surface there may be the feeling of depression, which is anger turned inward, or the opposite extreme, which is anger projected outward toward a person or situation that doesn't reflect the true source of your anger.

Beneath depression or projected anger lies true anger, and beneath true anger lies a fear or insecurity. Fears and insecurities are the foundations for all angers and resentments.

Please note that anger and some of the other negative feelings that come up during the grieving process are almost like emotional toxins. It's not that they are "bad"—in fact, anger can be healthy as a way of getting feelings out. But if you try to repress or "stuff down" the angry feelings, they will begin to build up like toxic waste.

In the first column, list things, events, or aspects of yourself that seem "depressing" to you. Remember, depression is anger turned back toward yourself; this boomerang effect can spur you toward self-destructive behavior, such as your food compulsion.

In the second column, try to get in touch with the underlying resentment, anger, or grudge that seems to fuel your depression.

In the third column, ask yourself about the fear or insecurity that is the foundation for the anger.

I AM DEPRESSED BY:	I AM ANGRY ABOUT:	I AM AFRAID OF:
(I feel unattractive due to weight.)	*(My husband doesn't give me physical or sexual attention.)*	*(What if he doesn't love me anymore and leaves me; I'm afraid of abandonment.)*
_____	_____	_____
_____	_____	_____

Keep in mind that the whole purpose of grieving is to get in touch with your feelings, since feelings that are denied rather than acknowledged are the stuff of which addictions are made.

After you get in touch with your feelings, allow yourself to feel them freely. Like lancing a boil to clean the pus out, grieving is similar to cleansing a festering wound. It's painful, but it's a healing pain.

As you get in touch with your feelings and give yourself permission to feel the accompanying pain, remind yourself that it's a healthy pain, signifying that the grief process is working as it should and that you are on the verge of life, not death. Grieving this toxic pain is a cleansing process that will lay the groundwork for entering into a more loving relationship with yourself and others.

DAY 3

Step 9. We made direct amends to such people wherever possible, except when to do so would injure them or others.

MAKING AMENDS TO YOURSELF

If there are relationships in which you have allowed yourself, knowingly or unknowingly, to be significantly victimized, you may indeed owe amends and restoration to an important person . . . but not the party who first came to mind. You may need to make a verbal apology to yourself for the wrongs that have been inflicted on you, either through your own choices, decisions, and mistakes, or through the choices, decisions, or mistakes of others.

Beyond the verbal apology, there may be further restorative action that you may need to make to yourself. This might be done by making a pledge to yourself regarding the new boundary you have established to ensure that you never permit this kind of victimization to take place again.

I need to make amends to myself for _____

In addition, I pledge to myself that _____

_____

_____

I need to make amends to myself for _____

In addition, I pledge to myself that _____

_____

_____

I need to make amends to myself for _____

In addition, I pledge to myself that _____

_____

_____

If the misuse of food has long been a form of self-damage, be sure to include that on this list. Common harms inflicted on self through compulsive overeating include: deterioration in physical health, social isolation, and feelings of low self-worth. Of all the relationships you seek to restore through the amends of recovery, your positive relationship with yourself is one of the most important.

Week 9

DAY 4

MENU FOR TODAY

Cheese Flounder Fillets
Carrots with Cilantro
Your Favorite Rice Pilaf Recipe
Calorie-free Beverage

Serves 4
Total calories per meal: 315

CHEESE FLOUNDER FILLETS

   Nonstick butter-flavored vegetable cooking spray
1 **pound flounder fillets**
2 **tablespoons lemon juice**
3 **tablespoons Parmesan cheese**
2 **tablespoons Romano cheese**
4 **tablespoons fresh parsley, minced**
1 **tablespoon shallot, minced**
½ **teaspoon butter-flavored sprinkles**
¼ **teaspoon garlic salt**

Spray a metal baking dish with butter-flavored cooking spray. Place four fish fillets in the pan. Pour lemon juice over the fillets. Combine the remaining ingredients and sprinkle over the top. Bake uncovered at 350° for 15 minutes. The top should be lightly browned.

Yield: 4 servings, 150 calories per serving, 22 percent fat.

CARROTS WITH CILANTRO

1 **pound carrots, peeled and cut into julienne strips**
1 **tablespoon olive oil**
¼ **cup fresh cilantro leaves, chopped**
   Dash of salt and pepper

Lightly sauté carrot strips in olive oil. When the carrots are slightly tender, add spices. Sauté for 1 minute more and serve immediately.

Yield: Six servings, 58 calories per serving, 28 percent fat.

Additionally with your meal, serve steamed broccoli with spices and herbs, and a noncaloric beverage such as an herbal tea (Cranberry Apple Zinger by Celestial Seasonings® is a wonderful choice).

TODAY'S COOKING REVIEW

Check the tips that might be useful to you in your own kitchen.

_____ Sautéing vegetables may be done in much less oil or other fat than most traditional recipes suggest. By using the coating sprays and keeping the temperature a little lower than normal, you can ensure that the food will not stick to the pan.

_____ Diet margarines work just as well as regular margarines for sautéing.

_____ When you have the option of using fresh herbs as opposed to dried, do so. They will brighten the flavor of most recipes and make them taste gourmet instead of routine. Many of these herbs may be grown easily in your own backyard with very little effort or expense. Examples of homegrown herbs you might try include basil, dill, mint, rosemary, and cilantro.

_____ Shallots provide a delicate balance between the taste of onion and garlic and work well with most fish recipes. It is rarely overpowering and saves you at least one preparation step.

DAY 4

THE FOURTH STAGE OF GRIEF: TRUE GRIEF OR SADNESS

Not everyone reaches this stage. Many people get hung up on an earlier stage in the grief process and remain in denial or shock or anger for weeks, months, or decades.

Yet if you have been working through each week in this workbook, you may well be experiencing a gut-level sadness by now. That sadness might be in regard to your food addiction, losses in your present and recent past, and especially things that might have occurred within your family of origin.

At this stage in the process you may experience childlike grieving or weeping. This kind of emotional response may occur over a period of days or even months. There is folk wisdom about the benefit that can come from just having a shoulder to cry on. The dynamics of that simple act apply nowhere as appropriately as they do here, in the fourth stage of the grieving process.

This is not the place for happy platitudes, for "fix-it" schemes, for lectures about the nature of things. This is the place where nothing feels as cleansing as a good, old-fashioned cry. Maybe more than once.

As the tears flow, imagine the pain and shock and denial and anger, little by little, being washed away in the process.

The next time you experience these waves of true grief washing over you, break away from the swirl of day-to-day activities and find a quiet place where you can let the feelings run their course. At that moment, take the opportunity to journal about your feelings. Don't edit as you write, but let your pen flow as freely as your grief as you give vent to the feelings. Consider exploring your feelings in the form of a letter to God. Remember the value of that shoulder on which to cry? Let God's presence provide that comforting place in which you can "let it all hang out" as you experience this fourth and pivotal stage of the grief process.

Please note that the stages of grief are not necessarily linear; you likely will find yourself flip-flopping between them. Even having experienced true grief and sadness, it's possible and even probable that at some point you will slip back into anger or denial. Just be aware of the shift when it happens. Follow the principles you've studied in this workbook to break beyond the denial or to peel back the layers of depression or anger until you uncover the fear that lies at the very core. These are the techniques that will move you beyond these emotions and into the more healing stages of real grief and even resolution and forgiveness, which make up the fifth stage of the grief process.

DAY 4

Step 9. We made direct amends to such people wherever possible, except when to do so would injure them or others.

REGARDING THOSE WHO SHOULD NOT BE CONTACTED

It may be your experience, as it has been the experience of others, that there are certain persons who should never be contacted. An example is found in the experience of a sex and relationship addict. He got very excited when he came to Step 9 and soon was making elaborate plans to go back and visit all of his seventeen former girlfriends and have a face-to-face discussion. We helped him realize that this might not be God's will for him, even though technically he would be, indeed, making amends. He eventually recognized that initiating person-to-person exchanges with relationships of that intensity would also reopen the door on many if not all of those codependent relationships.

In my relationship with _____, I was responsible for _____ and in many respects should make an effort to express my remorse and clear the air. Yet due to circumstances surrounding _____, contacting this person might result in more damage than good. The kind of damage or pain that might result from person-to-person contact includes: _____

_____

In my relationship with _____, I was responsible for _____ and in many respects should make an effort to express my remorse and clear the air. Yet due to circumstances surrounding _____, contacting this person might result in more damage than good. The kind of damage or pain that might result from person-to-person contact includes: _____

_____

Regarding relationships that it may prove unwise to reopen, there are two other methods that provide some form of experiencing the process of apology, without requiring that you physically reconnect with persons from your past. The empty-chair Gestalt method and the technique of journaling are examined in tomorrow's material. These two approaches, along with a third one covered tomorrow, are also valuable tools when you need to make amends with someone you are unable to contact, such as someone who is deceased.

DAY 5

MENU FOR TODAY

Western Style Eggs in Pita Pockets
Tomato Juice
Sliced Cucumbers
Hot tea

Serves 4
Total calories per meal: 200

WESTERN STYLE EGGS IN PITA POCKETS

2 medium pita pockets
1 large Idaho potato, washed and diced
½ cup red bell pepper, diced
¼ cup red onion, finely chopped
3 medium eggs or ¾ cup Egg Beaters®
3 tablespoons skim milk
Nonstick butter-flavored vegetable cooking spray

Cut the pita pockets in half and open each side to stuff. Parboil or microwave the diced potato until soft. Coat a nonstick pan with cooking spray and lightly brown the peppers and onions. Whip the eggs (or egg substitute) with the skim milk and then add to the pepper and onion mixture. Stir as they cook, scraping from the bottom of the pan. When the eggs are thickening but still contain some liquid, add the softened potato. Cook until completely done and add salt and pepper to taste. Fill each pita pocket with one-fourth of the egg mixture.

Yield: 4 servings, 175 calories per serving, 38 percent fat.

Serve your meal with sliced cucumbers and chilled tomato juice or vegetable juice cocktail and hot tea or coffee for a complete and satisfying breakfast.

TODAY'S COOKING REVIEW

_____ Using pita pocket bread for either breakfast or luncheon sandwiches is always a good choice since it is very low in fat. Whole wheat varieties are available.

_____ Egg Beaters® by Fleischmann™ is a wonderful no-cholesterol substitute for scrambled eggs. It is composed of 99 percent egg whites. Many of the other egg substitutes contain an additional five grams of fat per serving to mimic the fat content of a real egg. In this recipe you may use ¾ cup Egg Beaters® in place of 3 fresh eggs.

_____ Don't hesitate to serve sliced raw vegetables at breakfast or anytime as an accompaniment to your entrée. They fill the plate and your stomach and taste great with eggs or egg substitutes.

_____ Tomato juice in the morning instead of orange juice will save you calories and provide a lot of good nutrition.

Week
9

DAY 5

THE FIFTH STAGE OF GRIEF:
RESOLUTION, ACCEPTANCE, AND/OR FORGIVENESS

The final stage of the grief process is resolution, acceptance, and forgiveness. Biblically, stage five comes down to a peace that passes understanding. If you have experienced big hurts, losses, and disappointments, you are not saying you agree with what happened to you or are even glad that they happened—instead you simply are saying that you have gotten to the place where you can accept that it happened and—if other people were the perpetrators—you forgive them.

The Texas two-step is a country western dance, but it's also similar to what many people try to do with the grieving process. They will dance right from stage one, shock and denial, to stage five, which is forgiveness. Anger and grief are overlooked in the process of mouthing the words that everything is forgiven and forgotten. This kind of response may be well-intended, but it does not have emotional integrity. If you know what it's like to dance this step, you know that on one level you are saying, "I forgive," but on a deeper level, resentment lies and festers. This kind of leap can lead to a lot of passive/aggressive behavior. After all, if you have anger inside, being out of touch with that anger doesn't mean it goes away; that anger is still working on you and having a toxic effect, making itself felt in direct ways.

For example, going directly to stage five, bypassing stages three and four, sets up an ideal emotional environment in which your food addiction can survive and thrive. That ungrieved anger and sadness will demand indirect expression as well as something to push them back down whenever they begin to surface, and food is a likely candidate for both functions.

List your losses in the following spaces.

Hurt or loss:	*Anyone you have typically held responsible:*

In a quiet moment of meditation, take the time to calm yourself, then visualize the person responsible for the first loss on your list. Take a moment to fill in the details with your imagination: what does the person look like? What is the person wearing? Where is the person sitting or standing? Envision this person and remind him or her what the hurt was—maybe it was an uncle who sexually abused you as a child—and then say the words aloud, "I forgive you. I don't endorse what you did, but I release the pain."

Here's the key: Listen to your body language and your emotions as you say the words "I forgive you." If you experience a sense of peace, a happy calm, or a tingling sense of release, you will know that you are forgiving with emotional integrity.

However, if your words are accompanied by a knot in your stomach, the clenching of your teeth, or the return of old feelings such as bitterness or fear, you may rightly wonder if you're doing the Texas two-step. These emotions and body language may be indicators that you have not yet finished the grieving process.

Remember, it is okay to cycle and recycle back through the five stages. Don't be too hard on yourself if you discover the need to go back and work through previous stages such as anger or sadness before moving on into the forgiveness segment of the process.

DAY 5

Step 9. We made direct amends to such people wherever possible, except when to do so would injure them or others.

REGARDING THOSE WHO CANNOT BE CONTACTED

Finally, there are those who cannot be directly contacted, for whatever reasons. These people may be dead, or perhaps they've disappeared from your life or moved to an unknown area and you may not have access to them.

There are three important techniques that can be used, especially for important deceased persons like a parent. One is called the empty-chair Gestalt technique. That's where you talk to an empty chair and imagine the person is there. Express to him or her whatever is stored in your heart, going as far as to imagine responses made back to you. This kind of dialogue can be very helpful in resolving important issues.

Second, you may want to write letters to the deceased person or persons whom you cannot contact. Even though the letters will never be received, there is a kind of communication that occurs by this very writing process.

Finally, there is what is called a graveside dialogue, in which you go back and visit the grave of that person who was significant in your life and simply talk to him or her. Somehow, just the presence of being there at their place of rest can be a very powerful catalyst for emotional dialogue.

If there are those to whom you owe amends—amends which cannot logistically take place for whatever reason—write the names of the individuals in the space provided. Also indicate whatever method you will use to "bury the ledger" with that person.

If I could speak with _____, I would express my remorse and regrets regarding _____

Unfortunately, I no longer have access to this relationship due to _____

_____

As a means of addressing my personal need for some resolve to the pain in our relationship, I will adopt the previously described method of:

____ empty-chair Gestalt method

____ writing a letter

____ visiting the grave and "talking" to this person from my past

If I could speak with _____, I would express my remorse and regrets regarding _____

Unfortunately, I no longer have access to this relationship due to _____

_____

As a means of addressing my personal need for some resolve to the pain in our relationship, I will adopt the previously described method of:

____ empty-chair Gestalt method

____ writing a letter

____ visiting the grave and "talking" to this person from my past

WEEKLY FOOD AND EXERCISE JOURNAL

Date _____
Weight (First day of week only) _____

	Breakfast/ A.M. Snack	Lunch P.M. Snack	Dinner Nite Snack	Exercise	Feelings and Major Events of the Day
Day One					
Day Two					
Day Three					
Day Four					
Day Five					
Day Six					
Day Seven					

Week 9

DAY 1

UNDERSTANDING OBESITY

"Obesity is an old disease but can only be properly understood and managed in the light of new scientific information,"[1] says noted obesity research scientist Theodore Van Itallie of Columbia University. In past generations of physicians and other health care professionals, a great mistake has been made in oversimplifying the problem of obesity and even categorizing it as merely a character flaw. The classic example of treatment failures revolves around an impatient physician who tears off a one-page diet plan, sends the patient packing, and tells him to come back when he has lost twenty pounds.

It has become clear that obesity is driven by a multitude of factors including emotions, genetics, eating habits, and activity levels. A unidimensional approach for the treatment of obesity has never worked. In this workbook, we have already discussed most of the factors that will give you even a slight edge for increased success. In this section, we will take a closer look at the actual nature of obesity.

WHAT IS OBESITY?

Obesity can be defined as an excessive enlargement of the body's total quantity of fat or adipose tissue. Sometimes called overfatness, obesity begins when men are more than 120 percent of their ideal body weight or when women are more than 130 percent of their ideal body weight. In addition to the total percent body fat, obesity may be described further by the types and numbers of fat cells that make up the adipose tissue. When excess weight is gained later in life but weight was not a problem during the growing-up years, the fat cells tend to get larger but do not increase in number. This type of obesity is called *fat cell hypertrophy*, meaning that your existing fat cells simply filled up more. If you were overfat as a baby, child, or adolescent, then you probably have a greater number of fat cells, but they are usually not overly large. This is called *fat cell hyperplasia*. Regardless of which kind of obesity is present, when weight is lost, the number of fat cells does not decrease, the cell size merely becomes smaller.

WHAT IS A FAT CELL?

Fat cells are the body's fuel storage tanks. Even though you may not be too thankful for them right now, they are one of the major survival mechanisms of the human body. At a carnival you may have seen a balloon inside of another slightly larger balloon. If you imagine this, then you can understand the structure of a fat cell. The largest individual part of a fat cell is that inner balloon, which serves as a storage vesicle (a membranous and usually fluid-filled pouch) for a tiny droplet of fat. This feature takes up almost the entire cellular structure. The slightly larger outside balloon represents the cellular membrane which houses other cellular parts including the nucleus (control center) of the cell. When the body is deprived of energy (as on a weight-loss diet) the inner balloon which holds the fuel reserves is deflated as the fat that it holds is used for daily energy requirements. You can just imagine millions of those tiny balloons deflating as you become slimmer. That's a nice picture to hold in your mind on one of those days when you feel hungry.

The one piece of bad news is that once you have a fat cell, it never goes away. You do not lose fat cells when you diet, they merely deflate. The outside balloon (in our carnival illustration) will reduce in size as the inside balloon or droplet container becomes smaller. After you have lost weight, the remaining fat tissue looks like a bunch of little deflated balloons, if you were to look at them under a microscope. One thing further, don't take it for granted that you will be able to lose, gain, and lose again. Each time these little cells inflate again, it is metabolically more difficult for them to lose the fat droplet yet one more time. Researchers are not sure what causes this phenomenon, but it is clear that "yo-yo" dieting won't work forever.

DAY 1

SAYING HELLO TO NEW MESSAGES

In sections of previous weeks, you looked at negative existential messages to which you may have been exposed as a child, messages about who you are and what is your worth. In dealing with the old floodtide of negative messages, it was important to examine . . .

- messages you heard;

- messages you experienced despite contrasting verbal messages (actions that spoke louder than words);

- unspoken, felt messages;

- messages you witnessed;

- messages about feelings or needs.

One mistake people make is underestimating the power of these negative messages. In recent weeks, you've learned how to say good-bye to many of the hurts and losses and dysfunctions in your life. You've also learned how to grieve through the pain associated with these things. The third step in the process of fully freeing yourself from the influence of your past is to replace your old negative perceptions—of yourself, your body, your relationships, your world—with messages that are new and more accurate, and uniformly positive and uplifting.

One way to "input" these new messages is through positive "self-talk" or affirmations. Some people, when approached with the concept of positive self-talk, have raised the argument, "That's unrealistic. You're wanting me to just say good things about myself, but there are bad things about me too." To this we readily admit that, yes, we may be going to extremes, but for a purpose. The majority of people with food addictions suffer from an unrealistic, low self-esteem. At this stage in your recovery, focusing on positive self-talk serves as corrective balance. It takes this kind of imbalance toward the positive to counterbalance the old negative floodtide and result in a realistic view of self.

Take the rest of today or a good part of tomorrow and simply keep tabs of the messages—both negative and positive—that you receive. You'll want to keep track of verbal and nonverbal messages; the messages you receive from others as well as the messages that flow out of your own thoughts. If you are like most people, you will be surprised to realize how constantly you feed yourself depreciating, negative, or scary messages.

Negative thought or message from myself:

Examples:

Woke up wondering if I would fail my driver's license exam this afternoon.

Got stuck in traffic on way to important lunch and berated myself as I sat there steaming in traffic.

Made the mistake of watching one of the nighttime soaps and spent the hour comparing myself to all the thin, rich characters I saw on TV.

_____

_____

_____

_____

_____

_____

Negative thought or message from someone else (verbal):

Examples:

The kids poked fun at the way I was dressed as I headed out to work this morning.

My spouse yelled at me for not having the car gassed as we were running late for a social event.

Overheard coworker complain to my boss about the way I handled an office decision.

_____

_____

_____

_____

_____

Negative thought or message from someone else (nonverbal):

Examples:

When I mentioned the project's budget in the meeting with clients, my boss flashed me a look that made me feel this *small.*

Accidentally cut off another car on the way home from work; the other driver honked and yelled and gave me an obscene gesture.

Tonight I caught my dinner date flirting with someone at the next table.

_____

_____

_____

_____

DAY 1

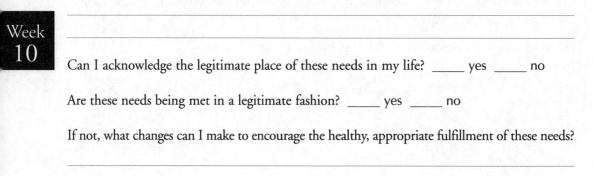

STEP 10: WE CONTINUED TO TAKE PERSONAL INVENTORY AND WHEN WE WERE WRONG, PROMPTLY ADMITTED IT.

Steps 10, 11, and 12 are sometimes called the maintenance steps. In ways, they repeat many of the things outlined in previous steps, but they are now given the sense—through daily practice—of the urgency and repetition that are so vital to the recovery process.

One of the daily inventories that is vital to recovery is an inventory of needs. God instilled in us a rich treasure house of needs: need to give and receive love; need to create; need to be productive; needs for safety and security; need to experience joy and ecstasy, and so on. Oftentimes the food addict is a person who has become disillusioned about the prospect of meeting many of these needs. The buried needs transmute into an exaggerated felt need for food, and thus the food addiction.

We all have needs; God made us that way. So you have a choice: you can continue trying in vain to meet your needs through the counterfeit means of your addiction, or you can get your needs met through healthy, God-directed means. If you, indeed, find healthy ways to get your needs met, you will be pleased to discover that over time, the gnawing sense of insatiable needs begins to recede. Finding legitimate ways to meet your needs is actually one of the most unselfish things you can do—it in essence "turns down the volume" on the love hunger that has kept you from living and giving freely.

Ask yourself the following questions every day as you continue your recovery process:

What are my needs, including basic needs such as love, acceptance, and security?

_____

_____

Can I acknowledge the legitimate place of these needs in my life? _____ yes _____ no

Are these needs being met in a legitimate fashion? _____ yes _____ no

If not, what changes can I make to encourage the healthy, appropriate fulfillment of these needs?

_____

_____

Week 10

DAY 2

GENETIC FACTORS

Fat cell distribution is definitely an inheritable trait. This is especially apparent when you notice families and whether they tend to add fat to the central part of the body or more to the peripheral portions. If parents are overweight, there is a much greater incidence of obesity in their children. This is especially true if both parents are overweight. Now, we know what you are thinking right about now. Everything else we have told you was at least meant to be encouraging—what about this piece of information? Does this mean that if both of your parents were overfat, you should just close the book now and forget about ever making permanent changes? Absolutely not! In fact, there are so many stories floating around in the media that we decided to confront this issue head on as an encouragement to you.

We have yet to meet a single patient with a perfect body or a perfect genetic code. No such human exists. We must all learn to accept who we are and be glad for the entire package. Some people are born with a predisposition to alcoholism. But not all of those people are alcoholics. Some people are born blind, but many of those enter the work force and have a normal and productive life. Some people will become diabetics because of their genetic makeup. But most of them are able to control this condition and also lead a normal life. No matter what you have heard, obesity is controllable, too. *Anyone who wants to lose weight and finds out how to do so properly can lose weight.* Granted, it will be more difficult for some to lose and maintain the weight loss than for others, but there is no justification in giving it all up and deciding that you must live with being obese. You, or anyone else, are capable of weight loss and weight maintenance.

Now let's look at some introspective questions about your family and weight control.

Were your parents overweight? Both or just one? _____

_____

What about your grandparents, aunts, and uncles? List them here. _____

_____

What about your brothers and sisters? List them here. _____

_____

For any of the relatives listed above, do you feel that they were overweight because of their eating habits or because of their genetic makeup? _____

_____

_____

Do you feel that they were overweight because of a combination of these two factors?
_____ yes _____ no

How do you feel about the reasons for your own problems with weight? What factors figure in? (Examples: emotional deficits, compulsive eating, genetics, lack of activity, others.)

_____

_____

_____

_____

If the genetic influence on your weight has bothered you in the past, affirm this statement:

> There are many reasons for gaining weight. I have studied most of those reasons over the last few months. I can control this thing from several angles which involve my whole being—body, mind, and soul. If I do have relatives with weight problems, it *does not* mean that I will follow in their footsteps. By using the complete lifestyle plan I have been studying, my weight can come under control now and stay under control in the future.

DAY 2

MESSAGES ABOUT YOUR HEALTH, BODY IMAGE, AND APPEARANCE

The following are examples of new, positive messages about your health, body image, and appearance.

Week
10

I deserve to look good.
I can reach the top.
I deserve to be healthy.
I deserve to be sexual.
My body is my friend.
My body is a gift from God.
My body is something I have control over.
I am happy to be the gender God created me to be.
I enjoy feeling good.
I enjoy looking good.

For a good number of years—particularly if you have been overweight as a result of your food addiction—you have been receiving negative messages about your body, health, and appearance. The tragedy is that for every negative message you may have perceived through the verbal or nonverbal communication of others, you may have sent yourself many more negative messages on your own. What are some of the negative messages you have often replayed or generated regarding your appearance, health, or body?

Sometimes I look in the mirror and think _____

_____

I seem to be always berating myself for _____

_____

When my scale goes up a notch, I usually think to myself, _____

_____

Even when other people give me compliments, I may discount their comments and think, instead, _____

_____

I most often think negative things about myself in the area of _____

_____

Week
10

DAY 2

Step 10. We continued to take personal inventory and when we were wrong, promptly admitted it.

A DAILY CHECK: COUNTERFEIT MEANS OF FULFILLMENT

A third component of your daily inventory needs to be a look at how you are meeting your needs. While it's okay to have the needs, you must now ask yourself if you are trying to satisfy those needs by bogus methods.

Am I overcontrolling others? ____ yes ____ no

If so, why? _____

What would be a better approach to meeting that need? _____

_____

Am I being perfectionistic or compulsive with myself or others? ____ yes ____ no

If so, why? _____

What would be a better approach to meeting that need? _____

_____

Am I attempting to win acceptance by playing the martyr or the victim role in relationships?
____ yes ____ no

If so, why? _____

What would be a better approach to meeting that need? _____

_____

Am I compulsively rescuing or enabling others? ____ yes ____ no

If so, why? _____

What would be a better approach to meeting that need? _____

_____

Am I using food as a substitute for other needs? _____ yes _____ no

If so, why? _____

What would be a better approach to meeting those needs? _____

_____

DAY 3

PREVENTING OBESITY

It may be too late for all of us who have already struggled with the weight issue, but the authors of this book feel that the best treatment for obesity or any other disease is the prevention of that disease. So why talk about it now? For the benefit of readers who have children at home or others over whom they may have influence.

The body is capable of adding new fat cells only at certain times of life. The first substantial addition of fat cells is in the last trimester of pregnancy. Studies have indicated that mothers who gain too much weight during this period of time produce babies who have greater numbers of fat cells. So be careful about that prenatal weight gain. You and your baby will be better off if you gain no more than twenty-five pounds.

The first years of life is another time when fat cells may be added. Don't overfeed those babies with arbitrary amounts of formula or baby foods. And, remember that it is always preferable to breastfeed infants and to delay solid foods and juices until the sixth month (as recommended by the American Academy of Pediatrics). Keep a close eye on the diet and growth charts as the child grows and never be satisfied with "he'll grow out of it" from your physician if your child starts becoming overweight. Statistics do not indicate that children will simply "grow out" of obesity. In fact, they indicate just the opposite. The longer a child is overweight, the greater their chances are of becoming an obese adult.

Another crucial time of life to watch those scales are the adolescent years. This is also a time of life when new fat cells may be added. This seems especially important for girls who have already reached their maximum height and now should slow down on their caloric intake (unlike many of their adolescent brothers who seemingly eat everything that is not glued down).

The major factor that has increased obesity among young Americans is the statistical fact that children are less active than they once were. They are doing more sitting activities instead of roaming the neighborhood on bikes. Encourage your children to play outside. Until your sedentary child reaches the point where playing outside is enjoyable, you may have to schedule a time and enforce outdoor play. Promote outside activities as a family and enroll your child in team sports. Developing and nurturing a love of physical fitness will be a lasting benefit that will help them for the rest of their lives.

KIDS ON THE COUCH

In an article entitled, "Little Couch Potatoes Keep Sprouting" (Tufts University Diet and Nutrition Letter, 8:5, July 1990), it was reported that by the time most of our children reach their seventies, they will have spent 10 percent of their lives in front of a television set. This activity will have used up more of their time than any other single activity except sleeping. Television time and pediatric weight gain seem to be increasing at the same rate. You can see it all across America—the TV sets are glowing. Little League is being ignored, and childhood obesity is rampant.

The American Academy of Pediatrics is more than a little concerned. When you consider the fact that watching the tube burns only a few more calories than does sleeping, you can imagine the damage to a growing body. Even youngsters must uncouple those associated eating behaviors that we talked about weeks ago. *When you eat, only eat,* and teach your children to do the same.

PREVENTING OBESITY RECURRENCE

Perhaps you cannot prevent obesity from affecting your life at this point. But you can prevent it from recurring. We will talk about this issue in next week's lessons. Today, we want to present a few key factors.

1. Every time you try to lose weight again after losing and regaining, it is metabolically more difficult. Keep this in mind if you ever again lapse into that "all or none" feeling that says "I'll eat everything I want, even to the point of becoming sick since I have already blown it today." Even occasional binges can cause fat cells to start refilling. Once a fat cell is formed, it does not go away. It simply inflates or deflates as extra calorie stores become available or unavailable.

2. Make permanent changes and continue the same routine you have begun in this program. Look for new, late-breaking ideas in magazines. Do not revert to the old habits, food selections, portion sizes, and exercise habits that contributed to the weight gain in the first place.

Week
10

3. Keep up your exercise. Most experts agree that this is the single most important factor in maintaining your newfound weight.

How do you feel about the lesson today? Can you live with the fact that you were once overweight without feeling burdened? Can you give up those negative feelings, knowing that you are on the road to recovery? _____

_____

_____

Who in your life can you help prevent obesity? Is there a child or a spouse you can influence? Can you do it in a loving and caring way, never being judgmental, but instead talking about proper eating habits from the medical perspective?

_____

_____

_____

Are you planning to keep up your exercise program even when you are the weight and size you want to be? ____ yes ____ no

DAY 3

NEW MESSAGES ABOUT RELATIONSHIPS

The following are examples of new, positive messages about your relationships.

> I want people in my life.
> I can enjoy healthy relationships.
> I can enjoy intimacy in my relationships.
> I deserve to be sexual.
> I have permission to ask people to help meet my needs.
> I can love and be loved.
> My spouse is my best friend.

A new, positive message that is critical is the message that you have permission to ask the people with whom you enjoy relationships to help meet key needs in your life. For many people who come out of a dysfunctional family, there are hidden messages that say needs shouldn't exist or should be ignored. Examples of this kind of thinking might include:

I don't have permission to ask my spouse to meet my sexual needs.
I don't have permission to ask my boss for a raise to meet my financial needs.
I don't have permission to ask my parents to meet my need for privacy.
I don't have permission to ask my friends to meet my need for greater intimacy.

In contrast, when you give yourself permission to ask your spouse, friends, colleagues, and family to meet your legitimate needs, you are less likely to try to meet these needs through a surrogate relationship with food.

Take a moment and think about some of the needs that you have a right to have met through your relationships with people.

I give myself permission to ask that my need for _____
_____ be met through the dynamic of relationship. In the past, I have sought to meet this need through the (circle one) legitimate/illegitimate means of

_____

I give myself permission to ask that my need for _____
_____ be met through the dynamic of relationship. In the past, I have sought to meet this need through the (circle one) legitimate/illegitimate means of

_____

I give myself permission to ask that my need for _____
_____ be met through the dynamic of relationship. In the past, I have sought to meet this need through the (circle one) legitimate/illegitimate means of

_____

DAY 3

Step 10. We continued to take personal inventory and when we were wrong, promptly admitted it.

A DAILY CHECK: GIVING AS WELL AS RECEIVING

There is an economy of relationships: The more you give, the more you will receive. Please note that this is not an economy based only on narrow cause and effect: "If I give two hours of attention to my spouse, the effect is that I will receive two hours in return" is a faulty equation. The fact is, your two hours spent may result in no visible effect whatsoever. Yet the principle of give and take in relationships is still valid, and your expenditures will reap generous returns in the long run. God has placed us in a bountiful needs economy in all our relationships. The love that you give and receive freely will be richly multiplied far beyond any linear equation.

A more accurate perspective on the economy in relationships would be: "Just as it is important to ask that my needs be met, it is important for me to help meet the needs of others." Yet it's critical that you give with an attitude that says, "I give because I choose to, not out of guilt and shame; I don't give out of fear that if I don't, I won't get anything back. I give because I enjoy it and choose to. I feel better when I give."

What are the relationships in your life in which there may exist an unbalanced economy? Are there relationships you may want to nurture with an investment of more of yourself? Name the relationship and describe how you might increase your investment in that relationship.

(With regard to my relationship with my daughter, I choose to watch my critical tongue and uplift her with positive phrases instead.)

With regard to my relationship with _____, I choose to

_____

_____

(With regard to my relationship with my boss, I choose to respond to his requests by really listening instead of letting everything go in one ear and out the other.)

With regard to my relationship with _____, I choose to

_____

_____

What about relationships in general? Are there any statements you need to make to yourself regarding the ways you are currently giving or intend to give in your relationships?

Example:
   I give myself permission to give emotional attention to my spouse.

I can enjoy encouraging the people I work with.
I can enjoy my relationship with my teenagers.

_____

_____

_____

_____

Regarding the key romantic relationship in your life, you may need to give yourself a lot of new messages regarding sexuality. For many adults with food addictions, there can exist an old shame base about sexuality and a denial of sexual feelings. Consider new messages specific to your sexuality that you may want to communicate to yourself.

_____

_____

_____

_____

DAY 4

UNDERSTANDING OBESITY: Q AND A

Over the next two days in the Body portion of the book, we will discuss the most commonly asked diet-related questions. The topics have arisen out of numerous patient consultations and seminar questions. We think you will identify with the patients who wondered about these issues.

Q. *What is the effect of eating only one meal per day instead of three or even more?*

A. Many patients report that they skip breakfast and/or lunch and then eat only one time per day. The result of this is a startling decrease in metabolism. The more meals you skip, the lower the metabolic rate declines. The other issue is that most meal skippers overcompensate for the calories they skipped earlier in the day, rationalizing that since they are only eating once they can make whatever food choices they care to. Many times, hunger will be so intense at this point that it is difficult to make wise or controlled decisions. Eating two times per day increases the metabolism over that of a person who consumes only one meal per day. The highest metabolic rate occurs when three meals are eaten every day.

Q. *Does it make a difference where body fat is located in terms of how fast or easily weight is lost?*

A. In the person who is more than fifty pounds overweight, abdominal fat cells reproduce very rapidly and these people can add fat easily to these areas of the body. When you begin to lose weight, the abdominal fat seems to come off easier as well. Fat that is stored around the buttocks and thighs seems more resistant to calorie restricted diets. Many experts feel that this fat is best lost with a combination of calorie restriction and a rigorous exercise program. Some of the fat found in these lower extremities has been added when women are pregnant, and was intended as a fat store for the production of breast milk. When those stores are not used up through lactation, they can be resistant to dieting. A serious walking program (a total of five hours per week at the rate of one mile per fifteen minutes) will help with this area.

Q. *Will spot reducing be effective if I have a particular problem area?*

A. Extra exercise for certain parts of the body (such as sit-ups for the abdomen or leg lifts for the thighs) is ineffective in terms of reducing the fat accumulation in these areas. They will definitely strengthen the muscles of that area and tone them, but the exercising of these areas will not cause you to selectively lose more fat. Aerobic exercise is the only type of exercise that can decrease fat tissues. It will decrease the fat stores in a fairly even manner throughout the body.

Q. *What is the perfect percentage of calories from fat that we should include in our diet? Should we be as extreme as the 10 percent Pritikin diet or can we get by with a 30 percent fat diet?*

A. The amount of fat in your diet should reflect your health goals. Are you trying to decrease your levels of blood cholesterol as well as lose weight, or are you simply looking for a way to take off a few pounds? The Pritikin-type diet is one that contains only 10 percent of its calories as fat. This diet, in combination with a rigorous exercise program has actually been shown to reduce plaque build-up in arteries. Previous to this, it was thought that once atherosclerotic plaques were present, the only thing you could do was either have them surgically removed or simply be on a health program that prevented increased accumulations.

Week
10

The Pritikin diet is not very easy to stay on since it is so low in fat. It also leaves you with that "I'm always hungry" feeling. A 25 percent fat program, which is what we estimate the Love Hunger Diet Plan represents, is far more satisfying and represents the type of diet that will work for maintenance. The American Heart Association supports that 30 percent or less of your dietary caloric intake should come from fat. Using this as the standard, the Love Hunger Diet Plan falls within the recommended range.

DAY 4

NEW MESSAGES ABOUT FOOD

The following are examples of new, positive messages about food.

> I give my body the most nutritious food I can.
> I stop eating when I am satisfied.
> I never eat in secret.
> My diet is a gift I'm giving myself.

When starting a food and weight program, a key message is that food is a friend and not an enemy. Often adults who are either anorexic or obese come to view food as an enemy because of what it does to them. When the relationship with food is perceived as a love/hate relationship with an enemy, it can fuel the self-destructive tendencies of the food addict. The new message that you want to foster is that food is a friend when used in moderation.

A second message about food is that food cannot serve in roles for which it was not created. Are you asking food to provide a function beyond physical nourishment? What are the roles food has been asked to play in your life? And what message can you give yourself about a better source for each need?

(I have tried to elevate food to be a tranquilizer for my pain. From now on, I will allow myself to feel the pain, say good-bye to the pain, and grieve past the pain.)

I have tried to elevate food to _____

From now on, _____

(I have tried to elevate food to the role of god in my life. From now on, I will nurture my relationship with the One true God.)

I have tried to elevate food to _____

From now on, _____

(I have tried to elevate food to become a substitute for romantic relationships. From now on, I will submit myself to the give-and-take dynamic of relationships with the opposite sex, giving permission to experience intimacy.)

I have tried to elevate food to _____

From now on, _____

DAY 4

Step 10. We continued to take personal inventory and when we were wrong, promptly admitted it.

A DAILY CHECK: SETTING NEW BOUNDARIES

As you think of new messages regarding your image of self, it's important to take these messages one step further and to translate them into new boundaries. In earlier weeks, we talked about the fact that a lot of abuse stems from boundary violations. Now, during the healing process, one of the most important ways to affirm your self-worth is to establish new boundaries for yourself. Boundaries are not barriers. They are the protective and shaping forms around which your new being and identity are shaped.

One woman who had been vulnerable to affairs outside of her marriage began to get in touch with her low self-esteem and all the negative messages she had been receiving and originating about her worth. She realized that she had been so hungry for affirmation of her worth that she had been unable to establish boundaries that protected herself and her marriage. She said, "My self-esteem was so bad that I prostituted my boundaries in return for attention, affection, and affirmation. I just couldn't say no for the fear that someone might not 'like me' for respecting my own boundaries."

There are other examples of old negative messages resulting in inappropriate boundaries, as in the case of the young man who was so convinced that he was unattractive and without worth that he built physical and emotional barriers against the first sign of intimacy in any relationship. His boundaries were just as inappropriate as those of the woman whose infidelity threatened her marriage.

Just as the negative messages resulted in inappropriate boundaries, new positive messages require a shift in boundaries toward the appropriate. For example, if one of your new messages is that you deserve to have equal financial authority in your relationship with your spouse, you will want to establish that corresponding new boundary. Perhaps the actual boundary is that you approach your spouse and make it clear that you will not support any large financial decision that you haven't made together.

There are several areas in which we encourage recovering food addicts to establish new boundaries. Are you a good gatekeeper?

SOCIAL AND RELATIONSHIP ISSUES

In conjunction with my new, positive messages regarding relationships, a new boundary that I would like to establish is _____

The first step toward establishing this boundary is to _____

_____

This boundary is important because _____

_____

SEXUAL ISSUES

In conjunction with my new, positive messages regarding my sexuality, a new boundary that I would like to establish is _____

The first step toward establishing this boundary is to _____

_____

This boundary is important because _____

_____

I would like to say 'no' to _____

I would like to say 'yes' to _____

FINANCIAL ISSUES

In conjunction with my new, positive messages regarding finances, a new boundary that I would like to establish is _____

The first step toward establishing this boundary is to _____

_____

This boundary is important because _____

_____

I will take care of myself financially by _____

_____

HEALTH AND PHYSICAL ISSUES

In conjunction with my new, positive messages regarding health and my appearance, a new boundary that I would like to establish is _____

_____

The first step toward establishing this boundary is to _____

_____

This boundary is important because _____

_____

I will take care of my body by _____

_____

FOOD ISSUES

In conjunction with my new, positive messages regarding food, a new boundary that I would like to establish is _____

The first step toward establishing this boundary is to _____

_____

This boundary is important because _____

_____

DAY 5

UNDERSTANDING OBESITY: MORE Q AND A

Week
10

Q. Do overweight people have slower metabolisms than thin people?

A. This is indeed a possibility. Scientific studies have shown that certain babies have a slower Basal Metabolic Rate (BMR) than others at only three days of age and gain more weight by the age of three months, even though they consume the same amount of food. In adult studies, it has been shown that many obese persons consume less food than their thin counterparts.

Obesity is a complicated, multifaceted problem. Perhaps some persons are indeed eating compulsively and not exercising. Then as a result of an inherited, slower metabolism, they find that they cannot get away with this lifestyle without gaining a lot of weight.

Q. *Why do so many people who make a decision to quit smoking then gain weight?*

A. As we have talked about earlier, it is very typical to have more than one addiction. Perhaps some of the people who gain weight after they stop smoking have not dealt with the core issues that have made them choose an addictive agent in the first place. However, other physiological factors do exist. There are three major theories that explain why smokers gain weight when they try to quit smoking. First, it is a fact that when smokers quit, they eat more. Heavy smokers (more than a pack a day) gain more weight when quitting than light smokers and they often experience increased hunger, which may be withdrawal from smoking's appetite suppressant effect. Some form of nicotine replacement, such as nicotine chewing gum, may not lessen or prevent weight gain.

Secondly, ex-smokers often report an improved sense of taste and smell. This may trigger an increased interest in food and new tastes. Some smokers often crave sugar upon quitting.

Thirdly, it is thought that the nicotine in cigarettes is responsible for the increased metabolic rates reported in some smokers. The precise mechanism is unknown, but the increased rate seems to translate into a 5 to 10 percent increase in the total number of calories burned per day. Some researchers speculate it is because nicotine decreases the circulating levels of insulin, which, in turn, decreases fat storage. When nicotine is cut off, sugar cravings are triggered.

The best way to handle smoking cessation is to have a plan. *Don't try to lose weight while attempting to quit smoking.* Smokers prone to weight fluctuations should simultaneously begin to exercise and to eat fewer calories before quitting. Eating healthier and taking greater care of one's body may indeed lay the groundwork for a later program that will lead to smoking cessation success.

Q. *Are the very low-calorie diets (protein-sparing fasts) really safe? Will my metabolism decrease as a result of going on a diet like this?*

A. Perhaps America's most celebrated weight loss was made known to the public on November 15, 1988, when Oprah Winfrey disclosed to her television viewers that she had lost 67 pounds in four months. From this point on, the meal replacement diets were all the rage. Since then many people have gone on these diets only to regain their weight or at least part of it. The real question, then, is "Can you lose weight on these types of diets and expect to keep that weight off?" The answer, as always, is yes and no. The hallmark of any weight loss program must center around permanent lifestyle changes in the kitchen and when eating out, and a change in activity levels. If you are not prepared to make these changes then your chances of success are almost zero. Also, as we have repeatedly pointed out in *Love Hunger* and again in this workbook, you must deal with the emotional reasons that may be driving a food addiction and keeping you from making the right choices. If the liquid meal replacement program you are on addresses all of these issues, then you can probably be successful with your program.

A patient once told us that if she could have a facelift, then her failing marriage could be restored. We, of course, told her that this line of reasoning was false and that only a healed relationship between her and her husband could restore her marriage. The same can be true of a dieter who only focuses on poundage. The focus should instead be on what is eating at me, what are my internal struggles, how can I cook better and make wise food choices, how can I control trigger foods and binge eating, how can I get to the point where I truly look forward to exercise and increased activity? If you are successful at losing fifty or more pounds on a liquid diet system, but have not thoroughly dealt with these other factors, you have only a slim chance of not regaining your weight.

Physiologically speaking, any diet will lower your metabolic rate. But those that are below 1,000 calories per day may lower the metabolism by as much as 45 percent. There have been many successes on the liquid diets (including Medifast®, Optifast®, Life Plus®, HMR®, etc.). This method seems well suited for some dieters. Research data is not yet available on the long-term effects of these programs. However, most have taken behavioral change seriously, and this is what you should look for if you desire to find a local group.

DAY 5

NEW MESSAGES ABOUT YOUR VALUE

The following are examples of new, positive messages about your value.

> I deserve to live.
> I deserve to succeed in my career.
> God loves me.
> God forgives me.
> I accept His forgiveness.
> God guides me.
> God gives me strength to enact my new decisions.

Week
10

YOUR RIGHT TO EXIST

The most basic category of messages regarding your worth as a person is simply statements regarding your right to exist. This may sound obvious, but it's not such a clear-cut issue for people with low self-esteem, which is a prominent problem for nearly any person with a food addiction. As a recovering food addict, you may have deep, inner questions about your legitimate place in your family, in your marriage, in society at large.

Now is the time to establish new messages—and an abundance of them—regarding your basic worth and your right to inhabit your body! Patterning your messages after the examples above, begin now to compile your new positive messages about your right to exist.

_____

_____

_____

_____

_____

YOUR RIGHT TO HAVE THOUGHTS AND FEELINGS

Also related to messages about your worth are statements that validate your thoughts and feelings. People don't have to agree with your thoughts, share your feelings, or mirror your opinions, but that doesn't change the fact that these things are important and that you desire to share these innermost aspects of yourself. Write several affirmations declaring your right to have and express thoughts and feelings.

_____

_____

_____

_____

_____

YOUR RIGHT TO HAPPINESS

A third and key category of messages is that you deserve a generous degree of happiness. Many food addicts may be unconsciously addicted to pain—often their self-esteem is so low and they have become so accustomed to pain in their lives that they will do things to sabotage themselves and to bring on emotional and physical pain. Write declarations of your right to create and enjoy the happiness that God intends for you.

_____

_____

_____

DAY 5

Step 10. We continued to take personal inventory and when we were wrong, promptly admitted it.

A DAILY CHECK: MAKING AMENDS FOR VIOLATED BOUNDARIES

Another component of your daily inventory is making amends for violated boundaries—yours or those belonging to someone else.

If you have recently violated your own boundaries, as defined in yesterday's segment, then you need to make amends with yourself; you may owe yourself an apology. If you are aware of violating the boundaries of someone else, you need to do what you can to make amends and ensure that the boundary infraction doesn't occur again.

One of the best ways to help prevent the trespass from recurring is to deal with the underlying fear or need that prompted the crossover in the first place.

Am I aware of instances in which I have violated my own boundaries or the boundaries of others? _____ yes _____ no

If so, what were the personal boundaries that I allowed others to cross? _____
_____

How did I feel when my boundaries were not respected? _____
_____

What were the boundaries belonging to others that I allowed myself to cross? _____
_____

How did violating those boundaries make me feel? _____
_____

How can I reset and reestablish new, proper boundaries?

For myself: _____

Week
10

For my relationship with others: _____

How can I make amends to those who have been harmed by my boundary violations?

_____

_____

What needs were the driving force behind the violation of my own boundaries? (Example: the need for acceptance, a fear of not being loved, a fear of rejection.) _____

_____

What needs were the driving force behind my violation of the boundaries of others? _____

_____

_____

How might I provide a healthier fulfillment of these needs? _____

_____

Week
10

WEEKLY FOOD AND EXERCISE JOURNAL

Date _____
Weight (First day of week only) _____

	Breakfast/ A.M. Snack	Lunch P.M. Snack	Dinner Nite Snack	Exercise	Feelings and Major Events of the Day
Day One					
Day Two					
Day Three					
Day Four					
Day Five					
Day Six					
Day Seven					

DAY 1

PREVENTING DISEASE THROUGH IMPROVED NUTRITION

PREVENTING STROKES AND HEART ATTACKS

I'm sorry, but your husband's had a heart attack." Fateful words, life changing and tragically common, this statement is repeated dozens of times daily to stunned family members across the country. If the patient survives, typically much effort is made by the new heart patient and his family to make changes in their lifestyle that they hope will prevent the recurrence of any future heart problems. Often these belated efforts at prevention include exercise, stress reduction, smoking cessation, and dietary changes. Wouldn't it be great if the heart disease and threat to your life or your loved one's life could be avoided altogether?

One of the real benefits of a new approach to eating is the disease prevention effects that come along with a healthier diet. Later this week you'll learn how a healthy diet can substantially lower your risk of cancer, diabetes, and osteoporosis. But now, let's see what can be done to lower the risk of the leading cause of death in American men and women—cardiovascular disease.

Strokes and heart attacks are the number one killers of men and women in the United States. Tragically, many of these deaths could be prevented if the nutritional principles you are learning would just be applied by more people and at an earlier age. Your dietary changes could well benefit others in your family as they adopt the healthy eating habits you are learning.

There are several well-identified risk factors for cardiovascular disease. Most of these risk factors can be modified if they are recognized. Dietary changes can positively affect several of these risk factors such as high blood pressure, cholesterol, diabetes, and obesity.

DIETARY CONTROL OF HYPERTENSION

By simply decreasing salt intake and controlling weight, many cases of high blood pressure can be well controlled without medication. Those requiring medication will find they need fewer pills and lower doses of medicine to keep their blood pressure where it ought to be. Studies have clearly shown that losing as little as eight to ten pounds can be just as effective at controlling mild hypertension as medication. So, if high blood pressure is a problem for you, keep the salt shaker off the table, watch that sodium intake, and work on keeping off those extra pounds.

Do you have high blood pressure? ____ yes ____ no

Do any of your close relatives have high blood pressure? ____ yes ____ no

Are you aware that high blood pressure is an inheritable disease? ____ yes ____ no

If high blood pressure is a problem for you now or becomes a problem later, would you rather control it by medications or improved health habits?

DAY 1

SUPPORT GROUPS AND MAINTENANCE

Many recovering food addicts report that membership in a recovery support group can provide the sense of community lacking from their own families of origin. Even recovering food addicts coming from nurturing families agree that recovery groups provide a crucial missing link.

Even if you are a member of a support group such as OA—and particularly if you are not—take time today to familiarize yourself with recovery groups in your community. The reason for this is twofold: There is a practical advantage of simply having the knowledge of names, locations, and phone numbers of area support groups. More than that, however, if you have not yet joined a recovery group, there may be a lingering resistance that is keeping you away. The sheer mechanical step of looking through the phone book for names and numbers can be helpful in breaking past any lingering resistance or denial.

Begin with the white pages in your neighborhood phone book. An obvious resource is Overeaters Anonymous®. Yet many recovering food addicts also benefit from groups such as Al-Anon for spouses and children of alcoholics; ACoA for Adult Children of Alcoholics;

Week

11

CoDA or Co-dependents Anonymous. Whenever you reach a representative of one support group, ask her if she is aware of any similar or different recovery groups she might recommend. List your findings in the space provided.

Name of group: _____ Phone: _____

Name of person you spoke with: _____

Time and location of meetings: _____

_____

Directions to get to meeting location: _____

_____

Miscellaneous information about group or meetings: _____

_____

_____

Name of group: _____ Phone: _____

Name of person you spoke with: _____

Time and location of meetings: _____

_____

Directions to get to meeting location: _____

_____

Miscellaneous information about group or meetings: _____

_____

_____

Now, call large churches in your area, especially churches with counseling centers or departments. Ask about any spiritually oriented self-help groups in your community. Many of the Twelve Step groups have religious counterparts where the dynamics and recovery are closely integrated with the traditions of your faith.

Name of church: _____ Phone: _____

Name of person you spoke with: _____

Week
11

Name, time, and location of meetings they were able to recommend:

_____

_____

_____

Directions to get to meeting location: _____

_____

Miscellaneous information about group or meetings: _____

_____

_____

Name of church: _____ Phone: _____

Name of person you spoke with: _____

Name, time, and location of meetings they were able to recommend:

_____

_____

_____

Directions to get to meeting location: _____

_____

Miscellaneous information about group or meetings: _____

_____

_____

A variety of roadblocks and obstacles may have delayed you from actively seeking out a recovery group. You may have a seemingly legitimate reason such as: "I don't have time," "I can't find a baby-sitter," "I don't know how to locate a group," "I wouldn't know what to say if I showed up at one of these meetings." If you have yet to hook in with a recovery support group, what are the barriers that have so far kept you from making that connection?

I haven't linked up with a recovery group because _____

_____

_____

_____

Alcoholics Anonymous
P.O. Box 459, Grand
Central Station
New York, NY 10163
(212) 870-3400

Al-Anon/Alateen Family
Group Headquarters
Inc.
1600 Corporate Landing
Parkway,
Virginia Beach, VA
23454-5617

Debtors Anonymous
General Service Office
P.O. Box 920888
Needham, MA 02492-0009
(781) 453-2743

Emotions Anonymous
P.O. Box 4245
St. Paul, MN 55104-0245
(651) 647-9712

Gamblers Anonymous
P.O. Box 17173
Los Angeles, CA 90017
(213) 386-8789

Narcotics Anonymous
World Service Office
P.O. Box 9999
Van Nuys, CA 91409
(818) 773-9999

National Association for
Children of Alcoholics
11426 Rockville Pike
Suite 100
Rockville, MD 20852
(888) 554-2627

Overcomers Outreach
P.O. Box 2208
Oakhurst, CA 93641
(800) 310-3001
(Alcoholics and Adult
Children Claiming
Christ's Promises and
Accepting His Healing)

Overeaters Anonymous,
World Service Office
P.O. Box 44020
Rio Rancho, NM
87174-4020
(505) 891-2664

National Clearinghouse for
Alcohol Information
P.O. Box 2345
Rockville, MD 20847-2345
(800) 729-6686

Adult Children of
Alcoholics
ACA WSO
P.O. Box 3216
Torrance, CA 90510
(310) 534-1815

Incest Survivors Anonymous
P.O. Box 17245
Long Beach, CA
90807-7245
(562) 428-5599

Be advised these organizations exist also. Seek them out locally.

Adult Children
Anonymous

Alatot

Alcoholics Victorious
(Christian recovery
support group)

Bulimics/Anorexics
Anonymous

Child Abusers
Anonymous

Cocaine Anonymous

Codependents of Sex Addicts

Parents Anonymous

Pills Anonymous

Sex Addicts Anonymous

Sexaholics Anonymous

Sex and Love Addicts
Anonymous

Smokers Anonymous

Spenders Anonymous

Victims of Incest Can
Emerge

Workaholics Anonymous

DAY 1

STEP 11: WE SOUGHT THROUGH PRAYER AND MEDITATION TO IMPROVE OUR CONSCIOUS CONTACT WITH GOD, PRAYING ONLY FOR KNOWLEDGE OF HIS WILL FOR US AND THE POWER TO CARRY THAT OUT.

No assessment of relationships in your life is complete without an assessment of your relationship with God. Critical to your maintenance success is a daily effort to not only evaluate that relationship, but also to yield and surrender your will. Bill Wilson's caution for the addictive or the codependent personality—since willfulness is a major part of your addictive illness—is that you may have to daily surrender yourself back to God, reyield your life back to Him. This kind of daily surrender will probably need to go on for a lifetime.

There are several guidelines you may want to consider for Step 11.

Reserving a certain time to seek God and to engage in prayer should be a daily practice. This time usually should involve some sort of stillness, relaxation, or meditation. Particularly for the obsessive-compulsive personality—such as perfectionists or workaholics—it is especially important to slow down. Slowing down is one way to take yourself out of the driver's seat, which is, of course, an integral part of your Step 11 prayer as you daily ask God to take your will off center stage and to replace it with His will and the power to carry out that will.

Is there a special time of day when you might carve out a niche of time in which to spend time alone with God? If so, that time might be _____

_____

What can you do to protect that time from being crowded out by the hustle and bustle of your many responsibilities? _____

_____

Is there a special place you would like to spend these moments in prayer? If so, describe that place here _____

_____

Are you willing to make the commitment to begin today spending daily time alone with God in prayer? ____ yes ____ no

If you said yes, it's important to realize that there may still be days when your schedule manages to squeeze out your allotted time with God. When that happens, don't let shame and guilt set in—instead, simply make up your mind to pick up the following day with the quiet time you are in the process of establishing.

DAY 2

LOWER YOUR CHOLESTEROL BY EATING LIGHT

Over 60 percent of Americans have a cholesterol problem, and high cholesterol accounts for up to 30 percent of strokes and heart attacks. Usually dietary changes can take care of this problem without resorting to the use of medications. The Love Hunger Diet Plan will not only help you control your weight, but will also help lower and control your cholesterol as well. Perhaps you might be one of the estimated three hundred thousand lives who could be saved every year if people would just lower their cholesterol.

Cholesterol in the bloodstream has two sources—that which is produced within the body (endogenous cholesterol) and that which is introduced into the body through food sources (exogenous cholesterol). Some people have the ability to break down large amounts of cholesterol in their liver, thus keeping serum levels of cholesterol in the body low. Other people do not have as many of the specialized cellular sites where the cholesterol is broken down; therefore, they can experience a build-up of cholesterol in their bloodstream. Since you have no real control over your endogenous cholesterol, your next best chance of control comes from decreasing the amount of cholesterol you consume in your foods.

Mastering a low cholesterol diet is really quite easy. You can still have cheese cake, pizza, French fries, and chips—*if the ingredients and recipes follow certain guidelines.* Look at the chart on page 206, which shows you low-fat and low-cholesterol food alternatives. By using these simple methods, losing weight, and getting regular aerobic exercise, your cholesterol level may return to normal.

Elevated levels of serum cholesterol, diabetes, and heart disease are all genetically linked. Now, don't panic! Almost all of us have someone in our families who have had problems with one or all of these diseases. And since Americans are living longer, we are now seeing that these are the major health problems instead of viral and bacterial infections. As Dr. Sneed said in her women's health book, *Prime Time* (Word Books, 1989), "Our goal is not that you should live longer, but that you should live better."[1] Who wants to live in an incapacitated state in their retirement years? No one. And if you do have a genetic link to one or all of these diseases, then you have all the more reason to protect yourself through preventive medicine. You can change the course of events by taking care of the intricate body that God gave you.

Reflect on these questions:

I may have a genetic link to the following diseases: (list) _____

_____

Circle the ones that you can control through improved health practices.

DAY 2

THE LOGISTICS OF ATTENDING MEETINGS

In our experience, logistical barriers such as those regarding babysitting, distance, time, or schedule typically are a form of denial, covering the *real* reasons for not going: reasons related to fears about becoming vulnerable to a "chosen family" recovery group.

Particularly if you've experience pain in your family of origin, current family, or marriage, you may have a lot of fear about opening up and diminishing the isolation that, in some sense, seems to protect you. When you first look behind the logistical barrier keeping you from a recovery group ("I don't have the time"), you may find a reason similar to, "Don't open up, because you'll just get burned." Beneath that, you may find the real fear motivating the delay: "I'm not sure those people would accept me or like me; I'm afraid to let any group of people see the real me behind the mask, and if I went I'm afraid they would come to see the real me."

Take a few moments now to explore any fears that may be motivating a delay in making a recovery support group a key part of your life.

If I were active in a recovery group, other people might think _____

_____

If I were active in a recovery group, I might have to talk about _____

_____

If I were active in a recovery group, I'd have to admit to myself that _____

_____

If I were active in a recovery group, people in the group might _____

_____

Taking a second look at these fears, respond with a series of affirmations emphasizing how much you deserve the benefits that come with belonging to a recovery group. Your statements might be similar to these: "I deserve to have a support and recovery family," "I deserve to have my feelings heard by other people," "I deserve a safe setting in which to experience emotional intimacy," "I deserve to receive encouragement in my recovery journey."

I deserve _____

I deserve _____

I deserve _____

DAY 2

Step 11. We sought through prayer and meditation to improve our conscious contact with God, praying only for knowledge of His will for us and the power to carry that out.

THE SIMPLICITY OF PRAYER

If you are not experienced with prayer, you may want to begin in a simple fashion. Begin right now putting away perfectionist expectations about how to pray the "right way." If prayer is unfamiliar, we often suggest that patients pray as if they were little children. Just talk to God as a father. Make it simple; make it childlike. Don't worry about what you should or should not say in the prayer—just talk about whatever is on your heart. God is concerned about all aspects of your life, even those that do not seem related in any way to your food addiction. "Knowledge of His will and the power to carry that out" has implications reaching into every aspect of your life. And by all means, don't feel as though you need to take on airs or pray in a form of speech that is any different from the way you would talk to your neighbor, parent, or best friend.

Completing the statement suggestions below will help you develop a conversational, natural manner of talking with God. Read this statement aloud in today's quiet time, completing each blank with whatever comes to mind.

Dear God,

Approaching You in prayer makes me feel _____.

One reason for that might be _____.

I'd like to start by saying that I'm really thankful for _____ _____. I can see how You are involved in this because _____.

One of the concerns I'm facing right now in my life has to do with _____ _____. I've thought about approaching it by _____; another alternative would be to _____. I would really like to know Your will for me concerning this.

God, sometimes knowing Your will doesn't mean it's easy to find the power to carry it through. Like the matter of _____; I know that Your will for me in this area would be to _____, but I'm having a hard time responding like I know I should. I'm really struggling with _____, and even though I know what I should do about it, it's easier said than done.

Give me the strength to _____. I know that You have all power, and I need to rely on Your power regarding _____ _____. Aspects of my life, like my food addiction, have run out of control. I invite Your empowerment into the center of my being, and through that power coming alive in me, I ask that Your divine order be manifest in every dimension of my life. Thank You for hearing this prayer. I know that You will answer it. Help me to recognize Your answers when they come. Amen.

DAY 3

PREVENTING OSTEOPOROSIS

Slowly and gradually the nicely dressed, white-haired woman made her way across the room to greet a friend she had recognized. We couldn't help noticing the careful way she supported herself on furniture as she passed by or kept the wall within an arm's reach. No doubt this woman who looked like someone's grandmother was just being careful not to fall—not to fall and break her hip, that is. She had good reason to be concerned as osteoporosis, or the weakening of the bones, had become a reality in her life. We now understand that if preventive measures are taken early, this potentially disabling or even deadly disease is preventable.

Over twenty million people have osteoporosis and one in four women will develop curvature of her spine due to this progressive weakening of her bones. A largely unknown fact is that osteoporosis is the twelfth leading cause of death among women. This is due to the fact that two-thirds of the people who sustain a hip fracture ever regain normal activity and as many as 15 percent of these hip fractures lead to premature death.

YOU'RE NEVER TOO OLD FOR MILK

Even though many adults gave up milk long ago, you really do still need milk. It is an excellent source of dietary calcium. Of course, having just learned about the habits of cholesterol, you will want to use skim milk and nonfat dairy products exclusively. In fact, adequate calcium in your diet is important to build up the calcium stores in your bones throughout your adult life because your bone density will never be greater than it is at age thirty-five.

After thirty-five, it's a holding battle. Women, especially, need to do all they can to develop strong bones. Unless preventive measures are taken, a woman's bone mass will rapidly and progressively decline after menopause, and she can expect to lose up to 50 percent of her bone density by age seventy-five. Without pain or obvious symptoms, osteoporosis silently leeches away vital bone mass until spontaneous fractures begin to occur, often with only trivial trauma.

PREVENTION AND TREATMENT

Prevention begins with adequate amounts of dietary calcium early in your life and continuing throughout. For those who cannot or will not consume dairy products, a calcium supplement becomes vital. Men and premenopausal women need about 1,000 milligrams of calcium daily or the equivalent of three cups of milk. Skim milk is just as rich in calcium as whole milk but without the cholesterol-laden fat.

Both men and women need adequate dietary calcium, but women after menopause should strongly consider estrogen therapy to help prevent osteoporosis. Ideally, the postmenopausal woman takes estrogen replacement, consumes twelve hundred milligrams of calcium either from food or supplements, and engages in twenty to forty minutes of weight-bearing exercise three times a week. Osteoporosis is now both treatable and preventable.

Does anyone in your family have a curved spine that has occurred with old age?
____ yes ____ no

Have you taken calcium and milk intake seriously as an adult? ____ yes ____ no

Week
11

Which risk factors for osteoporosis apply to you?

____ Low calcium intake

____ White race and fair skinned

____ Genetic link to osteoporosis

____ Inactivity

____ Smoking

____ Postmenopausal, not taking estrogen replacement

____ Alcohol abuse

Circle the factors above that you can change.

Are you getting enough calcium now (three to four servings of milk per day or some milk and a calcium supplement)? ____ yes ____ no

Consider taking a calcium supplement.

DAY 3

REPARENTING

Reparenting plays an important role in the normal course of adult life. Whether you left home years ago or are just preparing to leave the nest now . . . whether your experience was that of a warm, loving home or a cold, dysfunctional family . . . the nurturing role normally played by parents must be filled by other means now that you are an adult.

The primary source of "reparenting" comes from within, as you learn how to walk alone, nurturing yourself as a good parent would. Yet many food addicts—perhaps because they come from dysfunctional families where they didn't see good role models for healthy parenting—don't know how to be good parents to themselves. Instead of building their own confidence, they berate themselves, filling their own minds with negative, abusive self-talk. Instead of providing nutritious food for themselves, they punish themselves with unhealthy food or fad diets that do little to take care of the body. Instead of protecting themselves with constructive discipline and boundaries, they allow themselves to be ruled by crises and emergencies and the whims of others.

Week
11

Reparenting yourself begins with nurturing the "emotional child" within you—the part of you that still feels and responds as a child. Especially if you harbor hurts from your days in your family of origin, this emotional child is the part of you that is most in touch with the old pain. In fact, for this child, the pain is as fresh as the day it was experienced. If your emotional child is hurting, nursing shame and anger and insecurities still fresh from the past, your feelings, decisions, responses, and self-esteem as an adult will be impacted.

Reparenting must include some level of healing for your "child" within. To do this requires the following three steps.

1. Extend compassion to the inner child. Say, "I know that you are experiencing emotional pain. Even the process of grieving through the old pain and letting go of old hurts creates a new sense of pain—it's a healthier hurt, this pain of cleansing festering wounds of the past, and it will heal with only a scar to mark the place. But it still hurts to go back and remeet the old wounds, even if it is for the last time. I understand. I can't make the hurt go away; I can't fix everything with a word or phrase or make it all better with a kiss. But I do know that this pain will heal, and that you can find healing and freedom from the wounds of the past."

2. Give your "inner child" assurance that you will never abandon the child or subject the child to further abuse.

While I don't have the power to magically erase all the old hurts—healing is a process that takes time and is often accompanied by discomfort—I do have the power to protect you from further abuse in the future. I vow to protect you from _____

_____

3. Give your "child" permission to trust again.

Say, "Yes, you've been burned in the past—like when _____

_____ and _____ and

it has caused you to fear the act of trusting in anticipation of being hurt again. But it's not going to be that way any longer. You now have new permission to trust. I can't say you'll never be hurt again—when you trust there's always that possibility. But living a life of trusting—despite occasional setbacks—is still a richer, happier, more fulfilling experience than living isolated and bitter. You can begin to trust people again, and begin to trust God. It's okay to be vulnerable, to allow emotional intimacy to grow. It's scary. I understand that. But it's healthy and right and good, and the rewards will be greater than you can, at this point, imagine."

Healthy parenting—and this applies to the parenting you might have received as a child, the reparenting you're giving yourself today, or the parenting you're giving to your children—requires a blend of nurturance and discipline.

New nurturance or permissions that you will want to provide for your "emotional child" include:

- Permission to express anger;
- Permission to be vulnerable;
- Permission to be relatively happy;
- Permission to be creative and productive;
- Permission to have and express sexuality;
- Permission to have emotionally intimate relationships;
- Permission to have and use a chosen support family.

Just as you are responsible to be a good parent to yourself, you can select other people to provide alternative reparenting models to provide nurturance and accountability as you progress through the recovery progress. You may want to consider approaching someone who can provide this kind of guidance and asking them to play this important role in your journey.

Candidates for reparenting include:

- trusted friends
- support group sponsor
- pastor
- spouse*
- biological parents*

- support group members
- therapist
- mentor or "adopted" parents
- siblings*

*Caution: If you rely on members of your family of origin or family of procreation to supply reparenting, you are at risk of reactivating old codependent family patterns. It is not uncommon for married persons to attempt to reparent each other. However, while your spouse may provide some aspects of the guidance, nurturance, and accountability necessary in the reparenting process, there is a danger of codependent spouses becoming even more entrenched in their codependency if they attempt to reparent each other. It is usually best to look to other persons outside of your immediate family or your family of origin as you look for reparenting candidates.

Week
11

As you choose an individual or individuals to help you reparent, be sure to select persons who know how to nurture. Especially if you grew up in a home with distant or critical parents, you may be drawn toward parental figures today who are cold and distant. Instead, select someone who can encourage rather than condemn.

Finally, consider turning to God for aspects of reparenting. The Bible is quite clear about God's availability to us as a heavenly Father who loves us dearly. And to enter into this kind of familial relationship with God, we must become as eager, expectant children, being "born again" into a relationship with our spiritual Father. For many people, this kind of intimacy with God satisfies like no earthly relationship can.

DAY 3

Step 11. We sought through prayer and meditation to improve our conscious contact with God, praying only for knowledge of His will for us and the power to carry that out.

PRAYER TURNED INTO DIALOGUE

Over time, allow your prayer experience to develop into a dialogue with God. Talk to Him—and expect Him to respond—as with a trusted friend. Allow God to be that spiritual Person with whom you can conduct a daily inventory of grief issues and confession issues.

Is there any aspect of your life you feel uncomfortable broaching in prayer?

_____ yes _____ no

If so, what are these areas? _____

Why do you think these areas are difficult to discuss with God?

_____

_____

If you were to spend an hour in indepth conversation with your closest friend, what are some of the issues in your life that would come up during your conversation?

_____

_____

Week
11

Have you told—or have you considered telling—God about these same issues?

____ yes ____ no

If not, why not? _____

_____

Would you consider doing so this week? ____ yes ____ no

True communication thrives on honesty. As you seek to develop intimate dialogue with God, honesty will play an important role. You've already seen how significant honesty is in your recovery process: honesty scatters denial; it enables you to deal with core issues and not just with their symptoms; it helps break down isolating barriers in your relationship.

Your relationship with God deserves no less. Being honest with God means getting past perfectionistic and unrealistic concepts of how things "should be" and refocuses your perspective on how things are. By contrast, attempts to avoid honesty and thus nurture denial in your relationship with God are exercises in futility since God is all-knowing. As He already knows your darkest secrets and deepest needs, uninhibited honesty is the only approach that makes any sense at all.

For moving examples of the kind of open dialogue to which God is inviting you, take a moment now and find the book of Psalms in the Bible. This book is comprised of poems and songs and prayers written primarily by a man named David. As you thumb through this book, randomly selecting sections to read, you may be struck by his honest approach to God. David's words, thousands of years later, make it clear that he sought communion with God through candor and intimate discourse.

DAY 4

THE DREADED DIAGNOSIS

Ask ten people which disease they fear the most and cancer would be right at the top of the list. There are about thirteen hundred different types of cancer, but just a few types are extremely common. Lung, breast, colon, and prostate cancer account for more than fifty percent of all reported cancers. Amazing as it may seem, one of the best ways of reducing the incidence of these feared diseases is with a good diet.

The American Cancer Society says that diet can be a primary line of defense against cancer.

A poor diet is believed responsible for up to 35 percent of cancers and all of the four major cancer sites can be favorably affected by dietary changes.[2] Diet has long been associated with the potential of certain food additives causing cancer. Now there is scientific data that suggests that less than 1 percent of all cancers are caused by food additives. Although certainly important, it is apparently not the red food dye, but the high-fat cheeseburger laden with mayonnaise that is the more likely culprit in dietary-induced cancer.

AMERICAN CANCER SOCIETY DIETARY GUIDELINES
FOR CANCER PREVENTION

A very brief review of the dietary recommendations for cancer prevention will show you that with the exception of avoiding nitrates, nitrites, and smoked or pickled foods your Love Hunger Diet Plan is oriented toward cancer prevention as well. The recommendations are as follows:

- Avoid obesity.

- Reduce total fat in your diet.

- Eat more high-fiber foods.

- Eat more foods rich in vitamins A and C.

- Eat more cruciferous vegetables such as cabbage, broccoli, and cauliflower.

- Reduce your consumption of alcohol.

- Reduce the amounts of salt-cured, smoked, and nitrite-cured foods.

DAY 4

TAKING HEALTHY NEW RISKS

While decisions and new permissions are great, they are academic until they are translated into actions. For every new permission you have given yourself, there needs to be a corresponding action. These actions are, indeed, risks, because there's no guarantee for any of us that any of our actions will turn out precisely the way we predicted and hoped for. But even in the face of seeming uncertainty, we will often find the seeds of a future success.

Now is the time to begin putting life to some of your decisions by turning them into

Week
11

actions. For each new permission you've given yourself, describe an accompanying action. Let this be your commitment to taking healthy risks; allowing yourself to step out in each of the ways you are about to indicate.

Permissions	Actions
Examples:	
I have permission to be sexual.	*Buying new clothing that properly reflects this aspect of myself.*
I have permission to admit when I'm angry.	*I will tell my spouse that what she said last night hurt my feelings and made me angry.*
I have permission to eat—and enjoy eating—healthy food.	*I'm going to begin tonight experimenting with some of the healthy recipes in this book.*
I have permission to enjoy emotional intimacy.	*I'm going to take the plunge and share my most secret fear with my support group tonight.*
_____	_____
_____	_____
_____	_____
	_____

DAY 4

Step 11. We sought through prayer and meditation to improve our conscious contact with God, praying only for knowledge of His will for us and the power to carry that out.

RECOGNIZING GOD'S RESPONSES

Now is the time to grow sensitive to answers that you may begin to receive from God. These answers will probably not be written in stone or echoed from a burning bush, but as a rule—if you practice honest dialogue with God—over time your prayer life will develop beyond a seemingly one-way experience. You will begin to feel, intuitively, God's direction coming back to you.

God instructs us via several methods, and it is a fact of Scripture that He never sends us messages that conflict one with the other. In fact, look for confirmation among the different sources whenever you feel God leading you in any direction.

INTUITION

The first way God will communicate with you is through what some may call intuition. What you may initially think of as a "gut feeling" is often God speaking to you through your spirit or soul. As you grow in your relationship with God, you will become more proficient at using your spirit to discern God's will for your life. You will begin to develop increasing levels of trust in your spirit's ability to hear from God.

OTHER PEOPLE

A second method God will use to communicate His will to you is through other people. If you sense God telling you something through your spirit, look for confirmation of this direction through messages from other people, particularly other people who also have committed their lives to God. You might hear a sermon in which the pastor echoes the message you are getting through your spirit from God. Or you might be in the middle of a conversation with a friend or family member when suddenly something that is said strikes home as you realize the comment dovetails with what God is already showing you. As other persons in recovery groups or spiritual communities share their spiritual journeys, you may discover that you are able to grow and gain from their experience. OA members often say during or after a meeting, "Sounds like you've been reading my mail. I can really identify with what you shared today."

SCRIPTURE

Most importantly, God has revealed His will to you through Scripture. This book of God-inspired verses will always remain your final authority on God's will for your life. Always compare messages you are receiving via intuition or other people with the Scriptures. If these messages are indeed from God, they will be confirmed in the pages of the Bible.

How is God responding to you? For the remainder of this week and weekend, look for moments—during prayer or at times of quiet meditation—when you feel close to God. These moments are the building blocks of communication from God to you. What are your feelings during these moments when God seems near? What are some of your thoughts?

This week, take a few minutes out of each day to read a page or more from the Bible and to converse with God. Describe any moments when God seemed near or you gained some new insight as a result of your time with Him:

_____

_____

_____

At least twice in the coming week, allow an opportunity for God to respond to you in the setting of nature. Take a walk beneath the stars or spend half an hour out of your weekend beneath breezy trees in your local park. Think about your relationship to God, talk to Him there amid the setting He created for your enjoyment, and spend more than a few quiet moments receiving His response back to you. Describe what it was like to spend these moments with God:

_____

_____

_____

DAY 5

DIETARY EFFECTS ON CANCER

OBESITY AND CANCER

With more than thirty-four million overweight American adults, the link between cancer and obesity becomes even more important. Obesity increases the risk of cancers in the uterus, gallbladder, kidney, stomach, colon, and breast. Simply put, obese persons will have as many as 30 to 50 percent more tumors than persons of normal weight.

DIETARY FAT AND CANCER RISK

If you eat less fat you will be less likely to develop cancer of the breast, colon, and prostate. People in Japan, where the diet is much lower in fat, have significantly less cancer. The typical American diet consists of almost 40 percent fat and the Love Hunger Diet goal of 30 percent or less fat in your diet is heartily endorsed by the American Cancer Society. The low-fat diet is good for your waist, good for your heart, and also a potent means of cancer prevention.

VITAMINS AND CANCER

Scientific researchers believe that vitamins A, C, and E may be cancer protective. Cancer prevention by these vitamins appears to occur due to a blocking action on specific cancer-causing agents. Because of the risk of toxicity from oral vitamin A supplements, it is recommended that this nutrient be obtained from food sources including the dark-green and deep-yellow vegetables. Cruciferous vegetables such as cabbage, cauliflower, broccoli, and brussels sprouts may reduce the risk of colon and respiratory cancers.

ALCOHOL AND CANCER

The more a person drinks alcohol, the greater his or her risk of cancer of the oral cavity, larynx, and esophagus. This relationship is particularly enhanced if the individual smokes as well. Excessive alcohol use leading to cirrhosis can increase the risk of liver cancer.

SUMMING UP THE WEEK

This week, in the Body portion of your workbook, we have talked about some ultimate decisions you can make to take care of your body and prevent disease from occurring. As we all know, human nature does not always allow us to do what we know is good and helpful for ourselves or others. As you work through all three sections of the workbook, exploring the body, mind, and soul, it is our sincere desire and plan that you will find that powerful combination of balance in which your healed mind and soul allow your body to do what it needs to do to promote your own best health.

DAY 5

DAILY MAINTENANCE

Maintenance of your commitment to food recovery is a day-by-day process. It's a commitment you make every morning, praying for God to provide the strength for you to uphold that commitment for twenty-four hours. At the end of those hours, you begin the next morning with a fresh commitment and a fresh prayer.

Because of the daily nature of maintenance, there are several steps or routines for you to consider incorporating into your daily schedule. Even though you are busy, these steps are key elements to your full recovery from food addiction and play a major role in preventing relapse. You can't afford not to take the time to make a daily commitment to these maintenance activities. Besides, these six steps can be customized to fit your precise circumstances. Complete each of the following statements by customizing the step to fit your lifestyle (the first step is completed for you as an example).

SIX DAILY RECOVERY ACTIVITIES

1. *In the course of my maintenance, I commit to taking a brief inventory every day.* Specifically, I will implement this step in my life by taking ten minutes at the end of every lunch break to evaluate my life.

This daily inventory will need to include the following three categories of questions:
What am I feeling? Identify and list feelings without judging them.

_____

_____

_____

What are my needs? Just to make it through this day, do I need a lot of encouragement from someone or do I need time alone or need stimulation from outside . . . ?

_____

_____

_____

Have I hurt anyone else or been hurt? If I've hurt someone else, I may need to make amends. If I discover I'm consistently being hurt and this surfaces in my inventory, this may tell me where I need to set new boundaries.

_____

_____

_____

2. *In the course of my maintenance, I commit to enjoying some daily quiet time and meditation every day.* Specifically, I will implement this step in my life by _____

_____

3. *In the course of my maintenance, I commit to praying to God every day.* Specifically, I will implement this step in my life by _____

_____

Week
11

I also will not get hung up on whether or not I am praying the "right" way. I realize that a childlike prayer will do: the only aspect of any importance is whether or not I am connecting with God.

4. *In the course of my maintenance, I commit to enjoying inspirational reading every day.* Specifically, I will implement this step in my life by _____

_____

One book I may want to consider is *Serenity: A Companion for 12-Step Recovery*. This devotional book ties the Twelve-Step process with Bible verses.

5. *In the course of my maintenance, I commit to daily contact with people who are special to me.* Specifically, I will implement this step in my life by _____

_____

6. *In the course of my maintenance, I commit to a daily food plan.* Specifically, I will implement this step in my life by _____

_____

DAY 5

Step 11. We sought through prayer and meditation to improve our conscious contact with God, praying only for knowledge of His will for us and the power to carry that out.

MAKING THE COMMITMENT FOR LIFE

The central theme of your prayer life should be twofold:

1. Yielding completely to God's will.
2. Empowerment to know and to carry out His will.

Many recovering persons use their Twelve Step recovery group—such as OA or AA—and the recovery literature as a stepping stone toward spiritual growth. Often, these men and women reach a place in their long-term spiritual maturation where they experience a hunger for even deeper communication with God. This is where both the organized church and sacred and spiritual literature can be a very valuable asset.

If you are looking for deeper, richer spiritual growth, consider tapping into a legacy that is thousands of years old—the Old Testament and New Testament. One of Bill Wilson's favorite books—one which he read over and over again—was Oswald Chambers's *My Utmost for His Highest*. Bill Wilson and Dr. Robert Smith, the cofounders of Alcoholics Anonymous, were both devout spiritual seekers. Consider the following questions as you continue your spiritual pilgrimage.

Do you have friends or coworkers who are involved on a regular basis in a spiritual community? _____ yes _____ no

Would these friends be individuals you would feel comfortable approaching regarding matters of faith? _____ yes _____ no

Do you have any questions or doubts regarding your faith or your participation in organized religion? _____ yes _____ no

Statement of question or doubt:

> Example:
> *(All religious people are overly emotional and I'll become like them if I join.)*

_____

_____

_____

Is there anything you've seen or heard that refutes that doubt?

> Example:
> *(My friend Rich belongs to a church and yet he's as level-headed as they come.)*

_____

_____

_____

_____

Am I willing to take steps toward greater involvement with spiritual communities and spiritually inspired recovery groups? How can I begin to implement these action commitments?

Week 11

_____

_____

_____

WEEKLY FOOD AND EXERCISE JOURNAL

| Date
Weight (First day of week only) | Breakfast/
A.M. Snack | Lunch
P.M. Snack | Dinner
Nite Snack | Exercise | Feelings and Major Events of the Day |
|---|---|---|---|---|---|
| Day
One | | | | | |
| Day
Two | | | | | |
| Day
Three | | | | | |
| Day
Four | | | | | |
| Day
Five | | | | | |
| Day
Six | | | | | |
| Day
Seven | | | | | |

DAY 1

THE MAINTENANCE DIET

Single-focused diet programs of the past could only claim that 5 percent of the people who started a diet program would actually lose weight and keep it off for more than a year. Programs that focus on the entire person, as we have attempted to do with the Love Hunger Diet Program, show much better maintenance results because the person has been working on a new lifestyle that will help him or her keep that weight off for the rest of his or her life. We have never talked about anything that wasn't permanent. We will be asking you to journalize a lot of feelings, impressions, and thoughts this week as you examine what this program has meant to you.

Have you lost as much weight as you need to? _____ yes _____ no

Are you now within your ideal bodyweight range? _____ yes _____ no

If not, how many more pounds do you need to lose? _____

At your current rate of loss, how long do you anticipate that it will take you to reach your ideal body weight? _____

How do you feel about your new weight and yourself?

_____

_____

_____

_____

_____

What has happened in your life that might not have otherwise been possible without the weight loss? (Examples: I can wear old or new clothes, feel better; my serum cholesterol has declined; I can now exercise without discomfort.)

_____

_____

_____

IMPORTANT! READ THIS FIRST

If you have not reached your ideal weight goal yet, we recommend that you save this chapter until you are at that point. If you are working with a group, go ahead and read it. There is nothing here that should alter your progress. If you have the option, however, you might want to save it until your goal is reached so that the information will be fresh on your mind.

WHAT HAVE YOU LEARNED?

Let's do a little reviewing. Consider this an open-book quiz! At any time look back to other sections of the book so that you can summarize the information you would want to commit to memory right here in this chapter.

Name five new food products you are using as a result of this program:

1. _____
2. _____
3. _____
4. _____
5. _____

How much exercise are you doing now that you have reached your weight goal?

_____

Do you realize that you still need about three hours of aerobic exercise per week to not regain weight? _____ yes _____ no

What type of activity do you plan to use to fulfill this need? _____

List some of the other health benefits you will receive by exercising regularly and eating right. What types of diseases are you preventing? _____

_____

_____

How has the daily food and exercise log helped you to see what your true habits really are?

_____

_____

Should lapse and relapse ever bother you, can you see the value of beginning a new log? How might this help? Be specific. _____

_____

_____

_____

What's your favorite new recipe? _____

_____

Have you tried most of the suggestions for lower calorie cooking in the workbook? ____ yes ____ no

Which ones do you still want to look into? _____

_____

Can you see how it is easy to save 300 to 400 calories per day through improved, low-calorie cooking methods without much effort at all? ____ yes ____ no

DAY 1

RELAPSE

As psychiatrists and psychologists, we walk a delicate balance in helping recovering food addicts to deal with the possibility of relapse—without programming them into the idea that they *have* to relapse, we also want to prepare them to be resilient and self-forgiving when temporary relapses do occur.

Relapse is nothing to be ashamed of. It's important to understand that it is a distinct possibility so that if and when it happens to you, you won't be so traumatized by relapse that you can't get back into food management. At the same time, you don't want to program yourself with the notion that you will invariably and consistently relapse.

What are your chances of relapse? Think for a moment about the degree of seriousness of your food addiction. Did you catch it in its early stages? For some people who see their food addiction as being caught in early stages—this was the first time they've been overweight and they caught it in time—the battle against relapse may not be great.

At the other extreme, if someone has struggled with his or her weight for twenty years and been on countless diets and lost and regained numerous times, the greater the battle against relapse. Remember that without vigorous recovery, addictions tend to be chronic, progressive, and potentially relapsing. The more entrenched and long-term the addiction has been, the greater the possibility of relapse. For some recovering food addicts there has to be a daily vigilance against relapse, and the food management program becomes a lifetime endeavor.

The fact is, if you are one of the many who have struggled with a serious, engrained addiction, we can almost guarantee periods of temporary relapse. As a word of reassurance, if you find yourself sliding off your long-term food goals and emotional recovery, don't panic. This doesn't mean your recovery hasn't worked. It simply means that you are experiencing what amounts to a predictable and temporary phase of your recovery—relapse.

The chances are great that while this workbook may very well be your last diet, it was not your first. In the past, when you tried a new diet and then abandoned it to resume old eating patterns, what was it like? Begin by remembering some of the excuses, rationalizations, or denial messages that allowed relapse to occur in the first place.

Name some of the events that have triggered past relapses: _____

_____

What were some of the excuses or rationalizations you told yourself as you approached relapse? (Examples: I've been strict with my diet for two months—I deserve this piece of cake; or I can't continue my diet right now—there's too much stress at the office. I'll resume my diet when things slow down.) _____

_____

_____

_____

Week
12

What did you stop or start doing that broke your healthy patterns and allowed food abuse to reenter your life? _____

_____

_____

After the relapse, what were some of the messages you gave yourself about shame? (Examples: I've been a bad person; I'll never be thin. See, I knew I couldn't do it.)

1. _____
2. _____
3. _____
4. _____

The first thing that has to go is the old shame base regarding relapse. For each of the negative shame messages you have given yourself regarding past relapses, write a positive affirmation about yourself and your success on your diet to date.

1. _____
2. _____
3. _____
4. _____

DAY 1

STEP 12: HAVING HAD A SPIRITUAL AWAKENING AS THE RESULT OF THESE STEPS, WE TRIED TO CARRY THIS MESSAGE TO OTHERS AND TO PRACTICE THESE PRINCIPLES IN ALL OUR AFFAIRS.

This is perhaps one of the most intriguing of all the paradoxes of Alcoholics Anonymous and the other recovery groups—in a sense, the healing of your addiction is actually only a stepping stone to a much more important goal; spiritual transformation and renewal.

There is a phase that is part of the oral tradition of AA and other Twelve Step groups by which people in meetings will introduce themselves this way: "Hi, I'm Frank. I'm a grateful, recovering alcoholic."

Week
12

What is meant is that these men and women have actually reached a place of gratitude for the addiction, dependency, or affliction that propelled them into Twelve Step recovery and the resulting spiritual awakening.

YOUR SPIRITUAL AWAKENING

You, too, may be able to look back with appreciation for the way your addiction brought you to crisis and a spiritual turning point in your life. What discoveries have you made about yourself as an indirect result of your food addiction?

Examples:

My food addiction, through the recovery process, has indirectly prompted my discovery of a closer relationship with God.

My food addiction, through the recovery process, has indirectly prompted my discovery of the dysfunctional role I played in my family of origin, and how that role was continuing to stunt my spiritual and emotional growth.

My food addiction, through the recovery process, has indirectly prompted my discovery of

_____

_____

My food addiction, through the recovery process, has indirectly prompted my discovery of

_____

_____

My food addiction, through the recovery process, has indirectly prompted my discovery of

_____

_____

Some sort of spiritual awakening may well be the most important discovery that has resulted from the recovery process. It certainly has more eternal implications than any other discovery you may have made. If the spiritual awakening referred to in this step is still a vague concept rather than a reality in your life, consider the following information.

Part of the oral tradition of AA includes this example: If you have a drunken horse thief and sober him up, what do you have? The answer is "a sober horse thief." Sobriety—or the capping of any addiction—is not the goal of recovery. It is only the beginning. Once your

Week
12

food addiction is put in balance, you can begin the real journey of spiritual growth. Can you envision unlimited new vistas of spiritual challenge, growth, and maturity? Can your life be remade?

Spiritual growth is a lifelong process, one goal of which is to move toward a more personal and intimate understanding of God. Even though Bill Wilson welcomed people at any point in their spiritual journey with the words, "It's God as I understand Him," both Bill Wilson and Dr. Bob maintained lifetime commitments to their own Christian spiritual pilgrimages.

DAY 2

ON AN EVEN KEEL

It usually takes about six months for a successful dieter's metabolism to pop back up to normal (or close to normal) after an extended period of calorie restriction. You indeed are successful, but you are also vulnerable. You will need to monitor your weight and food intake carefully for another few months to make sure your weight remains steady. Weigh yourself once or twice a week as a means of determining your maintenance progress.

One reason it is difficult to keep that weight on an even keel is that your body was once accustomed to your old weight and now it must physically get used to the new weight. You have a new set point—a new normal. You may be used to it, but your body will take a little longer to feel that this weight is normal for you.

HAS MY METABOLISM CHANGED?

This question is common among dieting patients throughout the nation. Your metabolism should be functioning as it previously did within a few months, but the thing that has changed is how many calories you need per day. Your previous weight required that you haul a lot of extra baggage around—continually. Think of it this way: If someone made you wear a thirty-pound backpack all day long, don't you think you would burn a few more calories by the end of the day? Now, at your thinner weight, you will be that person who no longer has to wear the backpack. Thus, you will use fewer calories to maintain your new weight than you did to maintain your old, heavier weight. Generally speaking, you will probably use somewhere in the neighborhood of twelve calories per pound per day. Just take your current weight, multiply it by twelve and you will find an approximation of the number of calories you need to consume each day in order to maintain your weight. Of course, if you are exercising more than three hours per week, that amount will be increased.

Week
12

AN AGE-OLD PROBLEM

One other problem we must alert you to is that as you age, your basal metabolic rate decreases. After the age of twenty-five, your metabolism decreases by 2 percent per decade. This is something you must be prepared for. Watch those scales in the years to come and be aware that there may be a need for reassessment if you have more than a five-pound gain.

One of the reasons this decrease may occur is that the lean body mass also declines with advancing age. This gives us all the more reason to keep up exercising and weight training to offset these tendencies.

DAY 2

CAUTION! DANGER AHEAD!

By now, you are probably several months into your food management program. It's possible that you have already begun to see red flags indicating possible relapse ahead. While the relapses may appear to happen suddenly and without warning, in reality they are the end product of a long line of minor infractions, stress, and warning signals.

Warning: Relapse can be insidious. Even though some of the signals we're about to discuss sound obvious and simple, if you are moving into relapse they won't be that obvious. Review the following checklist with someone else, like an OA sponsor, and avoid the temptation to respond with an immediate "Oh, I'm not doing *that.*" Denial is a strong factor with relapse—so examine yourself deeply with each of the following questions and statements.

FAULT FINDING

Are you doing a lot of fault finding with yourself or others? _____ yes _____ no

If so, who are you attacking and what surface reasons seem to be prompting your responses?

_____

_____

_____

Thinking about your confrontive attitude on a deeper level, what are you feeling inside that is leading you to be more hostile toward yourself or others? (Example: I've been pretty down on myself ever since the breakup with someone I was dating.) Look for any underlying negative

Week
12

feelings about yourself—if you don't catch them now they may end up prompting a relapse into food abuse.

_____

_____

_____

ACTIVITY LEVEL

Have you noticed a dramatic speed up or slow down in your overall activity level?

____ yes ____ no

A slow down can be an indication that you are moving toward depression; a dramatic speed up such as suddenly overcommitting yourself can indicate an emotional dynamic underneath and can also lead into stress. Even if your change in activity is not an *effect* of emotional issues related to relapse, could your change in activity become a *trigger for* relapse? For example, maybe your increase in activity is simply due to circumstances and not related to any emotional motivation: you aren't trying to prove your worth to your boss or cover up a sense of rejection from a recent break-up. Still, if your hectic schedule leads to stress, it could also lead to relapse as a way of coping with the stress.

What might the long-term effects be if you allow this altered activity level to continue?

_____

_____

ISOLATION

If you suddenly realize it's been two weeks since you've called your OA sponsor or that you recently canceled your plans for spending quality time with friends, you may want to stop everything, take a moment, and think through your reasons for pulling away from important people in your life. Remember, isolation is both a cause and effect of food addiction. When happening, it may seem circumstantial, but usually if we do something as important as pull back from others, it's not just circumstantial. Since you may be in denial, begin by examining your behavior before you try to analyze any motives that prompted the behavior.

Identify any recent events where circumstances have seemed to prevent you from getting together with important people in your life. Be particularly aware of any instances where you have reduced contact with people from your recovery support network.

Week
12

I seem to have lost or reduced my contact with _____

On the surface, the reason we have lost contact is _____

_____

Another reason for this sudden isolation might be _____

_____

Is there any shame involved when I think of renewing contact? ____ yes ____ no

If so, what is that shame regarding? _____

Is there anything I feel I would need to "explain" or justify at the moment of renewed contact?
____ yes ____ no

Explain. _____

_____

CRAVINGS

Have you experienced an intensification in specific food cravings or obsessions about food? It's pretty natural during the first few months of your diet to miss certain foods, and as you're dieting you may spend some time obsessing about food. But if, at the tail end of the process, you are hit with a new wave of intense cravings or obsessions, it may be a warning signal of a relapse just ahead.

How much time do you spend each day planning your meals or thinking about "illegal" foods? _____

Have you experienced any increase in your "thought life" regarding food?
____ yes ____ no

How has your attitude toward food changed during your recovery?

_____

_____

Have you recently felt your attitude slipping back toward some of your old thoughts and feelings about food? ____ yes ____ no

If so, in what ways? _____

_____

How does this make you feel? (Examples: scared, ashamed, guilty, rebellious.)

_____

_____

SIGNIFICANT INTERRUPTION OF YOUR DAILY RECOVERY ACTIVITIES

If you have gotten in the habit, as a part of your daily maintenance behavior, of reading devotional literature for twenty minutes and you suddenly realize that for the past five days you've had some excuse not to do it, you may be on the verge of a relapse. Or if you have built a routine of hitting the gym every morning at 6:30 for a half-hour workout with a friend, but suddenly find yourself too busy to meet that commitment, you may be on your way to relapse.

This is not to say that there aren't very acceptable reasons for disrupting your routine. Perhaps you've been running late to work or had to walk the dog. But whatever the reason, the net effect is that you've broken your daily recovery pattern, and that can be a very strong warning signal.

CONSISTENT WEIGHT GAIN AND/OR SIGNIFICANT CHANGE IN EATING PATTERNS

Finally, even if you are in denial about many of the warning flags indicating relapse, your scale will tell the story. Watch for a consistent increase over several weeks. It's normal during a long-term weight program for there to be some weeks when your weight seems to stand still even if you're exercising and staying right with your food plan. There may even be weeks when your weight seems to go up—but the gain will be temporary if you are indeed staying right with the program.

If you are charting your weight and discover you gained two pounds three weeks ago, a pound last week, and four this week, you are probably in relapse, even if you are telling yourself—in denial—that you have stayed on your diet.

The fact is, if your scale shows a consistent weight gain, your eating habits have changed, which probably indicates something going on deeper at an emotional level. You are starting to break out of boundaries you've set for yourself, and you are in the midst of relapse.

Have you experienced a gradual weight gain over a period of several weeks or longer?
_____ yes _____ no

DAY 2

Step 12. Having had a spiritual awakening as the result of these steps, we tried to carry this message to others and to practice these principles in all our affairs.

CARRYING THE MESSAGE TO OTHERS

Psychologists have long recognized the special empathy generated between persons who have had similar afflictions. For example, if you have walked in my shoes—if you know what it's like to struggle in the same manner I struggle—then you may have a very special key to reach me in a way that no other person could do with the same degree of effectiveness.

This is why Bill Wilson would ask alcoholics to help other alcoholics. And it's also why we now have such a proliferation of self-help groups—Alcoholics Anonymous®; Emotions Anonymous®; Gamblers Anonymous; Overeaters Anonymous®. Quite simply, it works. The dynamic of evangelism between persons with like-experiences is quite powerful.

You may be able to immediately think of people you know who fight an ongoing battle with food addiction. You may think—and rightly so—that you now have something to offer them in terms of hope for the future. This is not to say that you are now "perfect" or that you suddenly have all the answers. Rather, you have walked in their shoes and are familiar with the paths to the pitfalls as well as paths to healing.

Yet Step 12 is about more than proclaiming your journey out *of* addiction. It is about proclaiming your journey *toward* God. Your spiritual awakening is the good news; the news to which others—particularly those struggling with addictions—will find themselves drawn. The message is as simple as this: The steps out of an addiction crisis can lead to new spiritual life as well.

Are there people in your sphere of influence who would benefit from a message like this? Are there people you know—within your family, at work, among your friends—who are under the control of any type of addiction? (Examples: food, work, alcohol, drugs, destructive relationships, shopping, etc.) Identify the people, their addictions, how they have responded so far to the change occurring in your life, how they appear to be mostly adversely impacted by their own addictions, at least one of the emotions, fears, or voids that may be fueling the addictions, and how this recovery process/spiritual renewal could help them.

Example:

Person: Mom

Addiction: Compulsive Overeater

Response to my recovery: She thinks it's a phase; she doesn't seem to believe it could be a change for life.

Symptom of his or her own addiction: Mom's weight is starting to affect her heart.

Emotion that may be fueling the addiction: Unhappiness in marriage; no intimacy in relationship with Dad.

Week
12

How Twelve Steps and spiritual renewal could make a difference. Might help Mom see that she is substituting food for a marriage; plus a relationship with God could help fill some of the loneliness for her.

Person: _____

Addiction: _____

Response to my recovery: _____

_____

Symptom of his or her own addiction: _____

Emotion that may be fueling the addiction: _____

_____

How Twelve Step and spiritual renewal could make a difference: _____

_____

_____

Person: _____

Addiction: _____

Response to my recovery: _____

_____

Symptom of his or her own addiction: _____

Emotion that may be fueling the addiction: _____

_____

How Twelve Step and spiritual renewal could make a difference: _____

_____

_____

DAY 3

NUTRITIONAL NEEDS

We have talked a lot about maintenance of weight loss the last few days without even mentioning "food." There is a simple explanation for that. Quite frankly, you can now eat anything you want to, assuming the portions are suitable and in control. Can you really have a candy bar? Yes, indeed. Try to have a fun-sized one instead of the large, 300-calorie variety, though. Unless you have a medical restriction (such as diabetes or hypercholesterolemia), *there is no food you cannot have.*

We have learned a lot about nutrition, food preparation, and everything that will help make your weight loss permanent. Don't ignore the fact that there are a lot of unhealthy, "skinny" people out there who think that the only criteria for good health is being at your ideal weight. Not so! Let's review what the National Research Council says about good health through better nutrition:

1. Reduce the total fat intake of your diet to less than 30 percent of the total caloric intake. Eat lean meats only with an emphasis on fish.
2. Limit daily cholesterol to 150 mg.
3. Eat a lot of fruits and vegetables—at least three cups per day.
4. Eat six or more servings per day of bread, cereals, and other whole-grain products.
5. Get *regular* physical activity.
6. Alcoholic beverages are not recommended.
7. Limit your daily salt intake to less than four grams per day.
8. Maintain an adequate calcium intake.

Do these have a familiar ring to them? The entire Love Hunger Diet Plan was written with your long-term health in mind. What we are building up to is that all the new recipes, foods, and other discoveries you have made over the last twelve weeks should stay with you for the rest of your life. This is the way we should all be eating. So why did we say that you can also have whatever you want—including a candy bar? Because a few of these special treats thrown in with a larger version of the diet you have followed the last three months will serve you well as you maintain your weight.

DAY 3

THE DYNAMICS OF RELAPSE

Often when we encounter relapse, we find ourselves looking at the face value of the experience. "I've gone off my diet," we tell ourselves. Yet the experience of relapse has much more to offer us than that. As you bump up against the experience or threat or fear of relapse, ask yourself, "What is the relapse trying to teach me?"

Think of your relapse as an opportunity. Relapse is telling you that you need to focus back on some underlying dynamic that wasn't finished in recovery or is being neglected in recovery. Relapse provides you with a crossroad: you can either allow relapse to defeat and shame you, or you can use it as a teaching tool.

There are three major, underlying dynamics of relapse. Anytime you face the threat or experience of relapse, learn from the relapse by attempting to identify any of the following dynamics that may be going on in your life.

DYNAMIC ONE: SELF PUNISHMENT THROUGH SELF-SABOTAGE

Even though you are now months into recovery, you still may be responding at some level to the old shame base. At some deep level, you may be continuing to feed yourself messages that you deserve to be fat or unhealthy and/or unhappy.

Could this be one of the factors fueling your relapse? ____ yes ____ no

What negative messages about yourself are replaying over and over in your mind?

_____

_____

_____

Are you punishing yourself with your relapse? ____ yes ____ no

If so, why? _____

_____

Week
12

> **If self-punishment is indeed fueling your relapse . . .**
>
> . . . you might need to further grieve out the family of origin shame or trauma. If there are still some old negative messages or toxic emotional baggage, it may mean you haven't fully grieved through events from your past.
>
> . . . you might need to further affirm your self-worth and value. Writing positive messages to yourself is one way to affirm your self-worth.

DYNAMIC TWO: RESPONSE TO CONTEMPORARY MAJOR STRESS OR TRAUMA

Perhaps in the midst of your recovery journey, you experience an event that is a major stress producer. It might also be that the accumulation of small stresses grows past the threshold. Either of these scenarios can result in relapse.

The following is a brief list of common pressure-filled experiences that can contribute to the build-up of stress: financial pressures, conflict in romance or marriage, job reversal (firing, demotion, lack of expected promotion, declining sales), health crisis, relocation, death or health crisis of a loved one . . . then there is the gradual build-up of stress associated with the recovery process itself. People often forget that as positive and beneficial as recovery is, it is still a stressful process to go through.

Could stress be one of the factors fueling your relapse? _____ yes _____ no

Remember, even happy events—Christmas, a wedding, the birth of a child—are high on the stress scale. What are some of the recent major events in your life?

_____

_____

_____

What about small, everyday stress? (Examples: conflict at home; job pressure at the office; problems with the car; a broken dishwasher; frustration or fears regarding your diet or weight loss.) _____

_____

_____

How do you typically respond to stress? _____

_____

When you are under stress, what special efforts do you make to reduce that stress? (Examples: physical exercise; relaxing with soft music; canceling events from an overbooked schedule.)

_____

_____

_____

If you can't think of any stress-reducing techniques that you practice, consider the ones listed above, plus any of the following: calling a friend to talk out some of the feelings generated by the stress; a long walk in the park; making love with your mate; taking thirty minutes for something you really enjoy whether that might be reading a book or having a manicure; a craft or hobby that both distracts you and rewards you with a sense of accomplishment.

If stress is indeed fueling your relapse . . .

. . . inventory your major and minor stresses with a trusted friend or recovery program sponsor. Make specific action plans for how these stresses can be released or better managed. (Example: Take a temporary time-out from a volunteer project that is consuming too much time.)

. . . be accountable. After you have formulated a plan to reduce stress and introduce times of relaxation, ask your program sponsor to hold you accountable for the diligent execution of this revised plan of self-care.

DYNAMIC THREE: REGRESSION—A FALSE SENSE OF SAFETY

One of the most powerful of all psychological coping and defense mechanisms is regression. If you get scared, or if you feel overwhelmed, an automatic emotional response can be to move backwards to an earlier period when you still feel secure. An extreme example of regression is when people who have had a nervous breakdown regress into the fetal position and begin to suck their thumbs. In cases like this, these men and women have felt so overwhelmed that they've regressed all the way back to infancy. A more commonplace example can be found among kids. Even though little Susie is potty trained, if she gets under stress—maybe Mom and Dad have been fighting a lot or Mom just brought a new baby home from the hospital or Susie is being traumatized by a shift to a new preschool—she may suddenly start wetting the bed again.

In much more subtle ways, recovering food addicts will sometimes get two or three months into recovery and discover that even though much of the change in their lives is positive, it's also scary. Face it: recovery means venturing into unknown territory, and it's quite

Week
12

possible to get scared enough to say—even on a subconscious level: "I want to go back to the way it was." Even though "the way it was" was dysfunctional and unhealthy, it's familiar. This is an important dynamic motivating many people to sabotage their food recovery: the regression gives an illusion of being familiar and safe.

Is regression a factor fueling your relapse? ____ yes ____ no

Are you experiencing negative feelings connected with your diet? (Examples: fear, panic, restlessness.) ____ yes ____ no

What are recent regressive behaviors you noticed? (Examples: sneaking food or secretive eating.)

_____

_____

Are you experiencing the sense of a "looming black cloud" of fears, doubts, or anxieties that you can't seem to connect to any specific problem areas in your life?
____ yes ____ no

If regression is, indeed, fueling your relapse . . .

. . . you may need to do more daily emotional inventory work like the kind of work suggested in Steps 10 and 11. Some call it "doing the daily emotional inventory," meaning taking time every day to pause and look at what's going on inside. The premise is that if you are at least aware of the pressures, that gives you some chance to grieve them out. For many people who are food addicted, there is the automatic tendency to stuff feelings down, even in recovery. Part of the antidote is to stay in touch with feelings.

. . . you may need to have more contact with support persons with whom you can process and debrief these feelings.

DAY 3

Step 12. Having had a spiritual awakening as the result of these steps, we tried to carry this message to others and to practice these principles in all our affairs.

KNOWING WHAT TO SAY

When Bill Wilson was approached by an old drinking buddy—suddenly sober and in a growing, stabilizing relationship with God—Bill wasn't subjected to a lecture or a discourse on the steps he needed to take to reclaim his life. Instead, this former drinking buddy simply told Bill what had happened to him. He spoke of his own despair, his own near-destruction, his own hopelessness, and how God had made the difference in his life. He simply carried the message of what he had experienced in his own life. Now, that's powerful. That's recovery evangelism.

As you interact with people who are hurting as you are hurting, the most powerful key you have to their hearts is through the honest telling of your own journey. You don't have to preach; you don't have to point out all the problems in their lives; you don't have to appear to know all the answers. Your part is the simple retelling of the pain, struggle, and healing through which you have lived.

Yesterday you thought about people you know who might benefit from hearing your message of spiritual renewal and recovery from addiction. Today brings the opportunity to think through what you might say the next time you find yourself in an appropriate setting. What is your story?

Consider the following questions as you begin to journal about your recovery process.

- What prompted your addiction?
- What voids, disappointments, and dynamics in your family of origin helped create your original love hunger or helped fuel it once it was in place?
- What was it like to be controlled by food?
- How did God fit into all this?
- Were you ever angry at God for the way your life was turning out?
- How did your food addiction impact your life? What were its worse effects?
- Had you ever tried to "cure" yourself with a diet, perhaps, or other strict controls?
- What happened? What did it feel like to fail? What were your hopes and fears for the future?
- What were your eating habits? How did they impact your health or appearance?
- What was the turning point for you?
- What finally pushed you into a more comprehensive recovery program consisting of or including this workbook?
- What did it feel like to go through the early stages of recovery?

Week
12

- What feelings were unearthed as you dug deep in your past for festering hurts and disappointments?

- What changes have taken place in your spiritual life?

- What's the hardest thing about the recovery process?

- For what part of the recovery process are you most grateful?

- You came into recovery regarding food; but how has recovery impacted other parts of your life besides eating?

- How has the recovery process impacted or altered your perspective of God?

- Looking back over the past few months, what are positive changes, big and small, that you identify in your health, lifestyle, and relationships?

- When you look into the mirror (both literally and figuratively speaking), what is your excitement about the "new you" that is emerging physically, emotionally, and spiritually?

DAY 4

PLANNING A MAINTENANCE DIET

Yesterday we discussed the fact that the Love Hunger Diet Plan you have followed for the last eleven weeks will take you smoothly into a maintenance program as well. You should continue to use the same:

- ingredients and grocery store items

- recipes

- cooking methods

The one variation with the maintenance diet is that you will now use exchange menus in the *Love Hunger* book. This should prove to be a convenient way of providing you with the nutrients you need for maximal health as well as infinite food possibilities. Now here is the step-by-step procedure for using this method.

Week
12

1. DETERMINE YOUR DAILY CALORIC NEEDS

You will always gain back a few pounds after ending any type of calorie restricted program. Do not be alarmed if this happens to you. However, since your metabolism is still very likely depressed from the weight loss program and will take approximately six months to normalize, you should begin your maintenance diet in a modest way. The following calculation allows you to multiply your *current weight* (not the old weight) by twelve to give you the total number of calories you may consume per day.

12 x your current weight = initial maintenance calorie level

I should consume _____ calories per day as I begin my new maintenance diet program.

2. LEARN YOUR EXCHANGES

Find the calorie content below that best meets your caloric needs.

EXCHANGE DIET ALLOWANCES

Food List	Calorie Levels				
	1500	1600	1700	1800	2000
1—Bread/Starch	7	8	8	9	10
2—Lean Meat	4	4	5	5	5
3—Milk Products	3	3	3	3	3
4—Fruits/Juices	4	4	5	5	6
5—Vegetables	no limit; 2 cups per day minimum				
6—Fats	3	4	4	5	6

After you find the calorie level best suited to you, note how many food choices you may have from each of the food lists on pages 353–355. For example, if you were on the 1500 calorie maintenance diet, you would be allowed seven servings per day of some kind of bread or starch product. You may use the food lists for the purpose of finding out what the size of one exchange is for any particular food.

3. DESIGN YOUR OWN MENU

The only thing left is for you to now design your own maintenance menu. Divide up the different types of foods you are having throughout the entire day and distribute them among all of the meals.

Breakfast: _____

Week
12

Snack: _____

Lunch: _____

_____

Snack: _____

Supper: _____

_____

_____

Snack: _____

IN CASE YOU ARE WONDERING . . .

Q. *Will I have to stay on this system forever, just to maintain my weight?*

A. Absolutely not! This is just for starters. The exchange diet is meant to help you get a sense of what constitutes a healthy, balanced approach to weight maintenance. After using this system for a few months, you won't even have to write down or design a menu—you will know what you need for that day.

Q. *What about extra sweets, desserts, and snack foods?*

A. These may be worked in right now. You should eliminate a bread serving in place of a small dessert. However, you should know that it is a rare person (or a very active one) who can get by with eating a heavy dessert (pie, cake, several cookies, or ice cream) on a consistent basis without gaining weight. We do not recommend that you do this except on occasion—and when you do, enjoy every mouthful!

Q. *What if I continue to lose weight?*

A. If you lose weight on your maintenance diet, you should increase your calorie level estimate. Go up in small increments. If you exercise more than three hours per week, you may want to increase your calorie intake to fourteen calories per pound instead of the twelve we have suggested you begin with. Also, as time progresses and your body becomes accustomed to your new weight, you will probably have to increase your calorie level for that reason as well. We began your maintenance diet at a lower level to keep you from regaining weight during a vulnerable adjustment period.

Week
12

DAY 4

COPING WITH RELAPSE: PART 1

You may or may not have experienced relapse at this stage in your recovery program. If you have, the steps outlined today and tomorrow will help you work your way out of relapse and back into your program—and you can actually be stronger for the experience!

If you have not experienced relapse yourself, go ahead and walk yourself through the following steps. In this manner you will be prepared for the possibility of relapse. Remember: the possibility of relapse is a predictable stage of your recovery. How you prepare for relapse determines how soon you catch yourself, how long you remain in relapse, and whether the relapse strengthens or destroys the new directions you've chosen for your life.

1. DISMANTLE THE RELAPSE SHAME-BASE

Immediately forgive yourself for the relapse and do not shame yourself for having experienced this predictable and normal stage of recovery. Dismantling the relapse shame-base may also mean the existence of even deeper shame issues—relating back to your family of origin—that were somehow overlooked in the recovery process so far. If there are things from your past that are still generating undeserved shame, you will continue to court failure in your recovery process. Unprocessed shame feelings generate shame-inducing behaviors. Therefore, it is vital to root out old and contemporary shame sources.

Regarding the presence of immediate shame connected to my relapse,

Examples:
I forgive myself for not noticing the warning signals sooner.
I forgive myself for gaining six pounds.
I forgive myself for stuffing down my anger at Larry with six donuts rather than expressing it verbally.

I forgive myself for _____

I forgive myself for _____

I forgive myself for _____

I forgive myself for _____

2. RECYCLE THROUGH THE GRIEVING PROCESS AS NECESSARY

If there are unfinished shame issues from the past, then you may need to recycle through the grieving process. Consider going back to Week 9 where you examined the stages of grief and working through the process of "letting go" of the shame, anger, or hurt from the past.

For the immediate pain of the relapse, give yourself permission to grieve about whatever damage was done, or whatever feelings of failure were generated by the relapse. Simply scolding yourself won't do it. You may need to take time to have feelings of sadness and anger about the relapse. Even though the relapse is nothing to be ashamed of and is a predictable stage of recovery, your feelings of anger and shame about the experience are very real and deserve to be acknowledged. Trying to stuff these feelings down or deny them will only increase the urge to turn to food again. Take a moment now to explore your feelings regarding the relapse.

I'm embarrassed that I _____

_____

My big fear is that _____

_____

The thing that makes me angry about the whole experience is _____

_____

I feel that the relapse cost me _____

_____

I feel sad that my relapse damaged _____

_____

3. RECHANNEL YOUR ANGER

It's fine that you may have experienced anger about the relapse experience. The key now is to rechannel your anger toward mobilizing a renewed recovery program, rather than turning the anger on yourself or against others. For many recovering food addicts, the tendency is to turn anger back in themselves, resulting in depression and further self-sabotage. A second tendency is to blame others: "My mean boss made me relapse, and I can't change him so I guess I'm stuck in my relapse."

Anger can actually be your ally in recommitting to your program. Relapse can result in a sense of letdown, disappointment, and/or lack of energy. All these things can make pulling out of relapse hard. It's as if you're spiraling downward, and just when you need engine power to pull out of the nose dive, your engine feels weak and has lost power. Don't be afraid to use anger as the energy you need to restart your program. Get angry . . . but not at yourself and not at people around you. Get angry at the relapse itself.

DAY 4

Step 12. Having had a spiritual awakening as the result of these steps, we tried to carry this message to others and to practice these principles in all our affairs.

WHEN OTHERS DOUBT

In the course of sharing your recovery story to others, you may find yourself presented with the doubts and fears of a friend who has, indeed, come close to losing all hope. As you respond to the following statements, regarding food addiction and/or God, don't focus on how you might intellectually counter each one. Rather, respond out of the heart of your own experience. Has the negative doubt or fear proven true in your own life? Or has your experience been a more hopeful one? Once again, there is no approach more powerful than the simple telling of the uplifting course of events that has resulted in your changed life.

Statement	Response
That may have worked for you, but it seems I've been struggling all my life. Even God can't change that.	*I used to think God couldn't help me either. But look at me—I'm turning things around, and I know it's not me, but God in me.*
I'll never be thin. It's in my genes.	_____ _____ _____ _____ _____
There's no connection between my relationship with God and people and my relationship with food.	_____ _____ _____

Week
12

_____

_____

_____

I can beat this thing on my own.

_____

_____

_____

_____

_____

_____

The *Big Book* of Alcoholics Anonymous® summarizes the transforming power of your fellow-ship with other recovering persons:

> Life will take on new meaning. To watch people recover, to see them help others, to watch loneliness vanish, to see a fellowship grow up about you, to have a host of friends—this is an experience you must not miss. We know you will not want to miss it . . . .[1]

DAY 5

RED FLAGS

It was a brisk autumn morning when Valerie and Todd came back to Dr. Sneed's office for the last time. It had been twelve months since their first visit and both of them had been at their ideal weight for over six months. Valerie was a little anxious about breaking ties with the people who had helped her rediscover her true feelings and changed her outlook on life. But she was confident about her new size and her ability to maintain that size.

As they walked into Dr. Sneed's office, Valerie began to ask some questions. She felt that she was still having a problem with rebellion as she said, "I still feel rebellious in some ways because sometimes I want to go to the store and pack the shopping cart with high fat chips, cream cheese dips, rich ice cream, and cookies. I just don't like the thought of not having total freedom in what I choose. Am I just behaving like a spoiled brat? Tell me the truth, Dr. Sneed—these things are really bothering me."

Dr. Sneed approached this question with as much earnestness as Valerie and Todd: "The most important factor may be as you say, Valerie, the rebellious spirit. Do you know that when diabetics are first diagnosed there is a lot of rebellion with them as well? And the other part of what you're feeling is undoubtedly fear of regaining the weight. Let's look at a few "red flag" areas that should catch your attention, in case you find them arising in the future."

1. Are you changing your grocery shopping patterns? After three or more months of doing what is healthy for your body, you may be tempted to go back to putting some of those old comfort foods in that shopping cart once again. Make sure you are using the same lower fat alternatives you have used with this program and look for new products as they appear on the market.

2. Are you eating larger portion sizes? Take care that you do not revert to the old amounts of food you once consumed. Remember to eat slowly and enjoy each mouthful. Drink plenty of fluids while you are eating, and do not return to family style meals.

3. Are you going back to old recipes with greater frequency? Many of your old stand-by recipes probably use ingredients that do not fit in with your new eating plan. Have you designed lower fat alternatives for these recipes? Or do you find yourself going back to use the same ones and feeling deprived if you do not use them? Be realistic about what humans are supposed to eat and remember that American eating habits are abnormal by world and historical standards.

4. Are you allowing yourself to eat differently because of new and different situations? Perhaps a different way of saying this is "Are you seeking justification through any recent occurrences in your life to eat larger portions or different types of food from what has been called for in this book?" Has a crisis come up in your family? Has your work schedule changed? Stay alert—these types of tensions may make you think that you can change the rules to fit the game.

5. Have your exercise habits changed? While actively losing weight, you should have about three to six hours per week of aerobic exercise. While maintaining your weight, we have talked about three hours per week as being sufficient. As life becomes more hectic, the exercise program is often the first thing tossed overboard. Exercise is possibly the number one factor that will help keep your weight loss in check. Make it a top priority in your daily schedule, or you will find that it simply does not get done.

Week
12

6. Have you gained five pounds? A five-pound gain should have an emotional element attached in your mind that tells you it is time to get serious. Notice that we did not say it was a signal for panic, but only a technique to get your attention. It shows you that once again it's time to dust off the *Love Hunger* book or workbook and rediscover where those extra pounds are coming from. Don't let it go beyond this point.

Valerie and Todd left feeling confident and refreshed, knowing that the things they had learned were permanent in their lives. They were finished with their workbooks, now, as you will be finished in a few more pages. Nonetheless, they tucked those well-worn pages underneath their arms knowing they would be available for them on the bookshelf at home in case they were ever needed again in the future.

DAY 5

COPING WITH RELAPSE: PART 2

4. LOOK FOR THE FOOD MESSAGE IN THE RELAPSE

Typically a relapse can tell you one of two things—if you are going too fast, or if you are going too slow, with your weight loss. Either scenario can trigger relapse. If you've been losing more than your body can handle, you may find yourself beset with cravings for your trigger foods. If, on the other hand, your weight loss is too slow—for example, if you've only lost a pound or two in a month's time—emotionally, it can get so discouraging that you begin to wonder, "What's the use?"

A second food-related message that your relapse may be communicating is whether your diet is too restrictive or too indulgent. Either extreme can predispose a relapse. Let's say you were on a diet allowing you to eat turnip greens only—any highly restrictive food plan will set your body up for food cravings and relapse. On the other hand, if your plan is too lenient and allows you to eat even limited quantities of any of your trigger foods, you may be setting yourself up for relapse.

What is my relapse telling me about the speed of my weight loss? _____

In the past month, I've lost _____ pounds. In terms of the speed of this weight loss, I think _____

_____

What is my relapse telling me about the variety of foods allowed on my diet? _____

_____

Do I need to make further restrictions and establish additional boundaries regarding what I eat? ____ yes ____ no

If yes, what boundaries? _____

Do I need to enlarge my variety of "legal" foods to discourage boredom and enhance nutrition? ____ yes ____ no

If yes, what foods will I be adding to my diet? _____

_____

5. Quickly Recommit to a New Food Management Program

The key word here is *quickly*. There is a window of time following your relapse in which recommitment to your diet plan will be easier. The longer you stay in relapse, the harder it will be to move back into your program. Even if there's a part of you that still feels rebellious or lacking energy, you need to move quickly. Even if you've come to the conclusion that you need to change your diet or find a new diet, *don't stay in relapse while you gear up for this change.* Go back to your old diet for a week until you are prepared to launch your new diet.

Ask support persons to confront you on this recommitment to your food program. Call your OA sponsor or close friend and ask him or her to call tomorrow morning and ask if you're back on your program.

6. Write Out a Contract for Emotional and Spiritual Recovery Activities

This contract is one made with yourself, naming the recovery activities to which you are committing. Your daily agenda will probably include prayer, some sort of physical exercise, emotional inventory, contact with someone from a recovery support group. You might also include in this contract weekly activities such as attending an OA meeting or Bible study. Even if the contract repeats much of what you had been doing before your relapse, it's important to record your recommitment on paper and in contract form.

Week
12

I hereby commit to the following activities as the ways in which I am choosing to take care of myself.

Regarding my relationship with food: _____

_____

Regarding my relationship with God: _____

_____

_____

Regarding my relationships with friends and family: _____

_____

_____

Regarding my contact with other recovering persons: _____

_____

_____

Regarding new boundaries I have established for myself: _____

_____

_____

7. FINALLY, TAKE TIME TO REINVENTORY ALL OF YOUR CURRENT MAJOR
RELATIONSHIPS

At the very beginning of the book *Love Hunger* and also in the beginning of this workbook, you read that your relationships with people have more to do with your relationship with food than calories or carbohydrates.

As the crowning aspect of your journey out of relapse, go back to your relationships. Is there anything missing there? Are there some important needs that aren't being met? If there are, these voids will continue to feed your love hunger, greatly reducing your opportunity for full and lasting recovery.

Take a moment to list any needs that you are experiencing within your major relationships—needs that are not being met. Then take a step of action and ask from these relationships that these needs be better met.

Week
12

Example:

Major relationship: My relationship with my boss.

Unmet needs: He never says he appreciates me. I have a real need for affirmation from him.

Step of Action: This week I'll talk to him about the problem; I'll ask if he is, indeed, pleased with my work and if he is, could he let me know?

Major relationship: My relationship with my wife.

Unmet needs: She's always joking with other people about my weight; I have a need for her to be supportive—or at least neutral—about my appearance in front of other people.

Step of Action: Tonight after dinner I'm going to tell her that her joking embarrasses me and ask her to stop.

Major relationship: _____

Unmet needs: _____

_____

Step of action: _____

_____

Major relationship: _____

Unmet needs: _____

_____

Step of action: _____

_____

Major relationship: _____

Unmet needs: _____

_____

Step of action: _____

_____

As a rule, if you make this kind of request of someone who plays a major role in your life, that request will be met. It's possible, however, that even after asking to have these needs met, that

Week
12

the other person in your life will be unable or unwilling to accommodate your request. Yet if you've given yourself permission to ask and followed through with an actual request, you've gotten your needs out on the table. That lowers the pressure you might have felt to turn to food to "stuff down" the expression of your needs or to meet your needs.

If and when relapse occurs again, you *can* be prepared to catch it early, pull out quickly, and use it as an opportunity to learn more about yourself. While relapse can be prevented and should be avoided, it is not an uncommon occurrence nor is it a tragedy when it does occur.

DAY 5

Step 12. Having had a spiritual awakening as the result of these steps, we tried to carry this message to others and to practice these principles in all our affairs.

INTEGRATING SPIRITUAL REBIRTH INTO EVERY FACET OF YOUR LIFE

There is an emphasis in Step 12 regarding the practice of these principles in all your affairs. This means if you have been spiritually transformed, over time this transformation will permeate all arenas of your life: financial, family, relationships, sexual conduct, work life . . . the list goes on and on.

As you've discovered in the past twelve weeks, no area of your life is isolated from the rest. Something as simple as what you choose to put in your mouth can be powerfully linked to dynamics in your relationships, your career, your personal history. In fact, the key to the entire Love Hunger recovery program is in its comprehensive approach. There is no realm of your life that is "off" limits as you are encouraged to explore the paths to freedom from your addiction.

In light of the fact that every segment of your life is networked together, your spiritual awakening may impact you in deeper and more varied ways than you ever imagined. Just as a pebble dropped in a small glassy pond will ripple the surface to the water's edge, your spiritual renewal will cause ripples—perhaps even tidal waves—of change that will permeate your entire life.

In what ways has your growing awareness of God impacted the various areas of your life?

In what areas would you most like to see God continue His transforming work in your life? Are there relationships, personal struggles or situations that you wish you and God might work on together in the future?

More than anything, your recovery process out of food addiction can become a new lifestyle—not just a new lifestyle of healthier food management, but a lifestyle of healthier emotional and spiritual management as well. The same tools that have helped free you from food codependency can continue to serve you for a lifetime of freedom from the control of past, present, and future disappointments and hurts.

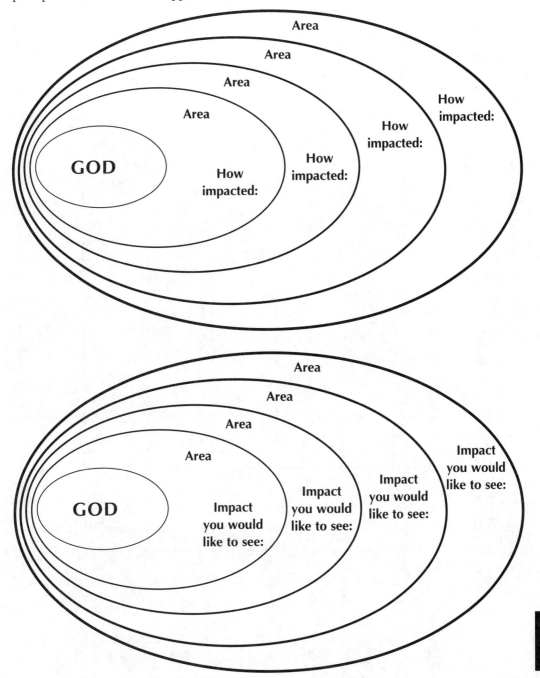

WEEKLY FOOD AND EXERCISE JOURNAL

Date _____
Weight (First day of week only) _____

	Breakfast/ A.M. Snack	Lunch P.M. Snack	Dinner Nite Snack	Exercise	Feelings and Major Events of the Day
Day One					
Day Two					
Day Three					
Day Four					
Day Five					
Day Six					
Day Seven					

PART THREE

THE MENU
AND FOOD
EXCHANGES

MENU EXCHANGES

BREAKFAST MENUS

(Each menu contains approximately 200 calories.)

GENERAL INSTRUCTIONS

1. *Choose any one* of the following menus for your breakfast each morning. If you do not anticipate having milk for snacks or at other times, it will be important to choose a menu with milk.

2. Beverages allowed include coffee, tea, herbal tea, mineral water, or ice water. Sugar or cream should not be added to these drinks. However, a sugar substitute may be used. We recommend that you use no more than two servings of a sugar substitute per day. For seasoning your food, salt, pepper, and other spices may be used.

3. Note that your lowest fat choices are the cereal or egg substitute entrées. The highest fiber, lowest fat, most nutritious choices are listed first and have a star (★) by them. The least recommended choices follow and do not have a star designation. If your doctor has recently told you that you have a problem with high cholesterol, do not eat the egg entrées unless they have been made with a cholesterol-free egg substitute.

HIGH FIBER CEREAL

(12 g fiber per serving)

½ cup Fiber One®, Bran Buds®, or other high fiber cereal	Calories	210
	% Protein	25
1 cup skim milk (drink the rest if not used on cereal)	% Carbohydrates	68
	% Fat	7
1 fruit selection (see Fruit Exchange List on page 354)	Cholesterol	4 mg
	Sodium	396 mg

OTHER CEREALS

1 serving of dry breakfast cereal (Approximately 100 calories—check the label; avoid high sugar varieties.)	Calories	225
	% Protein	23
	% Carbohydrates	71
1 rounded tablespoon Miller's® Bran	% Fat	5
1 cup skim milk (Drink the rest if not used on cereal.)	Cholesterol	4 mg
	Sodium	439 mg

YOGURT, FRUIT, AND BRAN

8 ounces light, nonfat yogurt (100 calories
    or less)
1 fruit selection (See Fruit Exchange List on
    page 354.)
3 rounded tablespoons Miller's® Bran

Calories	211
% Protein	29
% Carbohydrates	63
% Fat	7
Cholesterol	4 mg
Sodium	439 mg

Dice fruit and mix with yogurt and bran.

YOGURT BREAKFAST

8 ounces light yogurt (approximately 100
    calories)
¼ cup Grape-nuts®

Calories	210
% Protein	24
% Carbohydrates	74
% Fat	2
Cholesterol	4 mg
Sodium	570 mg

Add 2 to 4 tablespoons of Miller's® Bran if you would like to include a high-fiber supplement with this. Sprinkle Grape-nuts® over the yogurt and enjoy.

CHEESE TOAST AND FRUIT

2 slices light bread
2 slices 40-calorie or less cheese
1 fruit selection (See Fruit Exchange List on
    page 354)

% Carbohydrates	63
Calories	205
% Fat	8
Cholesterol	5 mg
Sodium	625 mg

Place cheese slices on the bread slices and toast together in the broiler.

★ LOW-FAT FRENCH TOAST

½ cup Egg Beaters®
3 tablespoons skim milk
2 slices light bread
    Nonstick vegetable coating spray
2 teaspoons diet margarine
1 teaspoon powdered sugar
1 tablespoon light syrup

Calories	215
% Protein	35
% Carbohydrates	49
% Fat	16
Cholesterol	3 mg
Sodium	432 mg

In a small bowl, combine the Egg Beaters® and skim milk. Beat until foamy. Dip the bread slices into the egg mixture. Spray a nonstick skillet with vegetable coating and preheat. Grill the dipped bread slices until golden brown. Serve hot, topped with the margarine, sugar, and syrup.

★ MUFFIN AND MILK

1 light bran muffin (no more than 120 calories per muffin, see *Love Hunger,* for recipe)	Calories	190
	% Protein	25
1 cup skim milk	% Carbohydrates	55
	% Fat	21
	Cholesterol	46 mg
	Sodium	305 mg

★ HOT CEREAL

¾ cup any hot-cooked cereal	Calories	209
1 teaspoon sugar	% Protein	25
Spices as desired	% Carbohydrates	55
1 cup skim milk	% Fat	21
	Cholesterol	46 mg
	Sodium	305 mg

★ CHEESE OMELET WITH EGG SUBSTITUTE

½ cup Egg Beaters®, 1 tablespoon skim milk, and sprinkle of dry butter substitute flavoring	Calories	200
	% Protein	37
1 slice light cheese (40 calories or less)	% Carbohydrates	32
1 slice light bread (40 calories per slice), toasted with 1 teaspoon diet margarine	% Fat	21
	Cholesterol	5 mg
Nonstick vegetable coating spray	Sodium	29 mg
Sliced tomatoes (See Fruit Exchange List on Page 354.)		

Use a nonstick pan sprayed with the vegetable coating spray. Whip the Egg Beaters®, milk, and butter substitute together in a bowl before pouring into the heated pan. Cook as you would an omelet, melting the cheese inside the omelet. Serve with fruit or juice for a complete breakfast.

★ BREAKFAST TACOS WITH EGG SUBSTITUTE

1 small flour or corn tortilla, 6-inch or smaller diameter	Calories	195
	% Protein	40
½ cup scrambled egg made from Egg Beaters®, no added fat	% Carbohydrates	38
	% Fat	22
½ cup plain boiled potato, precooked and diced	Cholesterol	3 mg
Nonstick vegetable coating spray	Sodium	285 mg
Picante sauce, onions, peppers, and spices (cilantro, parsley, chili powder)		

Make the scrambled eggs in a nonstick pan sprayed with nonstick vegetable coating spray and add sauce, onions, peppers, and spices if desired. Warm the tortilla in a microwave, place the cooked egg mixture in the tortilla and serve immediately.

★ Egg, Toast, and Fruit with Egg Substitute

½ cup Egg Beaters®, scrambled, no added fat
Nonstick vegetable coating spray
1 slice light bread with 1 teaspoon diet
   margarine
8 ounces skim milk

Calories	200
% Protein	45
% Carbohydrates	35
% Fat	20
Cholesterol	0 mg
Sodium	175 mg

Use a nonstick skillet sprayed with nonstick vegetable coating spray to prepare the Egg Beaters®. The bread may be toasted or grilled. Serve with milk.

★ Scrambled Egg and Breakfast Meat with Egg Substitute

½ cup Egg Beaters®
Nonstick vegetable coating spray
1 tablespoon skim milk
Dry butter substitute flavoring
1 ounce lean ham or 2 thin strips crisp bacon
1 slice light bread, toasted with 1 tablespoon
   diet margarine

Calories	200
% Protein	43
% Carbohydrates	34
% Fat	23
Cholesterol	60 mg
Sodium	622 mg

Combine the Egg Beaters®, milk, and butter substitute in a small bowl. Beat until light in color. Scramble in a heated nonstick, skilled sprayed with nonstick, vegetable coating spray. Grill the ham or bacon in the same skillet. Serve hot with toast.

Toast and Milk

2 slices light bread (or 1 slice of regular bread),
   toasted
2 teaspoons diet margarine (or 1 teaspoon
   regular margarine or butter)
1 cup skim milk

Calories	217
% Protein	21
% Carbohydrates	56
% Fat	22
Cholesterol	5 mg
Sodium	405 mg

Bagel and Cream Cheese

½ bagel, toasted, with 1 teaspoon diet margarine
1 ounce light cream cheese or 2 ounces of
   yogurt cheese
1 fruit selection (See Fruit Exchange List on
   page 354.) or 1/2 cup skim milk

Calories	195
% Protein	29
% Carbohydrates	47
% Fat	24
Cholesterol	15 mg
Sodium	394 mg

½ English muffin, toasted	Calories	205	
1 teaspoon diet margarine	% Protein	25	
1 teaspoon jelly or marmalade	% Carbohydrates	53	
2 fruit selections (See Fruit Exchange List on	% Fat	22	
page 354.) *or* 8 ounces skim milk	Cholesterol	11	mg
	Sodium	139	mg

WAFFLE OR PANCAKE BREAKFAST

1 toaster waffle or pancake	Calories	21	
1 teaspoon diet margarine	% Protein	22	
2 teaspoons light syrup	% Carbohydrates	55	
1 cup skim milk	% Fat	23	
	Cholesterol	32	mg
	Sodium	320	mg

Prepare a toaster or prepared mix waffle or pancake as suggested on the side of the box.

CHEESE OMELET

1 egg, whipped with 1 tablespoon skim milk and	Calories	213	
sprinkle of dry butter substitute flavoring	% Protein	26	
1 slice light cheese (40 calories or less)	% Carbohydrates	31	
1 slice light bread (40 calories or less) toasted,	% Fat	42	
with 1 teaspoon diet margarine	Cholesterol	251	mg
Nonstick, vegetable coating spray	Sodium	315	mg
Sliced tomatoes			

Make in a preheated nonstick pan sprayed with nonstick vegetable coating spray. Whip the egg, milk, and butter substitute together in a bowl before pouring into the heated pan. Cook as you would an omelet, melting the cheese inside the omelet.

SCRAMBLED EGG AND BREAKFAST MEAT

1 egg	Calories	206	
Nonstick vegetable coating spray	% Protein	27	
1 tablespoon milk	% Carbohydrates	24	
Dry butter substitute flavoring	% Fat	49	
1 ounce lean ham *or* 2 thin strips crisp bacon	Cholesterol	305	mg
1 slice light bread, toasted, with 1 teaspoon diet	Sodium	639	mg
margarine			

Combine the egg, milk, and butter substitute in a small bowl. Beat until light in color. Scramble in a heated nonstick skillet sprayed with the nonstick vegetable coating spray. Grill the ham or bacon in the same skillet. Serve hot with toast.

EGG, TOAST, AND FRUIT

1 egg cooked any style, no added fat	Calories	205
Nonstick vegetable coating spray	% Protein	20
1 slice light bread with 1 teaspoon diet	% Carbohydrates	37
margarine	% Fat	43
1 fruit selection (See Fruit Exchange List on	Cholesterol	249 mg
page 354.)	Sodium	326 mg

Use a nonstick skillet sprayed with the nonstick vegetable spray to prepare the egg. The bread may be toasted or grilled.

BREAKFAST TACOS

1 small flour or corn tortilla, 6-inch or smaller	Calories	186
diameter	Protein	18
1 scrambled egg, no added fat	% Carbohydrates	38
Nonstick vegetable coating spray	% Fat	44
Picante sauce, onions, peppers, and spices	Cholesterol	248 mg
(cilantro, parsley, chili powder)	Sodium	317 mg

Make the scrambled egg in a nonstick pan sprayed with the nonstick vegetable coating spray and add sauce, onions, peppers, and spices, if desired. Warm the tortilla in a microwave, place the cooked egg mixture in the tortilla, and serve immediately.

LUNCH AND DINNER MENUS

(Each menu contains approximately 300 calories)

GENERAL INSTRUCTIONS

1. Choose any one of the following menus for your lunch and another menu for your dinner each day. Try to preplan meals so that you will have a wide variety of foods to fulfill your nutritional needs for everything except calories.

2. Beverages allowed include coffee, tea, herbal tea, mineral water, or ice water. Sugar or cream should not be added to these drinks. However, a sugar substitute may be used. We recommend that you use no more than two servings of a sugar substitute per day. Spices, herbs, and seasonings of all types may be used as long as they do not contain fat, sugar, or a significant amount of calories.

3. Note that your lowest-fat choices are designated with a star (*). Other menu items are perfectly fine but do not provide as much good nutrition as the starred selections. Fast-food menus are included at the end of the list.

THE GENERIC MENU
(Use this basic menu and the menu selection examples below as a guide to help design any type of dinner.)

3–4 ounces lean, low-fat meat
> (Fish, chicken, beef, pork; this portion should not be fried or have any visible fat.)
> *Note:* Use 3 ounces for meat and poultry and 4 ounces for fish.

½   cup serving starchy vegetable or grain
> (potatoes, rice, corn, beans, peas, pasta, bread; see Starch Exchange List, page 353.)

2   cups low-calorie vegetables, no added fat

Examples of Menu Selections (using quantities listed above)

1. Meatloaf, mashed potatoes, green beans, sliced tomatoes
2. Roast turkey, low-fat gravy, dressing, steamed broccoli
3. Broiled red snapper, rice pilaf, green garden salad, low-calorie dressing
4. Grilled chicken (no skin), small baked potato, boiled carrots
5. Lean barbecued brisket, pinto beans, salad and/or sliced tomatoes
6. Baked ham, baked sweet potatoes, steamed cauliflower
7. Pepper steak, noodles, steamed vegetable medley

When adhering closely to the recommended quantities and to cooking methods that do not require extra added fat, the following nutritional analysis will apply to most menus:

Calories	300
% Protein	40
% Carbohydrates	41
% Fat	19
Cholesterol	60 mg
Sodium	146 to 1600 mg

(depending on seasonings used)

★ SANDWICHES

4 slices light bread (40 calories per slice)
2 slices lean meat (such as turkey breast, chicken breast, or ham)
2 slices light cheese (40 calories or less per slice)
Mustard, any variety that does not contain oil
Lettuce, tomato, sprouts, cucumbers, onions, etc.

Calories	317
% Protein	39
% Carbohydrates	45
% Fat	16
Cholesterol	44 mg
Sodium	767 mg

TACO SALAD

½ cup taco meat recipe (contains 3 ounces lean, cooked ground round made into taco meat using any commercial seasoning packet)
2 cups lettuce, shredded
½ tomato, sliced
1 green onion, chopped
½ carrot, grated
2 radishes, sliced
¼ cup picante sauce
2 tablespoons Catalina reduced-calorie salad dressing
1 6-inch corn tortilla, cut into julienne strips, *or* 5 baked tortilla chips

Calories	325
% Protein	37
% Carbohydrates	39
% Fat	25
Cholesterol	78 mg
Sodium	764 mg

Arrange the lettuce, tomato, onion, carrot, and radishes on a plate. Top with the taco meat, picante sauce, dressing, and tortilla chips.

★ CHEF SALAD OR OTHER SALADS

Unlimited low-calorie vegetables (Lettuce, tomatoes, sprouts, cucumbers, peppers, onions, broccoli; see page 354 for a complete list of low-calorie vegetables.)

⅓ cup diced meat, cheese, eggs, or other protein sources or 1/2 cup low-fat cottage cheese or tuna

¼ cup (or 4 tablespoons) low-calorie salad dressing (not to exceed 15 calories per tablespoon)

4 crackers (not to exceed 15 calories each; see grocery list for details.)

Calories	287
% Protein	30
% Carbohydrates	37
% Fat	33
Cholesterol	46 mg
	(more if egg yolk is used)
Sodium	671 mg

BROWN BAG SPECIAL

2 slices light bread (40 calories per slice)
1 slice lean meat (such as Danish ham)
1 slice low-calorie cheese (40 calories or less)
  Mustard, lettuce, tomato, sprouts, onion, etc.
1 serving fresh fruit (See Fruit Exchange list on page 354.)
1 package low-calorie chips (not to exceed 60 calories)
½ to 1 cup raw vegetable sticks

Calories	305
% Protein	20
% Carbohydrates	64
% Fat	16
Cholesterol	18 mg
Sodium	950 mg

PREPARED FROZEN DINNERS

Any dinner containing 300 calories or less. Add a large garden salad with low-calorie dressing as a side dish. (Many frozen dinners contain 250–270 calories; total caloric content in this menu is an estimate.)

Calories	325
% Protein	25
% Fat	30
Cholesterol	20 mg
% Carbohydrates	45
Sodium	932

MEXICAN FOOD

2 homemade tacos (using lean ground beef) and crisp taco shells) *or* 2 bean tostadas
Picante sauce

Calories	334
% Protein	29
% Carbohydrates	25
% Fat	47
Cholesterol	125 mg
Sodium	944 mg

Make tacos or tostadas as directed on seasoning packets. Use as much lettuce, tomato, and other vegetables as you like on both of these entrées.

CHINESE FOOD

1 cup of any chicken (or fish) and vegetable mixture (Moo Goo Gai Pan, Chicken Chow Mein. No fried choices.) ½ cup steamed rice (not fried rice)	Calories	315	
	% Protein	35	
	% Carbohydrates	47	
	% Fat	18	
	Cholesterol	76	mg
	Sodium	1296	mg

ITALIAN FOOD

1 cup spaghetti or other pasta ½ cup spaghetti sauce with meat (*or* use 1 ounce mozzarella cheese as a meat substitute) Large salad with reduced-calorie Italian dressing	Calories	313	
	% Protein	20	
	% Carbohydrates	50	
	% Fat	30	
	Cholesterol	18	mg
	Sodium	761	mg

GRILLED CHEESE SANDWICH, SOUP, AND SALAD

2 slices light bread 2 slices low-calorie cheese (40 calories or less) *or* 1 ounce low-fat mozzarella cheese 2 teaspoons diet margarine 1 cup tomato soup made with skim milk, or clear vegetable soup 1 cup green salad 1 tablespoon no-oil Italian dressing	Calories	300	
	% Protein	17	
	% Carbohydrates	44	
	% Fat	39	
	Cholesterol	18	mg
	Sodium	1353	mg

Melt the margarine in a nonstick skillet. Toast the cheese sandwich until golden brown. Serve hot with hot soup and fresh salad.

CHEF SALAD AND SOUP

A smaller version of the chef salad on page 350 (omit crackers) 8 ounces tomato or clear vegetable soup	Calories	315	
	% Protein	13	
	% Carbohydrates	70	
	% Fat	17	
	Cholesterol	5	mg
	Sodium	1432	mg

SNACK CHOICES
(100 calories or less per snack)

GENERAL INSTRUCTIONS

1. If you are on the 800 calorie diet plan, you should not use this list. If you are following the 1000 calorie diet plan then you may have two selections per day from this list. If you

are using the 1200 calorie diet plan, then you may have four selections per day from this list.

2. Try to make wise food selections. You will find a few junk food items on this list when you feel there is no other alternative.

- 1 slice light bread, 1 slice light meat (turkey, chicken, ham, etc.), 1 slice Borden's® Lite-line cheese, mustard
- 10 ounces of skim milk
- 2 pieces of toast made from light bread with 1 teaspoon of diet margarine
- ½ cup skim milk and ½ cup high fiber cereal
- A double serving of fruit based on the quantities recommended on the Fruit Exchange List (See page 354.)
- Example: 2½ cups of watermelon *or* 2½ cups of fresh strawberries, *or* ½ fresh cantaloupe
- Raw vegetable sticks and ¼ cup light dressing or dip made from low-fat cottage cheese
- 8 ounces of light yogurt (100 calories)
- 6 to 8 ounces of any fruit juice
- 12 ounces of tomato juice cocktail (very high in sodium)
- 3 cups of popped popcorn, without added fat (try cooking in a microwave and then spraying with a butter-flavored cooking spray.)
- ¼ cup cottage cheese and ¼ cup fruit cocktail or alternative
- 20 Mr. Salty® pretzel sticks
- 6 light tortilla chips with picante sauce
- 1 large rice cake spread with ¼ cup cottage cheese dip or ricotta cheese
- ½ cup light ice cream or frozen yogurt (100 calories)
- 2 frozen fruit juice bars
- 25 Goldfish® crackers or oyster crackers
- 1 slice angel food cake (1½-inch)
- 6 vanilla wafers
- 8 ounces of light Gatorade®
- 2 large graham crackers
- 2 Oreos® or other similar sandwich cookie

THE FOOD EXCHANGES[1]

1 STARCH/BREAD EXCHANGES

Bread (25–30 g.)		Grits (cooked)	½ cup
White (including French		Wheat germ	2 tbsp.
and Italian)	1 slice	Crackers	
Whole wheat	1 slice	Animal crackers	8
Rye or pumpernickel	1 slice	Arrowroot	3
Raisin	1 slice	Graham (2½" square)	3
Bagel	½ small	Oyster crackers	20
English muffin	½ small	Rye wafers	3
Frankfurter roll	½	Rounds, thin	6
Hamburger roll	½	Saltines (2" square)	5
Matzo (6" square)	1	Soda (2½" square)	3
Tortilla, corn	1–6"	Vanilla wafers	5
Tortilla, white flour	¾–8"	Flour	2½ tbsp.
Melba toast	4	Rice, grits (cooked)	½ cup
Lite bread (40 cal./slice)	2 slices	Spaghetti, macaroni, noodles	½ cup
Cereals		Beans, baked (no pork)	⅓ cup
Bran flakes	½ cup	Beans, lima	⅓ cup
Cooked cereal	½ cup	Corn	⅓ cup
Dry cereal (unsweetened)	¾ cup	Popcorn, ready-made	½ cup
Grape-nuts® and granola	¼ cup	Potato, mashed	½ cup
Puffed cereals		Potato, white	½ medium
(unsweetened)	1½ cups	Potato, sweet yam	¼ cup

2 LEAN MEAT EXCHANGES

Beef		Fish	
Veal, tenderloin, round (bottom,		Any fresh or frozen	
top), all cuts—rump, sirloin,		canned salmon, tuna, mackerel	1 ½ oz.
extra-lean ground round	1 oz.	Crab and lobster	¼ cup
Lamb		Clams, oysters	1 ½ oz.
Leg, rib, sirloin, loin		Scallops, shrimp, sardines (drained)	3
(no visible fat)	1 oz.	Cheese	
Pork		Low-fat cottage cheese	⅓ cup
Leg (whole rump, center shank),		Low-fat cheese	1 oz.
ham, smoked (center slices)	1 oz.	Dried beans and peas, cooked	½ cup
Poultry		Eggs and vegetarian alternatives	
Meat of chicken, Cornish hen,		Egg whites	4
and turkey without skin	1 oz.	Egg Beaters®	½ cup
		Whole egg	1

3 MILK AND MILK PRODUCTS EXCHANGES

Milk		Yogurt	
Skim, ½ of 1 percent	1 cup	Plain nonfat	1 cup
Low-fat buttermilk	1 cup	Cheese	
Evaporated skim milk	½ cup	Low-fat cottage cheese	½ cup
Dry nonfat milk	⅓ cup	Part-skim milk cheese	1 oz.

4 FRUIT AND JUICES EXCHANGES

Apple ½ medium		Mango	½ small
Applesauce, unsweetened	½ cup	Nectarine	1 small
Apple juice or cider	⅓ cup	Orange	1 small
Apricots	3 medium	Orange juice	½ cup
Banana	½ 6"	Papaya	⅓ medium
Blackberries, blueberries,		Peach	1 medium
or raspberries	¾ cup	Pear	1 small
Cantaloupe (6" diameter)	¼ medium	Pineapple	½ cup
Cherries	10 large	Pineapple juice	⅓ cup
Cranberries, no sugar	No limit	Plums	2 medium
Dates	2 medium	Prunes	3 medium
Figs	2 small	Prune juice	¼ cup
Fruit cocktail, peaches	½ cup	Raisins	2 tbsp.
Grapefruit	½ small	Rhubarb	No limit
Grapefruit juice	½ cup	Strawberries, fresh	1¼ cups
Grapes	15 medium	Tangerine	1 medium
Grape juice	¼ cup	Watermelon	1 cup
Honeydew melon	¼ medium		

5 LOW-CAL VEGETABLES AND FREE FOODS*

Use the following as desired. Eat at least 2 cups/day (four ½ cup servings per day).

Asparagus	Cucumber	Mustard	String beans
Bean Sprouts	Eggplant	Spinach	Summer squash
Beets	Green pepper	Turnip	Tomatoes
Broccoli	Greens	Mushrooms	Tomato juice
Brussel sprouts	Beet	Okra	Turnips
Cabbage	Chard	Onions	Vegetable juice
Carrots	Collards	Rhubarb	Zucchini
Cauliflower	Dandelion	Rutabaga	
Celery	Kale	Sauerkraut	

*Note: Starchy vegetables are found in the Starch/Bread Exchange List.

7 FAT EXCHANGES

Concentrated fats

    Oil, butter, margarine mayonnaise,

        salad dressings   1 tsp.

Low-fat alternatives

    Reduced-calorie margarine   2 tsp.

    Reduced-calorie mayonnaise   2 tsp.

    Reduced-calorie salad

    dressings 1–2 tbsp. (up to 20 cal./tbsp.)

Nuts

    All nuts   1 tbsp.

Others

Avocado	⅛ medium
Olives	10 small
Bacon	1 strip
Coconut, shredded	2 tbsp.
Nondairy creamer	1 tbsp.
Cream, light	2 tbsp.
Cream, sour	2 tbsp.
Cream, heavy	1 tbsp.
Cream cheese	1 tbsp.
Cream cheese, lite	1 tbsp.

SUMMARY WEIGHT LOSS GRAPH

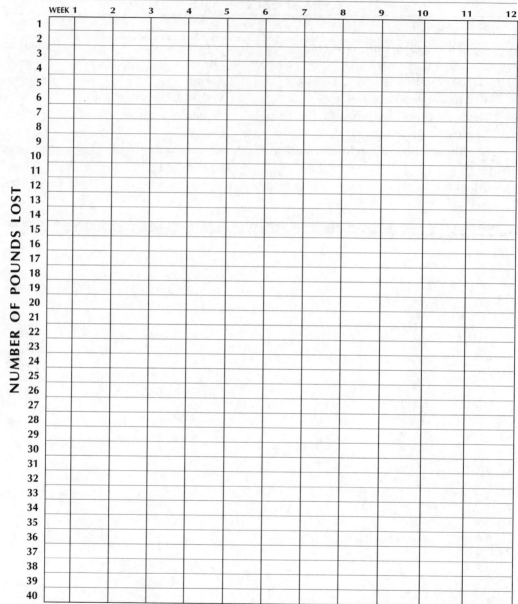

You can use the Summary Weight Loss Graph above to record your weight loss in two different ways. You can either record the number of pounds you lose each week (see the dotted line in the sample graph) or you can see the total number of pounds you lose as you progress through the Twelve-Week Weight-Loss Diet Plan (see the solid line in the sample graph). To see your total weight loss, record in the first column the number of pounds you lose the first week. Then move to the right for the second week and count down the number of pounds you lose that week.

THE TWELVE STEPS

1. We admitted we were powerless over our dependencies—that our lives had become unmanageable.

2. Came to believe that a Power greater than ourselves could restore us to sanity.

3. Made a decision to turn our will and our lives over to the care of God, as we understood Him.

4. Made a searching and fearless moral inventory of ourselves.

5. Admitted to God, to ourselves, and to another human being the exact nature of our wrongs.

6. Were entirely ready to have God remove all these defects of character.

7. Humbly asked Him to remove our shortcomings.

8. Made a list of all persons we had harmed and became willing to make amends to them all.

9. Made direct amends to such people wherever possible, except when to do so would injure them or others.

10. Continued to take personal inventory and when we were wrong, promptly admitted it.

11. Sought through prayer and meditation to improve our conscious contact with God, praying only for knowledge of His will for us and the power to carry that out.

12. Having had a spiritual awakening as the result of these steps, we tried to carry this message to others, and to practice these principles in all our affairs.

NOTES

WEEK 1—Preparing for Success
1. Bill Wilson, *Alcoholics Anonymous: The Story of How Many Thousands of Men and Women Have Recovered from Alcoholism* (New York, NY: Alcoholics Anonymous World Services, Inc., 1955), 11.

WEEK 2—Analyzing Your Eating and Buying Patterns
1. Wilson, *Alcoholics Anonymous,* 10.
2. Ibid., 49.
3. Ibid., 10.
4. Ibid., 11.
5. Chuck C., *A New Pair of Glasses,* (Irvine, CA: New Look Publishing Co., 1984).
6. Wilson, *Alcoholics Anonymous,* 12.

WEEK 3—Exercise and Metabolism
1. Wilson, *Alcoholics Anonymous,* 59.
2. Ibid., 13–14.

WEEK 5—Childhood Family Roles
1. Sharon Wegscheider-Cruse, *Another Chance: Hope and Health for the Alcoholic Family* (Palo Alto, CA: Science and Behavior Books, 1989).

WEEK 7—Nuts About Nutrition
1. Wilson, *Alcoholics Anonymous,* 76.

WEEK 10—Understanding Obesity
1. Theodore Van Itallie (Research Scientist, Columbia University), 256.

WEEK 11—Preventing Disease Through Improved Nutrition
1. Sneed, *Prime Time,* (Waco, TX: Word Books, 1989), 7.
2. National Cancer Institute: *American Family Physician,* May 1984.

WEEK 12—The Maintenance Diet
1. Wilson, *Alcoholics Anonymous,* 89, 93.

THE FOOD EXCHANGES
1. This material has been modified from *Exchange Lists for Weight Management,* which is the basis of a meal planning system designed by a committee of the American Diabetes Association and The American Dietetic Association. While designed primarily for people with diabetes and others who must follow special diets, the Exchange Lists are based on principles of good nutrition that apply to everyone. © 1989 American Diabetes Association, Inc., The American Dietetic Association.

ACKNOWLEDGMENTS

The authors are grateful to the friends, family members, and working companions whose contributions and assistance have made the publication of *Love Hunger* possible. We are especially thankful for Mary Alice Minirth, Jan Meier, and David Sneed. Many thanks also to Karen Scalf Linamen, whose writing craftsmanship transformed the authors' notes and transcripts into manuscript form; Janet Thoma, for her encouragement, support, and editorial expertise; Glenna Sterling Weatherly, for her friendship and her hours of typing; Vicky Warren and Kathy Short, for their assistance at all stages of copy. And finally, to those who participated in recipe formulations and testing: Ernestine Meadows, Shelly McAfee, Maxine McAfee, Pat Cavalier, Debra Evans (Director of Lake Austin Resort), and Georgia Butler (caterer, Austin, Texas); and Shannon, Lauren, and Jonathan Sneed, who tried many of the recipes as their evening meals—even with the recipes that weren't quite "bookers," they remained gracious and supportive.

ABOUT THE AUTHORS

DR. FRANK MINIRTH is a diplomate of the American Board of Psychiatry and Neurology and of the American Board of Forensic Medicine. Dr. Minirth has been in private practice in the Dallas area since 1975. He holds degrees from Arkansas State University, Arkansas School of Medicine, and Dallas Theological Seminary. He is president of The Minirth Clinic, P.A., in Richardson, Texas, and consultant to the Minirth Christian Program at Green Oaks Behavioral Healthcare Services. He is also Adjunct Professor in the Pastoral Ministries/Counseling Department at Dallas Theological Seminary.

DR. PAUL MEIER received an M.S. degree in cardiovascular physiology at Michigan State University and an M.D. degree from the University of Arkansas College of Medicine. He completed his psychiatric residency at Duke. Founder and medical director of Meier Clinics, Dr. Paul Meier is co-host of the national radio program, "New Life Live."

For more information, call 1-888-7-CLINIC or visit www.meierclinics.com.

Dr. Minirth and Dr. Meier have received degrees from Dallas Theological Seminary. They have also authored and co-authored more than forty books, including *Happiness Is a Choice, Worry-Free Living, Love Hunger, How to Beat Burnout, Safe Places, Sex in the Christian Marriage,* and *Beyond Burnout.*

DR. ROBERT HEMFELT, Ed.D., is a psychologist and marriage and family therapist in practice in Dallas, Texas, with emphasis on the treatment of compulsivity and eating disorders. Before entering private practice, he was an addictions specialist with a Fortune 500 corporation and the supervisor of therapeutic services for the Substance Abuse Study Clinic of the Texas Research Institute of Mental Sciences.

DR. SHARON SNEED is a registered dietitian and a practicing nutrition consultant. She has been an assistant professor at the Medical University of South Carolina and a postdoctoral fellow at the University of California at Berkeley. She has written more than a dozen research articles and books, including *Prime Time: A Complete Health Guide for Women 35–65.*

DR. DON HAWKINS holds a Master of Theology degree from Dallas Theological Seminary and a Doctor of Ministry degree from Calvary Theological Seminary. The author or co-author of over twenty books, he is president of Southeastern Bible College and is the host of the live nationwide call-in program *Life Perspectives.*